PUERTO RICAN WOMEN
AND WORK

Bridges in Transnational Labor

In the

PUERTO RICAN STUDIES SERIES

edited by

Luz del Alba Acevedo, Juan Flores,

and Emilio Pantojas-García

PUERTO RICAN WOMEN AND WORK

BRIDGES IN TRANSNATIONAL LABOR

Edited by
ALTAGRACIA ORTIZ

TEMPLE UNIVERSITY PRESS
Philadelphia

Temple University Press, Philadelphia 19122
Copyright © 1996 by Temple University. All rights reserved
Published 1996
Printed in the United States of America

Text design by Gary Gore

Library of Congress Cataloging-in-Publication Data
Puerto Rican women and work: bridges in transnational labor/edited by Altagracia Ortiz.
     p.   cm.—(Puerto Rican studies)
    Includes bibliographical references and index.
    ISBN 1-56639-450-3 (cloth).—ISBN 1-56639-451-1 (pbk.)
    1. Puerto Rican women—Employment—History. 2. Women—Employment—Puerto Rico—History. I. Ortiz, Altagracia, 1941– . II. Series.
HD6057.5.U5P84   1996
331.4′097295′0904—dc20

                            95-43822

To my daughter, Nicolè,
a new generation of Puerto Rican women workers

CONTENTS

PREFACE

his collection of essays tells the story of women workers whose
lives have been deeply affected by a colonial system of government and whose labor has been exploited throughout the
twentieth century by an expanding capitalist industrial economy. Collectively, these essays provide a historical portrait of women who
worked very long hours for little pay and few benefits—either in *talleres*
(shops or factories) or at home in Puerto Rico and on the U.S. mainland—to support themselves and their families. I am grateful to them for
sharing their experiences with us; this is their story.

One of these workers was my mother, Matilde Rodríguez Torres, a
woman whose life in many ways represents the spirit of this collection.
She was both a wage laborer and—as a wife and mother—an "unpaid
worker" in Puerto Rico and later in the United States, where she came
to live in 1951. Throughout her life, she worked from morning till night
at all kinds of jobs—some for pay (as a seamstress or garment worker),
others out of a sense of duty to her family. Although she often felt forced
to work because she had to help support her family, a few times, especially when she was younger and did fine needlework or gardening, I
sensed she also loved to work. I owe my interest in Puerto Rican women
workers to my mother, and I thank her for this gift. She was the inspiration for this book.

The actual collection of essays, however, came after a presentation
entitled "A Historical Appraisal of the Puerto Rican Female Labor Force
in the United States, 1900–1990," which I made at the annual conference
of the American Studies Association in Toronto on November 5, 1989.
My paper was presented as part of a panel on Puerto Rican women that
had been organized by Eileen Boris of Howard University, who was at the

time researching women needleworkers in Puerto Rico during the 1930s. Before I left for Toronto, Janet Francendese of Temple University Press saw the conference program and requested a copy of my paper; soon after, I received a letter from Temple's senior acquisitions editor, Doris Braendel, expressing interest in my work. I am grateful to Janet for recommending me to the press and to Doris for her unfailing support of this project. I also wish to thank Elizabeth Johns and Joan Vidal for their excellent editing of the manuscript.

Until I was contacted by Temple, my publications on Puerto Rican workers had focused exclusively on Puerto Rican women in the United States. But in June 1989 I attended a workshop on Puerto Rican women working both on the island and on the mainland. The workshop was held at the Universidad de Puerto Rico (UPR) in Río Piedras and was sponsored by Intercambio, the City University of New York–UPR academic exchange program. There I met with several scholars who were interested in doing collaborative research on Puerto Rican women on the island as well as in the United States. I then proposed to Temple the compilation of a collection of investigations on women workers. All of the contributors to this collection except for Eileen Boris were participants in the Intercambio women's studies workshops, which ran from 1989 to 1992 under the directorship of Antonio (Tony) Lauria and his assistant, Michelle Bloom-Lugo. I thank Tony for his efforts to obtain funding for our workshops and Michelle for her efficiency in administering this program. I also wish to thank the Centro de Estudios, Recursos, y Servicios a la Mujer of the Centro de Investigaciones Sociales at the Universidad de Puerto Rico in Río Piedras, especially Alice Colón-Warren, for organizing these workshops and for sharing invaluable monographs and materials with me. I am also indebted to the Professional Staff Congress and the City University of New York (CUNY) for granting me two separate Research Foundation Fellowships, which enabled me to complete the research for the introduction to this collection and for my article on garment workers in New York City. I owe Jacob Marini, John Jay College's research director, special thanks for his consistent endorsement of my grant applications; he has truly been a "lucky charm." My most sincere thanks go also to the Centro de Estudios Puertorriqueños (Center for Puerto Rican Studies) at Hunter College of CUNY for inviting me to be one of their Fellows during the 1994–95 academic year. This fellowship afforded me not only the time to edit this collection but also the opportunity to benefit from scholarly *charlas* (workshops) with my Centro colleagues: Juan Flores (Centro director), Camille Rodríguez, Roberto P. Rodríguez-Morazzani, Amilcar Tirado Avilés, and Blanca Vázquez.

I have also appreciated the confidence and support of Clara Rodríguez, professor of sociology at Fordham University; Judith P. Zinsser, president of the World History Association (1994–96); and Roberta Walker Kilkenny, my long-time friend and Caribbean studies colleague, who invited me to share this collection in panels at (respectively) Fordham University's Puerto Rican and Latin American Studies Institute (1993), the American Historical Association (San Francisco, 1994), and the Caribbean Historians' Association (San Germán, Puerto Rico, 1994). I am especially grateful to Sylvia Miranda and Yolanda Sánchez of the Puerto Rican Association for Community Affairs for inviting me to share a draft of the essays with the students of their Puerto Rican History and Culture course for high school students this past year.

To the librarians and staff of the Archivo General de Puerto Rico, Centro de Estudios Puertorriqueños, University of Puerto Rico at Río Piedras and Cayey, Interamerican University at San Germán, Puerto Rico, John Jay College of Criminal Justice and Hunter College of CUNY, and New York Public Libraries I owe a debt of gratitude for their diligence in locating sources for me. My most sincere thanks go to all of them, but most especially to Nélida Pérez, Amilcar Tirado Avilés, and Félix Antonio Rivera of the Evelina Antonetty Library of the Centro de Estudios Puertorriqueños; Tony Simpson, Marvie Brooks, and Dee Aikens of the John Jay Library; and Adriana Laborde of the Biblioteca del Instituto de Cultura Puertorriqueña of the Archivo General de Puerto Rico.

Without the constant love and support of my family, working on this collection would not have been nearly as pleasant. I am especially grateful to my daughter, Nicolè Anne Squillace, for her love and generosity, and to my companion, Henry Amiccé Soto, for his steadfast friendship and understanding. The honesty and friendly humor of my father, Benigno Ortiz Ramos, have always nourished me in very special ways. For this and much more I send to him in his home in Cayey, Puerto Rico, *un millón de gracias*. And I thank my sisters, Margaret Carlo, Socorro Maldonado, and Rose Ortiz, and my brother, Nelson Ortiz, for keeping alive our mother's lifelong dedication to work.

PUERTO RICAN WOMEN AND WORK

Bridges in Transnational Labor

Introduction

ALTAGRACIA ORTIZ

T|his collection of essays represents the work of ten contemporary feminist scholars investigating the work experiences of Puerto Rican women (*puertorriqueñas*) between 1920 and 1990. Although our essays emerge from different disciplines and use a variety of methodologies, each sheds light on a unique aspect of the labor history of Puerto Rican women in Puerto Rico or on the mainland United States. Collectively, they render a historical portrait of women who have worked in different time periods, geographic regions, occupations, economies, and labor markets, but whose struggles reveal continuities in a strong work ethic, in home and factory work, in a determination to survive the most oppressive and dangerous work conditions, and in the evolution of diverse strategies that have empowered them to challenge the forces limiting their lives. Specifically, our essays focus on the struggles of women in the home needlework industry in Puerto Rico from 1920 to 1945 (Boris); the gender and ethnic discrimination Puerto Rican migrant women encountered in the garment industry of New York City between 1920 and 1980 (Ortiz); the activities of Puerto Rican teachers anxious to create bicultural and bilingual educational programs in New York City's public school system from 1945 to 1967 (Sánchez Korrol); the impact of capitalist restructuring on the employment and socioeconomic status of migrating *puertorriqueñas* in the mid-Atlantic region during the 1970s (Colón-Warren); the survival strategies of women in workplaces (garment factories) and in their private spheres (households) in Puerto Rico at the beginning of the 1980s (Pérez-Herranz); the collective efforts of women seeking to make toxic workplaces safe in the mid-1980s (Muñoz-Vázquez); the controversial struggles of poor working-class Puerto Rican women, permanently out of the labor force, challenging gender ideologies and the state

1

for the right to use public assistance to support their families in New York City in the late 1980s (Torruellas, Benmayor, Juarbe); and the unsubtle mediation of gender and class ideologies in the fast-growing field of clerical services in Puerto Rico in the early 1990s (Casey). In this introductory essay I integrate these different investigations into a general history of Puerto Rican women workers ranging from 1900 to 1990. My purpose here is to show the connections among women's work and the origins of colonial capitalism in Puerto Rico, labor migration and community development in the United States, industrial development and capitalist reorganization both on the island and the mainland, and women's labor struggles in the twentieth century.

I have arranged our essays in a historical chronology that attempts to weave together the worlds of *puertorriqueñas* working in Puerto Rico and on the mainland in order to illuminate continuities and divergences in their labor experience in the twentieth century. Thus, this collection complements other studies seeking to break the dichotomy that in previous scholarship has fragmented the lives of the Puerto Rican people into two separate spheres—that is, the "island experience" or the "mainland experience"—and to present a more unified and comprehensive vision of the history of *puertorriqueñas* between 1920 and 1990.[1] The need for such an approach was made abundantly clear many years ago by Manuel Maldonado Denis in his *Puerto Rico y Estados Unidos: Emigración y colonialismo,* first published in 1976.[2] In this work Maldonado Denis advocated the study of Puerto Rican history (especially the economic transformations that have taken place in the twentieth century) from "the wider perspective of the problems and disorders that affect a society as an organic whole," and he passionately urged us to take into consideration in our historical investigations the entire Puerto Rican community, including its *emigrantes* (migrants).[3] As he pointed out:

> The Puerto Rican working class is in fact the object of a double exploitation that also has no geographic escape. This exploitation goes on both in Puerto Rico and in the metropolis, like the two faces of the same social reality. In Puerto Rico under a system whose necessary consequences are unemployment, marginalization and emigration; and in the United States, under a capitalist society where racism assigns the Puerto Rican workers to the "bottom of the social ladder."[4]

In spite of Maldonado Denis's pleas for more "global" perspectives in Puerto Rican working-class studies, few works by scholars on the island have fully included the migration experience or delved deeply into its impact on island workers. Similarly, investigations on Puerto Rican migrants in the United States often use the island experience merely as background to appraise the lives of *puertorriqueños* abroad, without exploring any further the connections to or differences between the history of workers in Puerto Rico and that of emigrants.[5] By intertwining the twentieth-century histories of Puerto Rican women workers on the island with those on the mainland, we create in this collection of essays a more holistic view of the work experiences of the Puerto Rican people that invites a comparative dialogue on workers whose lives have been intimately connected to developments within the U.S. capitalist system, both in Puerto Rico and on the mainland.

Women's Work and Colonial Capitalism

In Puerto Rico, the 1898 takeover of the island by the United States resulted in the expansion of colonial economic interests that incorporated large numbers of women into the insular paid labor force.[6] However, long before American capitalism began to transform Puerto Rico's economy, *puertorriqueñas* had already become involved in the production and service sectors of the island during the time it was a colony of Spain. Until the abolition of slavery in 1872, enslaved black women worked in the fields, planting and harvesting coffee, sugar, and other products, and as household servants, cooking, caring for children, sewing, washing and ironing clothes, and cleaning the master's or mistress's house.[7] Before and after 1872, free black women, as well as other white and racially mixed *jornaleras* (wageworkers), also earned their livelihoods in domestic service, selling home-prepared foods and candies or working in the fields for agricultural hacendados.[8]

Some women continued to work as farmhands in plantation agriculture (for example, coffee plantations) until the end of the nineteenth century, but the first U.S. employment survey (derived from the 1899 census of Puerto Rico) indicates that when the U.S. colonial capitalist economy got its start in Puerto Rico, women were concentrated in jobs that were simply an extension of their roles in the home: there were some 18,453 domestics, 16,855 laundresses, and 5,785 seamstresses.[9]

There were few *talleres* (workshops or factories) on the island at this time, and so the census of 1899 records only 60 factory workers, found exclusively in the tobacco industry.[10] The census does record the presence of women in teaching (563), nursing (64), and sales (25), and in the straw-hat making industry (387); but no women were recorded among office, needle, garment, and public service workers.[11] Yet by 1930 women were more than visible in these new and expanding job categories: there were 2,500 office workers, 3,635 needleworkers, and 6,383 garment workers. Additionally, there were now some 9,290 tobacco factory operators, 4,254 teachers, 34,345 seamstresses, 921 nurses, 828 sales "girls", and 691 straw-hat makers.[12] In contrast, by the same year the majority of the male labor force had been channeled into sugar cane production, which had come to dominate the island's economy in the first three decades of United States rule in Puerto Rico.[13] The incorporation of women into Puerto Rico's colonial labor force, therefore, was into a sex-segregated labor market that saw the rise of "female occupations," many of which were directly related to the needs of U.S. colonial capitalism on the island and which have exploited women's work in the twentieth century.

The tobacco and needlework industries starkly illustrate the gendered divisions and deplorable employment conditions affecting women workers in Puerto Rico's nascent industrial colonial economy at the beginning of the century. In the tobacco industry thousands of women worked excruciatingly long hours, for extremely low wages, and under dangerous health conditions as leaf strippers, sorters, and packers. Men were usually employed in the more skilled trade of cigar making, where they could earn higher wages. Perhaps because so many of the women who first entered the tobacco industry were young, unmarried, and still living in their parents' homes, these tobacco workers brazenly challenged their oppression by demanding that the male-led Unión de Tabaqueros (Tobacco Workers' Union) organize and represent them, and by participating in strikes and other work actions against the American tobacco companies that exploited their labor.[14] One of their most vocal supporters was the energetic socialist-feminist Luisa Capetillo, a *lectora* (reader) in cigar-making factories in Puerto Rico and the United States, who fought for their rights not only as workers but as women.[15] From 1905 until her death in 1922, Capetillo mobilized women workers in Puerto Rico, Tampa, Florida, and New York City, demanding their equal economic, legal, and political integration into society.[16] By 1919 Capetillo and other labor activists had won a minimum-wage law from the island's legislators; but the gains expected under this law were nullified during the 1920s by precipitous declines in the cigar-making industry caused by competition from cigarettes produced in the North American South. Throughout the early 1920s, while some women continued to work as leaf processors for the export trade, hundreds of others lost their jobs. Increasingly, as the decade progressed, *puertorriqueñas* looking for work emigrated to the United States or sought work in the needle trades, an industry also notorious for its exploitation of women.

In fact, we begin our collection with an essay on home needleworkers in Puerto Rico because, unlike tobacco workers—who mostly worked in factories and could take advantage of their collective labor experience to organize a sustained assault against North American industrialists— island needleworkers were so divided between those who worked in shops and those who labored at home that it was extremely difficult for them to develop and sustain a united front against U.S. manufacturers.[17] Thus they were probably the most exploited of all women wage workers during this period. Nevertheless, needleworkers did organize several unions and participated in labor strikes that at least challenged women's exploitation in the needle trades.[18] This exploitation began almost immediately after the U.S. occupation and, as Lydia Milagros González, María del Carmen Baerga, and Luisa Hernández Angueira have observed, involved the collaboration of national entrepreneurs.[19] Working together with foreign investors, native entrepreneurs—or *comisionistas* (contractors), as they were known in Puerto Rico—transformed this simple island industry into one of the United States's major colonial enterprises after World War I. As early as 1905, for example, Brígida Román and María Luisa Arcelay, two of the best-known *comisionistas,* began selling homemade workers' *calados* (finely embroidered and laced linens) and crocheted pieces to the crew and passengers on vessels of the United States–owned Puerto Rico Steamship Company during their calls at the ports of San Juan and Mayagüez.[20] Soon they were joined by North American white women, who saw in the export needle trade an acceptable occupation for their gender, and by religious humanitarians and public school educators, who were desirous of teaching needle skills to destitute women as a way to prevent "immorality" and idleness among the poor. By the 1920s these various interests had succeeded in influencing the colonial Department of Public Instruction in San Juan to implement a needlework curriculum to train female pupils in the few public schools scattered across the island.[21] Thus, when the needle trade between Europe and the United States was interrupted during World War I by commercial blockades, Puerto Rican and North American intermediaries were ready to deliver a highly skilled needlework labor force to the larger mainland entrepreneurs who greatly expanded the export trade in the next decade.

As the needle-trade market expanded in the 1920s, native entrepreneurial shops sprang up in urban centers such as Mayagüez, San Juan, and Ponce, easily drawing their labor force from the growing number of unemployed factory tobacco workers and rural women migrating from the nearby countryside—including those who had lost their jobs due to decreases in tobacco agricultural production. A few of these shops came to employ a sizable workforce (four had about one thousand workers) but most were just small producers, averaging about two to three hundred workers.[22] But as the island's economy worsened in the late 1920s and 1930s, shop owners increasingly acted as intermediaries for the fast-growing home needlework trades.[23] Some of these shop owners, as well as other well-placed maverick *comisionistas,* who operated out of their homes, unscrupulously exploited their home workers. According to Caroline Manning's 1933 study of women workers on the island, *comisionistas* often tricked women out of their meager wages by charging exorbitant commissions, sometimes as high as 50 percent of their earnings; others paid workers in kind (for example, in shoes or groceries).[24] Consequently, home needleworkers' wages never rose above survival levels since most women earned only about a dollar a day. Yet throughout the 1930s needleworkers in dingy *bohíos* (shacks) continued to slave over their bundles of garments using just a needle and thread or a tiny sewing machine, because their work was the only means of survival for their families in this period of crisis. It is within these well-established colonial production processes and the harsh economic realities of U.S. colonial capitalism at the time of the Great Depression that Eileen Boris places the enigma posed by Puerto Rican home needleworkers' struggles to prevent the elimination of an industry that was notorious for exploiting its workers.

In her essay, "Needlewomen under the New Deal in Puerto Rico, 1920–1945," Boris traces the ideological and political conflicts that ensued between home needleworkers, island political and business leaders, and the United States government when Congress attempted to apply the National Recovery Act (NRA) to Puerto Rico in 1934.[25] The NRA, a

New Deal measure passed in 1933 to stabilize the mainland economy, contained some 120 codes that regulated or eliminated many paid homework activities in the United States.[26] The law was applied to Puerto Rico in July 1934 because of mainland clothing manufacturers' fears concerning the great differentials in wages and production processes that existed between the North American and island needle trades. As Boris points out in her chapter, regulating the needlework industry in Puerto Rico therefore became essential for the survival of certain sectors of the manufactured clothes industry in the States; but for Puerto Rico, stringent regulation or complete elimination of the needle trades—especially homework—at this time would have spelled disaster. Thus, Puerto Rican needleworkers demanded that both shop and home needlework be continued but that the industry be regulated in order to guarantee better working conditions and higher wages. In her essay Boris shows how, despite differences in the rhetoric on gender roles and women's right to work, needleworkers established a coalition consisting of local officials, shop workers and owners, some union leaders, and homeworkers, which succeeded in getting the federal government to create a special code for Puerto Rico. The code called for a minimum wage of five dollars for shop workers; three dollars for home needle-workers; registration of *comisionistas* to safeguard against abuses; the determination of fair piece rates by commissions; the abolition of some needlecraft processes (including cutting, stamping, and washing); and an investigation of the possibility of establishing communal needlework centers in the future. Thus, the special NRA code for Puerto Rico enabled the needlework industry to continue to operate on the island, but as Boris notes, this code did not succeed in eliminating abuses in the trade. After 1945 the needlework industry entered an accelerated period of decline and has now almost disappeared as a result of the introduction of modern clothing factories since the 1950s.[27]

Women's Work and Labor Migration

Accompanying the integration of women into Puerto Rico's colonial economy during the first three decades of the twentieth century was the beginning of a labor migration that incorporated Puerto Rican migrant women into important sectors of the mainland economy. During these early years *puertorriqueñas* mainly emigrated to New York City, where they soon became a source of cheap labor for the city's needle and garment trades. At first they were mostly found in the home needlework industries, which at this time included—in addition to piecework in blouses, handkerchiefs, and undergarments, and the embroidery and crocheting of linens and garments—the decoration of lamps and flower making.[28] Although home-needlework wages were slightly higher in New York than on the island, conditions in the industry were no different: migrant Puerto Rican women spent long hours, after their house chores were done, finishing garments for a few dollars a week. By the late 1940s, however, campaigns by the International Ladies' Garment Workers' Union (ILGWU) against homework, and the brief post–World War II expansion of the clothing trades, had begun to harness the labor of migrating *puertorriqueñas* into garment factories throughout the city. Their experiences in these shops appear at first glance to duplicate those of their predecessors in the industry. Indeed, like earlier European immigrant women, they experienced gender-segregated workplaces, low wages, deskilled jobs, and limited opportunities for advancement both in the trades and in the trade's major labor organization, the ILGWU. Additionally, *puertorriqueñas* shared with African American women, and with other Hispanics in the trades, a history of discrimination, not only because of their race but also because of their ethnicity. In the case of Puerto Rican women, however, this gender and ethnic discrimination was compounded by increasing market and production changes that profoundly affected their lives, as the industry entered a period of modernization and globalization after the 1950s.

My own chapter, " 'En la aguja y el pedal eché la hiel': Puerto Rican Women in the Garment Industry of New York City, 1920–1980," therefore explores the history of Puerto Rican garment workers in New York City from the perspective of an industry already rigidly stratified by gender, ethnicity, and race; and it also attempts to examine the impact of capital and labor market transformations on the labor force participation of migrant *puertorriqueñas* in clothing manufacturing during those years. By the time migrant women from the island entered the city's garment industry in the 1920s, its gender divisions had been clearly established. With the expansion of the industry in the early 1900s, Jewish and Italian immigrant women, who constituted the bulk of the female labor force during these years, had been assigned to do "women's work" in the trades.[29] Those working for the better coat and suit makers usually only hemmed and sewed on buttons by hand; in the sectors that were experiencing standardization, such as the producers of cheaper women's dresses and suits, children's wear, and underwear, women were the sewing-machine operators, cleaners, and packers, while men carried out the designing, cutting, tailoring, and retailing operations. From 1920 to 1960, the most active years of Puerto Rican women's labor force participation in the garment trades, white women usually held the "women's jobs" in the better-paid shops. However, declines in white women's labor participation due to immigration restrictions imposed by World War I and the National Origins Act of 1924, opened up the medium- and lower-priced shops to *puertorriqueñas* after 1920. By 1950 they were the essential labor force in the dress and skirt industries (the most standardized items of production in the city's shops) but were also present in blouse, children's wear, and underwear manufacturing.[30]

Although Puerto Rican women encountered hostility from white workers in many of the shops, it was in the locals of the ILGWU, the largest of the clothing workers' organizations, that they came to feel the full impact of ethnic discrimination in the garment industry. In the 1930s and 1940s they had to wage a struggle with white union members for admission into Dressmakers' Local 22 and other low-wage locals, and in succeeding decades they never made it into the more prestigious locals—namely, Cutters' Local 10 (still a male domain), the Italian Dressmakers' Local 89, or the Italian Cloakmakers' Local 48. When they joined other Hispanic workers in petitions to organize their own local, they were hastily dismissed by ILGWU leaders with the excuse that the creation of other language locals would further splinter the union. Yet the Italian locals were permitted to function uninterrupted, even after the number of Italian women had dwindled in the trades and, perhaps more surprisingly, after ethnic locals were declared illegal by the state in 1948! In the meantime, the top leadership of the ILGWU—in the hands of Jewish male workers (whose numbers also had declined considerably since they helped organize the union in 1900)—controlled: all appointments to vacancies in the locals; an election process that denied challengers equal access to workers in the shops and union newspapers; the distribution of union funds; and all decisions regarding contracts.[31] This consistently patriarchal and undemocratic climate made it impossible for *puertorriqueñas,* who constituted the bulk of the ILGWU membership after World War II, to confront the industry-wide problems—especially those caused by technological and clothing style changes, foreign competition, and relocation of businesses to lower-wage areas—that eventually contributed to the decline of significant sectors of the industry in New York City in later decades.[32]

Even though the literature on other early twentieth-century Puerto Rican migrant women workers is scanty, a few sources note the presence of *puertorriqueñas* in New York's tobacco, confectionery, and meat-packing industries, as well as in domestic, laundry, and clerical services.[33] Recent studies have also located Puerto Rican migrant women among the city's professionals during the first decades of the century. Four women stand out in these works: Pura Belpré, a librarian and author; Victoria Hernández, a musician; Josefina Silva de Cintrón, a journalist; and Carmela Zapata Bonilla Marrero, a religious community organizer. Belpré, college educated in Puerto Rico and trained in library sciences in New York City, found employment in the city's public library system in 1924, and in the decades to follow she went on to recount Puerto Rican folktales in delightful children's books.[34] Hernández, an accomplished violinist and cellist, taught music and ran a music store in Harlem during the 1930s and 1940s, in order to support her brothers, Rafael and Jesús Hernández, who during these years won the hearts of the Puerto Rican community with their nostalgic songs, while Silva de Cintrón honed her journalism skills as editor of *Artes y Letras,* a Hispanic monthly publication that from 1933 to 1945 kept Latinos abreast of happenings in Latin America and the United States.[35] And Zapata Bonilla Marrero, or "Sister Carmelita," as she is best known in the Puerto Rican community, was the first nun assigned by the Catholic Church to work among Hispanics in New York City. From 1923 to the early 1970s, when she retired, Sister Carmelita developed and administered dozens of social and educational programs that enriched the lives of Puerto Rican children and adults.[36]

Through their work in factories, their neighborhoods, and other places in the city, these pathbreaking women contributed to the emergence of a Puerto Rican community that became a new home to thousands of *puertorriqueños* who emigrated after World War II.[37] Most of these newcomers were blue-collar workers in search of better employment opportunities created by the expanding postwar economy.[38] Although the number of post-1945 Puerto Rican migrants to the States has been difficult to calculate, Adalberto López and James Petras estimate that

between 1940 and 1950 an average of 18,700 Puerto Ricans
migrated to the United States annually. In the decade of the
1950s the average rose to 41,200 per year, and in the 1960s it declined to an average of about 14,500 annually. In 1953 alone,
when the migration reached its peak, about 69,000 Puerto Ricans left the island to settle in the United States mainland.[39]

Similarly, there are no complete accounts of the number of children who
came with these migrants, but by 1948 the Committee on Puerto Ricans
in New York City of the Welfare Council of New York instructed the city's
Department of Education to keep counts of the number of Puerto Rican
children in its various school districts. In January 1948 the Committee
reported: "There were 24,350 Puerto Rican children in the public
schools of the five boroughs and about 5,000 in the parochial schools."[40]
Because many of these children knew no English, the only language of
instruction on the mainland at the time, in 1949 the New York City Board
of Education created the position of a Spanish-speaking "substitute auxiliary teacher" to help integrate the new pupils into the city's school
system. Ana Peñaranda Marcial, a highly experienced teacher from
Arecibo, Puerto Rico, became the city's first substitute auxiliary teacher
(SAT). Using the story of this dedicated and gifted migrant woman as the
focus of her essay, "Toward Bilingual Education: Puerto Rican Women
Teachers in New York City Schools, 1947–1967," Virginia Sánchez Korrol presents a historical profile of the educational and cultural contributions of *puertorriqueñas* employed as SATs in the city's public schools
during the 1950s and 1960s.

Originally hired to teach English to Spanish-speaking children in the
elementary and intermediate grades, SATs quickly reconceptualized this
role. First, they challenged the idea that the most effective way of teaching the English language to their pupils was through the "immersion
method" (the use of English only in the classroom), maintaining that by
using the Spanish and English languages together, the Puerto Rican migrant child would learn English faster and better. With the support of
Puerto Rican community leaders and liberal educators throughout the
city, SATs eventually developed bilingual and bicultural curriculum materials and implemented teaching pedagogies in their classrooms that,
Sánchez Korrol believes, laid the foundation for bilingual and multicultural education in the United States. SATs also worked very closely with

other community leaders on issues of great concern to Hispanics through-out the city. They struggled with the Board of Education for the employment of more Puerto Rican professionals in the school system and sought the licensure of bilingual teachers as "regular" staff members, not just as substitutes. They contributed to the organizational life of the community by creating the Society of Puerto Rican Auxiliary Teachers, the Puerto Rican Educators' Association, and the SAT chapter of the United Federation of Teachers. Together with parents and other individuals in their school districts, SATs celebrated Hispanic cultural events, disseminated information on important topics such as education and health, and engaged in empowerment struggles to better the lives of Hispanics in the United States. By illustrating the work of SATs in New York's Spanish-speaking *barriadas,* Sánchez Korrol demonstrates the strong presence of working *puertorriqueñas* in the construction of their communities in the United States.

Unfortunately, the story of the Puerto Rican SAT in New York City also serves as an example of the integration of educated women into what has generally been classified (both on the United States mainland and in Puerto Rico) as a woman's profession. Since the 1830s single women (and in later years married ones) were readily granted teaching licenses in the States, but they were poorly paid in comparison to other professions.[41] In Puerto Rico economic and social conditions under Spanish colonial rule denied women a similar access to the teaching profession, although they were present in some of the few public and private schools on the island during the nineteenth century.[42] With the extension of the U.S. educational system to Puerto Rico after 1900, many more women were hired as teachers; by 1920 their numbers had jumped from 563 (as noted earlier) to 2,636.[43] Soon they became the majority of the teachers in the island's public school system, predominating most especially in the elementary grades. Yet, as in the United States, women teachers until recently were paid less than their male counterparts, were not widely considered for supervisory or administrative positions, or elected to school boards.[44] Although most teachers' salaries have remained low in relation to other professional salaries, both in Puerto Rico and the United States, the teaching profession has continued to attract *puertorriqueñas.* In 1980, in spite of a variety of other occupational opportunities generated by the postwar economy, over half of all professional women on the island were counted as teachers.[45] In the United States the institutionalization of the position of bilingual teacher in 1960 and the implementation of bilingual, Puerto Rican studies, and affirmative action programs in the last twenty-five years also created new openings for Puerto Rican women in education.[46]

Women's Work and Industrial Capitalism

As these few educated Puerto Rican women were moving into the teaching profession in New York City, many blue-collar workers began losing their jobs as a result of the economic transformation affecting the entire mid-Atlantic region during the 1960s and 1970s. The nature and impact of this transformation on Puerto Rican women was first systematically researched by Rosemary Santana Cooney of Fordham University, who in the late 1970s examined the published census data on women in some fifty-six cities, including mid-Atlantic industrial centers, to compare seven significant variables (labor market conditions, education, age, family size, marital status, female-headed households, assimilation) applicable to Puerto Rican women in ten of these cities. In her study, published in 1979, Cooney corroborated emerging government reports (for example, the 1973 Manpower Report of the President) indicating a low labor force participation rate for Puerto Rican women—that is, the percentage of workers fourteen years and older in the labor force—compared to other women throughout the country.[47] However, when examining the labor force participation rates of Puerto Rican women in the previous two decades, Cooney also found that while in 1970 this rate was 29.8 percent (compared to 44.5 percent for African American and 38.9 percent for white women), in 1950 the labor force participation rate for Puerto Rican women had been 38.9 percent, but that by 1960 this rate had dropped to 36.3 percent. Cooney argues in this pioneer study that Puerto Rican women's declining labor force participation was not only localized to the northeast region of the nation (since in some Midwest and West Coast cities the participation of *puertorriqueñas* showed an upward trend) but that

> the variable changes that were responsible for a declining Puerto Rican female participation rate in New York [and its environs] were the loss of nondurable operative [i.e., sewing-machine] jobs, the dramatic increase in the number of females

heading families, and a more favorable industry mix for more
highly educated females even after controlling [for] the loss of
nondurable operative jobs.[48]

In the next few years, working with a group of dedicated co-re-
searchers, Cooney continued to explore the relationship between the
economic changes in the mid-Atlantic region and the unique demographic and social characteristics affecting Puerto Rican women workers
in the area.[49] One of these researchers was Alice Colón-Warren, who in
this volume updates her investigations of the factors that persistently
contributed to lower labor force participation rates among Puerto Rican
women between 1970 and 1980 in New York, New Jersey, and Pennsylvania.[50] In her chapter, "The Impact of Job Losses on Puerto Rican
Women in the Middle Atlantic Region, 1970–1980," Colón-Warren notes
that by 1980 Puerto Rican women's labor force participation had increased to 37 percent in the Northeast, yet this participation rate still
lagged behind those of African American and white women (58 and
48 percent respectively). Searching for an explanation, Colón-Warren
closely correlates education to labor market conditions in the mid-
Atlantic region and finds that *puertorriqueñas* have been disproportionally disadvantaged, as members of the "lower strata of the working class,"
in the region's educational opportunities, which she believes ultimately
limited their participation in the expanding professional, clerical, and
sales occupations in the 1970s. Because white and African American
women were highly concentrated in these occupations during this period, Puerto Rican women also experienced greater competition in the
labor market. Meanwhile, the loss of jobs in the manufacturing sector
did not abate. Since this sector had been the most important source of
employment for Puerto Rican women in the past, they were, of course,
the most affected by its demise: by 1980 for the first time in U.S. history
there were fewer Puerto Rican women employed as sewing-machine operators than as clericals.

Colón-Warren's essay draws our attention to yet another critical research issue initiated by Cooney—that is, the relationship between
Puerto Rican women's work, the incidence of female-headed households, and poverty, one of the most controversial topics in Puerto Rican
women's studies in recent years. For Colón-Warren the rising rate of
poor families headed by women is attributable to two factors: women's

exclusion from gainful employment and their lower levels of earnings when they do obtain employment. She also believes that factors such as English-language skills, presence of children, access to family networks, and home ownership may have affected the labor force participation of single women more than married ones. In her final analysis, however, Colón-Warren reiterates Cooney's assessment of the effects of labor market conditions for Puerto Rican women following their employment apogee in 1950—specifically, that the decline of industrial jobs in the mid-Atlantic region placed *puertorriqueñas* in a highly vulnerable economic position. Without adequate educational opportunities and secure sources of employment, many Puerto Rican women, especially single heads of households, were thus forced to turn to public assistance in order to support themselves and their families. Colón-Warren, although critical of the welfare system in general, sees the use of welfare benefits (which are sometimes supplemented by informal economic activities) as a form of "resistance" to further deterioration in employment and economic conditions in the Middle Atlantic region. Yet, she recognizes that this resistance is extremely limited, only offering Puerto Rican women basic survival at the poverty level.

Women's Work and Economic Development

Recent transformations in the Puerto Rican economy have led to similar labor and life patterns among women workers on the island. Clearly, since the mid-1970s women workers in Puerto Rico have also been experiencing greater job losses, unemployment and underemployment, and increasing difficulties supporting families on the low incomes provided by their wage labor.[51] This is in sharp contrast to the previous two decades when women's employment opportunities, labor force participation (at least in some sectors), and wages had experienced notable increases as a result of the implementation of Fomento, the island's post–World War II economic development program.[52] Conceived in the early 1940s as a strategy for increasing employment opportunities for men, Fomento had succeeded by the 1960s in bringing to Puerto Rico mainly industries that were heavily dependent on women's labor. Most of these industries came to Puerto Rico in response to various incentives promoted by the island's new commonwealth government, namely, generous long-term tax exemptions, a renovated infrastructure (including electric and water plants, better transportation facilities, more schools), and the promise of an abundant low-cost labor force. Thus, during this first stage (1950–65) of economic development, Manos a la Obra (or Operation Bootstrap, as Fomento is popularly called in English) attracted many labor-intensive industries from the United States, such as the garment, textile, and leather companies that provided employment to thousands of women workers on the island.[53] Although in the 1960s and throughout the 1970s Fomento attempted to shift Puerto Rico's economy to more capital-intensive, high-technology enterprises (petrochemicals, pharmaceuticals, electronics, electrical equipment and appliances), with hopes of generating more jobs for men, most of the major industries that were created or expanded during this period hired more women than men also.[54] More significantly, until the early 1970s the garment industry continued to be an important source of wage work for women on the island.[55] As Puerto Rican workers' demands for higher wages increased in the 1980s, however, many of these enterprises, notably the garment businesses, began reducing operations in Puerto Rico and relocating to lower-wage areas in Latin America and Asia.[56]

A historical assessment of the impact of these economic changes on Puerto Rican women's lives has yet to be made, but a number of studies have prepared the way for a greater understanding of the relationship of women's work to the island's industrialization process and of the effects of Operation Bootstrap on women workers in recent years.[57] For example, the anthropological analyses of a 1980 survey of 157 garment workers in the western part of Puerto Rico, designed by Helen Icken Safa and conducted by her graduate research assistant, Carmen Pérez-Herranz, have provided important information on the impact of economic development on women factory workers. In her interpretation of this survey Safa notes that employers in Puerto Rico preferred hiring women workers between the ages of twenty and twenty-four for their production jobs, but worsening conditions in the garment industry in the early 1980s (and the availability of clerical jobs for younger women) resulted in the employment of an older (aged thirty and over) workforce in some plants.[58] Many of these older women had little formal education, yet they tended to be more assertive than younger women—most of whom had high school degrees—concerning workers' rights in the factory. This obviously was one of the reasons why employers sought younger women. Safa also points out that, unlike workers in the "global factory" of the multinational corporations, many garment workers in Puerto Rico tended to be married with children. Another unique pattern among Puerto Rican garment workers was the presence of an increasing number of women heads of households. In general, whether single or married, most of these women were part of large households and kin networks that served as support systems or problem-solving mechanisms in the factories, at home, and in the community. Just as *puertorriqueñas* in the garment industry in New York City were forced to, garment workers in Mayagüez struggled with low wages, occupational segregation, paternalistic management-union relations, and plant closings, while at home they were beleaguered by their "double-shift" responsibilities. Although Safa has noticed an increased awareness of these work and gender issues among women in Puerto Rico, she concludes that they "remain quite apathetic in their responses to these problems."[59]

Pérez-Herranz's essay, "Our Two Full-Time Jobs: Women Garment Workers Balance Factory and Domestic Demands in Puerto Rico," generally corroborates Safa's findings, but her detailed account of these workers' lives depicts women actively and earnestly seeking solutions to their workplace and household problems. To cope with the more stressful demands of their garment jobs, women brought their mothers, daughters, sisters, cousins, and close friends to the factory, where as co-workers they could support one another whenever such help was needed. On occasion, attempts were made to incorporate management into these kin and affinal relations. Even though, as Pérez-Herranz points out, the introduction of these personal relations into the modern factory is reminiscent of the *peón-patrón* relationship under the island's old hacienda system, she adds that the presence in their workplaces of relatives and friends gave women, especially older ones, a great sense of security and empowerment. Because they saw the ILGWU as a "company union" (in fact, the union had been invited by the company to organize them), women rarely brought their grievances to their union representatives and—either individually or through their kin relations—preferred to resolve conflicts themselves.[60] Pérez-Herranz believes that women did not resort to more organized and confrontational tactics because they considered these "too aggressive" or "manly" and because, for the most part, their "subtle strategies" yielded the results they expected. In their "private worlds" women also employed a variety of strategies to carry out their family, household, and community responsibilities: women efficiently routinized their work schedules, enlisted the aid of relatives and friends, and sought husbands or mates to help with chores. At home women workers also expected greater participation in decision making and information sharing.[61]

New Voices in Women's Labor Struggles

Other investigations of the strategies Puerto Rican women have used to confront their personal and work-related problems indicate that *puertorriqueñas* have explored a variety of alternatives for resolving these issues. The last three essays in our collection document the different modes of resistance and action that have empowered Puerto Rican women to challenge restrictive gender and work ideologies on the island as well as the mainland. The chapter by Marya Muñoz-Vázquez, entitled "Gender and Politics: Grassroots Leadership among Puerto Rican Women in a Health Struggle," deals with a group of women workers in the Guanajibo-Castillo Industrial Park in Mayagüez who between 1983 and 1989 helped organize El Comité Pro-Rescate de Nuestra Salud (CPRNS) (Committee to Rescue Our Health). The aim of this committee was to force employers to establish a safer work environment and compensate workers for damage to their health after toxic gas emissions repeatedly contaminated their workplace. In "Negotiating Gender, Work, and Welfare: *Familia* as Productive Labor," Rosa M. Torruellas, Rina Benmayor, and Ana Juarbe record the demands of poor Puerto Rican migrant women in the late 1980s for public funds and services to help raise their families—a responsibility they viewed as significant work as well as a cultural right. The last chapter in our historical chronology, "New Tappings on the Keys: Changes in Work and Gender Roles for Women Clerical Workers in Puerto Rico" by Geraldine J. Casey, evaluates the efforts of clerical and secretarial workers on the island to combat the workplace problems they have encountered in recent years. Although their various strategies have not produced all of the results Puerto Rican women have expected, they stand as courageous examples of attempts to overcome the oppressive socioeconomic conditions that today threaten the Puerto Rican working class.

One of the most crucial battles in this struggle has pitted women workers against U.S. transnational corporations operating in the Guanajibo-Castillo Industrial Park of Mayagüez over issues of occupational safety and environmental health. The battle began in 1980 when residents living near the industrial site complained to governmental authorities of a stench emanating from the park.[62] In the next few years several large gas emissions occurred, and after each incident workers in the complex, as well as their neighbors, experienced a variety of symptoms including headaches, dizziness, vomiting, and diarrhea.[63] Convinced that there was a correlation between their illnesses and the toxic discharges in the industrial park, workers demanded that the companies in the complex and governmental agencies investigate the emissions, but their pleas were ignored.[64] In the fall of 1983 workers—mainly women from the garment factories in the site—and residents in the nearby barrios organized themselves into the CPRNS and began to push for a quick resolution to the environmental problems in the Guanajibo-Castillo area. From its inception the group functioned as a collective and routinely asked labor organizers, doctors and other scientists, and lawyers for advice in planning strategies. Muñoz-Vázquez was one of the psychologists who participated in the collective from 1986 to 1988. In her contribution to this volume, Muñoz-Vázquez evaluates the origins, decision-making process, and impact of the CPRNS on women's health struggles in Puerto Rico during the two years she worked with the organization. Muñoz-Vázquez believes that in establishing a collective decision-making process, committee organizers made it possible for women to participate more actively in the organization's activities. Thus, the CPRNS encouraged women to challenge doctors' false diagnoses of their symptoms (for instance, their illnesses were attributed to "hysteria" about possible emissions in the future, problems with husbands, or menopause); to insist on on-site investigations of their physical conditions and work environments; and to bring suit against the companies suspected of the contamination.[65] Although the committee did not succeed in obtaining indemnity for the workers, Muñoz-Vázquez urges us to appreciate the fact that as a result of the committee's efforts, governmental agencies such as the Department of Health conducted several studies that led to production changes inside the Guanajibo-Castillo Park. On a broader scale, as Muñoz-Vázquez's essay well illustrates, the CPRNS also symbolizes women's capacity for developing effective grassroots leadership and collective political action in the workplace in modern-day Puerto Rico.

Another contested issue in the contemporary survival struggles of the Puerto Rican working class concerns the use of public assistance programs (welfare, food stamps, Medicaid) by *puertorriqueñas* on the mainland. Joining critics of the welfare state, Linda Chávez, a conservative Mexican American Republican, has argued that welfare has created a perennial dependency on the state among Puerto Rican women heads of households—a life pattern that she believes has undermined "patrimony," family support systems, and the "responsibilities of autonomous adults" within the Puerto Rican community.[66] Discounting the deteriorating socioeconomic conditions in the Northeast (where the bulk of the Puerto Rican population has resided) since the 1970s and the effects of racial and ethnic discrimination, which may account for women's participation in welfare programs, Chávez has implied that Puerto Rican women are on public assistance because they have a "surprisingly strong family attachment," a "propensity" to have children out of wedlock, a desire to care for school-age children themselves, and a lack of a "strong work ethic."[67] The chapter by Torruellas, Benmayor, and Juarbe, based on the detailed life histories of thirteen migrant *puertorriqueñas* on public assistance in New York City in the late 1980s, reaches a very different interpretation of the connections between Puerto Rican women and the welfare state. As other studies of welfare recipients have shown, Torruellas, Benmayor, and Juarbe demonstrate that, far from lacking a work ethic, the *puertorriqueñas* they studied considered work an integral part of their lives.[68] As child laborers many had contributed to their families by doing "women's work"—babysitting, home needlework, and the like. Too, their decision to migrate was made with the expectation of doing wage work to better their poor economic status. Once in the States, most had worked until declining economic conditions in the mid-Atlantic region in the 1980s—combined with their lack of formal education, training, or skilled-work experiences—caused some of them to lose their jobs and eventually to withdraw permanently from the labor force. Other women found themselves with unemployed or disabled husbands, became widows, or separated from mates, becoming heads of households as the result. Therefore, these women turned to welfare for a variety of reasons and only after exhausting other income-generating possibilities.[69] Even then they did not become passive "dependents" of the state, for by 1986 all of them were enrolled in the El Barrio Literacy Education Program, a project designed for the Spanish-speaking community in East Harlem by the Language Policy Task Force of the Centro de Estudios Puertorriqueños (CEP) (Puerto Rican Studies Center), a research institute located at Hunter College of the City University of New York.

Working closely with a group of CEP staff members, which included Torruellas as director of the program, Benmayor, and Juarbe, these welfare recipients were to transform the CEP's literacy program in the next five years into an adult-learners collective that encouraged them to explore the important issues affecting their lives.[70] One of these concerned compliance with the Family Support Act of 1988, requiring women on welfare with children aged one year and older to participate in educational or work programs intended to help them become economically self-sufficient.[71] In compliance with this act, *puertorriqueñas* in the CEP literacy collective were assigned to such menial, low-wage, part-time jobs (for example, cleaning abandoned lots) that they concluded that the government was not interested in bettering their lives but in humiliating them because they were poor working-class mothers. The indignation that explodes in Torruellas, Benmayor, and Juarbe's recounting of these women's "workfare" experiences takes on greater meaning as these women's gender and work expectations are placed in perspective. Because as *puertorriqueñas* they had been socialized into a culture that values motherhood and recognizes family and household responsibilities as work, they had grown up believing that being mothers was their most significant social responsibility as "autonomous adults." Now they argue that, as migrants from a United States territory and thus as American citizens, they are entitled to exercise their "cultural citizenship rights" to motherhood—even if they must depend on public assistance to do so. Unfortunately, welfare claims based on the cultural rights of motherhood have long been under attack by feminist and other critics, who see the origins and evolution of the modern welfare state as a product of "maternalist politics" that failed to address women's independence from state patriarchy and their rights as workers in the twentieth century.[72]

Geraldine J. Casey's essay on *oficinistas* or clerical workers in Puerto Rico returns us again to the world of wage work and to women's constant struggle against negative gender and class images in the workplace.[73] In this article Casey specifically examines how gender and class mediated the lives of women working in offices at the Río Piedras campus of the University of Puerto Rico (UPR) in the early 1990s and how these *oficinistas* responded to the challenges that these issues have posed. As Casey vividly demonstrates, traditional gender assumptions regarding women's performance, attire, and speech still permeate the office environment at UPR. Thus, women workers are perceived as sexy, "fluffy-headed females" who must render personal services to management and dress and speak "appropriately" in the office. This usually means that women are seen as incapable of using the ever-changing computerized technology of clerical work, are often asked to take care of male bosses' personal needs (such as buying gifts for wives), and must wear fashionable clothes and avoid the use of slang in the office. *Oficinistas* themselves perpetuate traditional gender images in their workplaces by celebrating, through parties and gift giving, "women's holidays," especially Mother's Day and St. Valentine's Day, which incidentally were both imported from the United States. Casey found that class was not as significant as gender in relations between workers and management at UPR, but—as part of the working class on the island and more specifically as employees in the public sector—clerical workers are daily being affected by changing work conditions. In recent years, for example, cutbacks in federally funded programs, technological innovations, and "scientific" office management have led to reduced training programs, underemployment, and unemployment.

How have Puerto Rican women clerical workers addressed these problems? The 167 women interviewed by Casey between 1990 and 1992 provided multiple and sometimes opposing responses to this question. While some *oficinistas* have simply accepted existing work and labor market conditions, others—either as individuals or as members of workers' associations—are determined to create a workplace that is more responsive to women's concerns. Many have joined their trade union and other professional organizations. They also have begun to celebrate their art and poetic work or their labor struggles in place of the commemorations of women's traditional roles. To counter the perception that women are incapable of mastering the new technology, and also because they need to maintain a competitive edge in an already flooded labor market, *oficinistas* at UPR attend workshops to update their secretarial and computer skills. Additionally, they have joined groups to learn to cope with stress, improve their self-esteem, and deal with health and safety issues. But because they have not been able to halt deteriorating work conditions or improve their low salaries, employed clerical workers often engage in "moonlighting" activities (selling clothes, jewelry, cosmetics, foods) to supplement their incomes or help support unemployed family members.[74] Casey notes that the problems of underemployment and unemployment have also led to an exodus of women clerical workers to the United States.[75]

Women's Work and Transnational Labor

Puerto Rican Women and Work: Bridges in Transnational Labor traces the changing nature of women's work in the twentieth century as it has responded to the insatiable demands of a major capitalist nation. The first essays in this collection demonstrate that between 1898 and 1940 women workers in Puerto Rico responded by working for American businesses (mainly tobacco and garment), either at home or in factories, under dire work conditions for miserable wages. During this period they also migrated to the U.S. mainland, where their work experiences were not much different. These essays show how *puertorriqueñas* were integrated into a colonial migrant labor force that since the United States occupation of Puerto Rico in 1898 has been shifted from island to mainland to meet the needs of an expanding modern capitalist system. Other essays in the collection focus on the problems of working women in Puerto Rico after 1945 in an effort to appraise the impact on women of Operation Bootstrap, one of Latin America's most aggressive and controversial development programs. The collection thus introduces Puerto Rican women into a scholarly debate that began in 1970 with the publication of Ester Boserup's *Women's Role in Economic Development*—a debate to which many feminists have contributed—regarding the differential effects of twentieth-century industrialization and modernization schemes in less-developed countries.[76] Essays in this collection indicate that women's work experiences under Puerto Rico's economic development program since the 1950s anticipated those of other workers (most of them women) in export-processing zones or in *maquiladora* (assembly) plants in other parts of the world in recent years. In this sense the collection recognizes the preeminence of Puerto Rican women workers as forerunners of today's transnational labor force, considered by many as the basis for the globalization of capitalism in the last three decades.[77]

But, Puerto Rican women's experiences are not only an example of the exploitation of workers by multinational corporations but of the labor migrations that have resulted from this process of exploitation. By focusing on women who are forced to emigrate from a developing nation that has undergone such rapid industrialization, the authors in this collection further the research on the role of women in labor migration movements and their place in expanding capitalist economies since World War II. In the case of Puerto Rican women, this role has been extended to include population-control programs that have resulted in extremely high sterilization rates among *puertorriqueñas* both in Puerto Rico and in the United States, thus putting into question the ethics of using such population control programs to expedite a nation's economic and social development.[78] Moreover, since Puerto Rican migrant women were among the first Latin American women after 1945 to help meet the labor needs of this country's growing economy, and because in many ways their experiences parallel those of other Spanish-speaking Caribbean and Latin American nations, essays in this book may provoke comparative analyses of contemporary Hispanic immigrant workers' lives in North America. Scholars engaged in the study of gender, ethnic, and racial stratification within the American immigrant labor force will also benefit from its probing of discrimination issues among Puerto Rican migrant women.

This collection of essays also seeks to contribute to the growing body of knowledge on Latin American women workers. While many Latin Americanists perceive the Puerto Rican nation, economy, and labor force as extensions of the United States, Puerto Rican women are an integral part of Latin America's labor history and experience. Indeed, before the U.S. occupation of Puerto Rico, *puertorriqueñas* shared in the legacy of exploitation found in the forced-labor systems (*encomienda,* slavery, and peonage) that harnessed women's work in Latin America during the Spanish colonial period. The labor history of Puerto Rican women in the twentieth century also suggests strong parallels with the work experiences of other women throughout Latin America.[79] Some of the essays in this collection show, for example, that Puerto Rican women workers are linked to women in Latin America by common bonds inherent in their household responsibilities, assembly-plant work, labor migrations, and forms of resistance. Throughout Latin America, as in Puerto Rico, the home as the site of unpaid and sometimes wage-labor production is a universal phenomenon. Like Puerto Rican women, workers in many Latin American countries are suffering from the process of integration into the gender segregated, low-wage factory work of multinational corporations. And the migration of women workers is a fact of life that has affected all Latin American societies.[80] We, therefore, hope this collection on Puerto Rican women's work, migration, and labor struggles speaks to the realities of Latin American women workers, and serves as a bridge for understanding transnational labor not only in Latin America but in other parts of the world.

NOTES

1. See, for example, Edna Acosta-Belén, ed., *The Puerto Rican Woman: Perspectives on Culture, History, and Society* (New York: Praeger, 1986); Adalberto López and James Petras, eds., *Puerto Rico and Puerto Ricans: Studies in History and Society* (New York: John Wiley and Sons, 1974).

2. Manuel Maldonado Denis, *Puerto Rico y Estados Unidos: Emigración y colonialismo: Un análisis socio-histórico de la emigración puertorriqueña* (Mexico: Siglo Ventiuno, 1976), 27–46.

3. Citations are from the English-language edition: Manuel Maldonado Denis, *The Emigration Dialectic: Puerto Rico and the U.S.A.* (New York: International Publishers, 1980), 29.

4. Ibid., 43.

5. Exceptions to this are Centro de Estudios Puertorriqueños, History Task Force, ed., *Labor Migration under Capitalism: The Puerto Rican Experience* (New York: Monthly Review Press, 1979); Alba N. Rivera-Ramos, "The Psychological Experience of Puerto Rican Women at Work," in *Hispanics in the Workplace*, ed. Stephen B. Knouse, Paul Rosenfield, and Amy L. Culbertson (Newberry Park, Calif.: Sage Publications, 1992), 194–207; Havidán Rodríguez, "Household Composition, Employment Patterns and Economic Well-Being: Puerto Ricans in the United States and Puerto Rico, 1970–1980" (Ph.D. diss., University of Wisconsin–Madison, 1991).

6. See, for example, Juan S. Marcano, "Páginas rojas: Unidos venceremos," in *Lucha obrera: Antología de grandes documentos en la historia obrera puertorriqueña*, ed. Angel Quintero Rivera (Río Piedras: Centro de Estudios de la Realidad Puertorriqueña, 1971), 66–67; Yamila Azize, *La mujer en la lucha* (Río Piedras: Editorial Cultural, 1985), 40–60; Marcia Rivera, "The Development of Capitalism in Puerto Rico and the Incorporation of Women into the Labor Force," in Acosta-Belén, *The Puerto Rican Woman*, 30–45.

7. Luis Díaz Soler, *Historia de la esclavitud negra en Puerto Rico* (1953; Río Piedras: Editorial Universitaria, 1970), 155; Guillermo Baralt et al., *El machete de ogún: Las luchas de esclavos (Siglo 19)* (Río Piedras: Centro de Estudios de la Realidad Puertorriqueña, 1989), 25; James Dietz, *Historia económica de Puerto Rico* (Río Piedras: Editorial Huracán, 1989), 39.

8. Dietz, *Historia económica de Puerto Rico*, 52; Baralt et al., *El machete de ogún*, 108.

9. Rivera, "The Development of Capitalism in Puerto Rico," 35. See also Olga Jiménez de Wagenheim, "Mujer y sociedad en el Puerto Rico del siglo XIX," *Boletín del Centro de Estudios Puertorriqueños* 2, no.7 (Winter 1989–90): 13.

10. Rivera, "The Development of Capitalism in Puerto Rico," 35.

11. The absence of needleworkers in this count obviously refers to the fact that the census did not take into consideration home workers; thus, as in other historical periods and societies, women involved in informal economic activities were excluded from census records.

12. Rivera, "The Development of Capitalism in Puerto Rico," 35.

13. Victor S. Clark et al., *Porto Rico and Its Problems* (Washington, D.C.: Brookings Institution, 1930; New York: Arno Press, 1975), 13–14.

14. For profiles of women tobacco workers, see Fernando Picó, "Las trabajadoras del tabaco en Utuado, Puerto Rico, según el censo de 1910," *Hómines* 10, no. 2 (1986–87): 173–86; María del Carmen Baerga, "Las jerarquías sociales y las expresiones de resistencia: Género, clase y edad en la industria de la aguja en Puerto Rico," in *Género y trabajo:*

La industria de la aguja en Puerto Rico y el caribe hispánico, ed. María del Carmen Baerga (San Juan: Editorial Universidad de Puerto Rico, 1993), 9. For descriptions of tobacco workers' struggles, see Azize, *La mujer en la lucha,* 50, 70; and Amilcar Tirado Avilés, "Notas sobre el desarrollo de la industria del tabaco en Puerto Rico y su impacto en la mujer puertorriqueña, 1898–1920," *Centro de Estudios Puertorriqueños Bulletin* 2, no. 7 (Winter 1989–90): 23–27.

15. For examples of Capetillo's radical feminist ideology, see Luisa Capetillo, *Ensayos libertarios: Dedicado a los trabajadores de ambos sexos* (Arecibo, P.R.: Imprenta Unión Obrera, 1904–7); Luisa Capetillo, *Influencias de las ideas modernas: Notas y apuntes: Escenas de la vida* (San Juan: Tipografía Negrón Flores, 1916); Luisa Capetillo, *La humanidad en el futuro* (San Juan: Tipografía Real Hermanos, 1910); Luisa Capetillo, *Mi opinión sobre las libertades, derechos y deberes de la mujer: Como compañera, madre y ser independiente (La mujer en el hogar, en la familia, en el gobierno)* (San Juan: Times Publishing, 1911).

16. Norma Valle, *Luisa Capetillo: Historia de una mujer proscrita* (Río Piedras: Editorial Cultural, 1990), 59–133.

17. Note that this militancy did not help preserve the industry in Puerto Rico because by the late 1920s the tobacco industry began to experience a decline from which it never recovered. See Clark, *Porto Rico and Its Problems,* 456; James L. Dietz, *Economic History of Puerto Rico: Institutional Change and Capitalist Development* (Princeton, N.J.: Princeton University Press, 1986), 116–17.

18. Blanca G. Silvestrini, "La mujer puertorriqueña en el movimiento obrero en la década de 1930," in *La mujer en la sociedad puertorriqueña,* ed. Edna Acosta-Belén (Río Piedras: Ediciones Huracán, 1980), 83–86. See also Blanca G. Silvestrini, "Women as Workers: The Experience of the Puerto Rican Woman in the 1930s," in Acosta-Belén, *The Puerto Rican Woman,* 66–71.

19. Lydia Milagros González, *Una puntada en el tiempo: La industria de la aguja en Puerto Rico (1900–1929)* (Santo Domingo, D.R.: Editora Taller, 1990), 4–6, 18, 64, 72, 76–77; María del Carmen Baerga, "La articulación del trabajo asalariado: Hacia una reevaluación de la contribución femenina a la sociedad puertorriqueña (El caso de la industria de la aguja)" in *La mujer en Puerto Rico: Ensayos de investigación,* ed. Yamila Azize Vargas (Río Piedras: Ediciones Huracán, 1987), 97; Luisa Hernández Angueira, "El trabajo femenino de la aguja en Puerto Rico, 1914–1940," in Baerga, *Género y trabajo,* 86–87.

20. González, *Una puntada en el tiempo,* 11–12, 18–19, 35.

21. In some cases, public as well as religious schools and orphanages became a source of child labor, as teachers and school administrators forced young girls to churn out needlework pieces for local intermediaries. Ibid., 14, 20–21, 34–35, 69–70.

22. Ibid., 5, 68.

23. Lydia Milagros González, "La industria de la aguja en Puerto Rico y sus orígenes en los Estados Unidos," in Baerga, *Género y trabajo,* 60–77.

24. Caroline Manning, "The Employment of Women in Puerto Rico," United States Department of Labor, Women's Bureau, *Bulletin of the Women's Bureau* 118 (Washington, D.C., Government Printing Office, 1934), 11–13.

25. A slightly different version of this essay appears in Eileen Boris, *Home to Work: Motherhood and the Politics of Industrial Homework in the United States* (New York: Cambridge University Press, 1994), 231–39.

26. For a detailed discussion of the application of the NRA to the mainland needlework trades see, ibid., 210–24.

27. A 1984 study of the Needle Trades Association indicated that homework still existed in Puerto Rico in the form of *marquesina* (carport) operations. Alice Colón, "La participación laboral de las mujeres en Puerto Rico: Empleo o sub-utilización," *Pensamiento crítico* 8, no.44 (May–June 1985): 87.

28. Lawrence R. Chenault, *The Puerto Rican Migrant in New York City* (New York: Columbia University, 1938; New York: Russell and Russell, 1970), 76.

29. Elizabeth Ewen, *Immigrant Women in the Land of Dollars: Life and Culture on the Lower East Side, 1890–1925* (New York: Monthly Review Press, 1985), 243–52. See also Alice Kessler-Harris, *Women Have Always Worked: A Historical Overview* (New York: Feminist Press, 1980), 76–77; Alice Kessler-Harris, *Out to Work: A History of Wage-Earning Women in the United States* (New York: Oxford University Press, 1982), 127, 138; Miriam Cohen, *Workshop to Office: Two Generations of Italian Women in New York City, 1900–1950* (Ithaca: Cornell University Press, 1992), 78–82, 147–54.

30. Roy B. Helfgott, "Puerto Rican Integration in the Skirt Industry in New York City," in *Discrimination and Low Incomes: Social and Economic Discrimination against Minority Groups in Relation to Low Incomes in New York State*, ed. New York State Commission against Discrimination (New York: New School for Social Research, 1959), 255–56; Roy B. Helfgott, "Women's and Children's Apparel," in *Made in New York: Case Studies in Metropolitan Manufacturing*, ed. Max Hall (Cambridge, Mass.: Harvard University Press, 1959), 21–134.

31. For an account of Jewish politics in the garment industry, see Robert L. Laurentz, "Racial/Ethnic Conflict in the New York City Garment Industry, 1933–1980" (Ph.D. diss., State University of New York at Binghamton, 1980), passim. See also Robert Asher, "Jewish Unions and the American Federation of Labor Power Structure, 1903–1935," *American Jewish Historical Quarterly* 40, no. 3 (March 1976): 215–27.

32. For an excellent analysis of the market and structural problems in the garment industry after World War II, see Laurentz, "Racial/Ethnic Conflict in the New York City Garment Industry," 181–334.

33. Centro de Estudios Puertorriqueños (CEP), Oral History Task Force Project, interview with Gregoria Lausell by Suzana García and Ana Juarbe, New York City, April 2, 1984; CEP, interviews with Margarita Sánchez by Blanca Vázquez, New York City, January 18, 1984, and February 3, 1984; Chenault, *The Puerto Rican Migrant*, 62, 70, 73, 75; Virginia Sánchez Korrol, "On the Other Side of the Ocean: The Work Experiences of Early Puerto Rican Migrant Women," *Caribbean Review* 8, no. 1 (March 1979): 26–27.

34. Columbia University, Oral History Project, interviews with Pura Belpré by Lillian López, New York City, April 4, 1976; Lillian López and Pura Belpré, "Reminiscences of Two Turned-On Librarians," in *Puerto Rican Perspectives*, ed. Edward Mapp (Metuchen, N.J.: Scarecrow Press, 1974), 83–96.

35. Ruth Glasser, " 'Que Vivio Tiene la Gente Aquí en Nueva York': Music and Community in Puerto Rican New York, 1915–1940" (Ph.D. diss., Yale University, 1991), 37–38, 177–82, 302–10, 332–38; Virginia Sánchez Korrol, "The Forgotten Migrant: Educated Puerto Rican Women in New York City, 1920–1940," in Acosta-Belén, *The Puerto Rican Woman*, 171–73.

36. Federico Ribes Tovar, *La mujer puertorriqueña: Su vida y evolución a través de la historia* (New York: Plus Ultra, 1972), 231–33; Virginia Sánchez Korrol, "In Search of Unconventional Women in Religious Vocations before Mid-Century," *Oral History Review* 16, no.2 (Fall 1988): 50–55.

37. For more information on early Puerto Rican migrant women, see Altagracia Ortiz, "The Lives of *Pioneras:* Bibliographic and Research Sources on Puerto Rican Women in the United States," *Boletín del Centro de Estudios puertorriqueños* 2, no.2 (Winter 1989–90): 41–47.

38. López and Petras, *Puerto Rico and Puerto Ricans,* 318–22; Centro de Estudios Puertorriqueños, *Labor Migration under Capitalism,* 150–51.

39. López and Petras, *Puerto Rico and Puerto Ricans,* 318–19.

40. Committee on Puerto Ricans in New York City of the Welfare Council of New York City, *Report of the Committee on Puerto Ricans in New York City* (New York: Welfare Council, 1948), 6.

41. Hunter College Women's Studies Collective, *Women's Realities, Women's Choices: An Introduction to Women's Studies* (New York: Oxford University Press, 1983), 412–19.

42. Juan José Osuna, *A History of Education in Puerto Rico* (Río Piedras: Editorial de la Universidad de Puerto Rico, 1949), 43, 88; Marcia Rivera, "El proceso educativo en Puerto Rico y la reproducción de la subordinación femenina," in Azize, *La mujer en Puerto Rico,* 121.

43. Azize, *La mujer en la lucha,* 44.

44. Rivera, "El proceso educativo en Puerto Rico," 117–18, 132; Azize, *La mujer en la lucha,* 46.

45. Luz del Alba Acevedo, "Industrialization and Employment: Changes in the Patterns of Women's Work in Puerto Rico," *World Development* 18, no. 2 (1990): 242–43.

46. There are few works on Puerto Rican women teachers in the United States, but two interesting unpublished studies have discovered a high degree of job satisfaction among Puerto Rican women. See Patricia Cintrón de Crespo, "Puerto Rican Women Teachers in New York: Self-Perception and Work Adjustment as Perceived by Themselves and by Others" (Ph.D. diss., Columbia University, 1965); and Elizabeth Iglesias, "Human Islands of Success: Professional Puerto Rican Women in Higher Education" (Ph.D. diss., Pennsylvania State University, 1988).

47. Rosemary Santana Cooney, "Intercity Variations in Puerto Rican Female Participation," *Journal of Human Resources* 14, no. 2 (Spring 1979): 222–35.

48. Ibid., 231.

49. Rosemary Santana Cooney and Alice E. Colón-Warren, "Declining Female Participation among Puerto Rican New Yorkers: A Comparison with Native White Nonspanish New Yorkers," *Ethnicity* 6, no. 3 (1979): 281–97; Rosemary Santana Cooney and Kyonghee Min, "Demographic Characteristics Affecting Living Arrangements among Young Currently Unmarried Puerto Rican, Non-Spanish Black, and Non-Spanish White Mothers," *Ethnicity* 8, no. 2 (1981): 107–20; Rosemary Santana Cooney and Vilma Ortiz, "Nativity, National Origin, and Hispanic Female Participation in the Labor Force," *Social Science Quarterly* 64, no. 3 (September 1983): 510–23.

50. In addition to the above reference see Rosemary S. Cooney and Alice Colón, "Work and Family: The Recent Struggles of Puerto Rican Females," in *The Puerto Rican Struggle: Essays on Survival in the U.S.,* ed. Clara Rodríguez, Virginia Sánchez Korrol, and José Oscar Alers (New York: Puerto Rican Migration Research Consortium, 1980), 58–73.

51. Isabel Picó Vidal, "La mujer puertorriqueña y la recesión económica," *Avance* 2, no. 145 (May 1–15, 1975): 5–8; Alice Colón, "La participactión laboral de las mujeres en Puerto Rico," 28; Acevedo, "Industrialization and Employment," 250; Rodríguez, "Household Composition, Employment Patterns and Economic Well-Being," 280.

52. Increases in women's labor force participation after 1950 must be qualified by the fact that in 1940 Puerto Rican women's labor force participation rate was higher (24.9 percent) than in 1960 (20 percent). For an analysis of this phenomenon and for comparative labor force participation rates between 1940 and 1980, see Palmira N. Ríos-González, "Work and Industrialization in Puerto Rico: Gender Division of Labor and the Demand for Female Labor in the Manufacturing Sector, 1950–1980" (Ph.D. diss., Yale University, 1990), 117–23.

53. For an excellent account of the integration of women into these industries, see Luz del Alba Acevedo, "Género, trabajo asalariado y desarrollo industrial en Puerto Rico: La división sexual del trabajo en la manufactura," in Baerga, *Género y trabajo*, 161–212. See also Palmira Ríos, "Export-Oriented Industrialization and the Demand for Female Labor: Puerto Rican Women in the Manufacturing Sector, 1952–1980," in *Colonial Dilemma: Critical Perspectives on Contemporary Puerto Rico*, ed. Edwin Meléndez and Edgardo Meléndez (Boston: South End Press, 1993), 89–101.

54. This period has been classified by some scholars as *Fomento*'s second stage. Acevedo dates it between 1963 and 1982 and Ríos places it between 1963 and 1977. Acevedo, "Industrialization and Employment," 238; Ríos, "Work and Industrialization in Puerto Rico," 208.

55. Helen Icken Safa, "Female Employment and the Social Reproduction of the Puerto Rican Working Class," in Acosta-Belén, *The Puerto Rican Woman*, 90.

56. Safa, "Female Employment," 91–92.

57. In addition to the works of Acevedo and Ríos, see Isabel Picó de Hernández, "Estudio sobre el empleo de la mujer en Puerto Rico," *Revista de ciencias sociales* 19, no. 2 (June 1975): 141–64; Helen Icken Safa, "Class Consciousness among Working-Class Women in Latin America: Puerto Rico," in *Sex and Class in Latin America: Women's Perspectives on Politics, Economics, and the Family in the Third World*, ed. June Nash and Helen Icken Safa (South Hadley, Mass.: Bergin Publishers, 1980), 69–85. For a general treatment of the impact of economic development in Puerto Rico, see Emilio Pantojas-García, *Development Strategies as Ideology: Puerto Rico's Export-Led Industrialization Experience* (Boulder, Colo.: Lynne Rienner Publishers, 1990).

58. Safa, "Female Employment," 94–98.

59. Helen Icken Safa, *The Myth of the Male Breadwinner: Women and Industrialization in the Caribbean* (Boulder, Colo.: Westview Press, 1995), 95.

60. For more information on the relationship between Mayagüez garment workers and the ILGWU, see Safa, *Myth of the Male Breadwinner*, 73–78, 95.

61. In her updated study of this community of workers (1986), Safa notes that younger married women workers have continued to demand greater participation in decision making, especially in financial matters, but she warns that "this shift in authority patterns" may not only be due to women's paid employment. Other factors that she believes need to be taken into consideration in analyses of changing gender roles in Puerto Rico include: the presence of return migrants; Puerto Rico's transformation into a more urban society; high

levels of male unemployment, which have "weakened the economic role of the man but strengthened the importance of women as key contributors to the household economy"; and women's increased use of federal transfer payments (e.g., Social Security, food stamps), which also have lessened their economic dependence on men. Safa, *The Myth of the Male Breadwinner*, 87–88, 96.

62. Neftalí García Martínez, "El estado, el pueblo y las emisiones de gases en Mayagüez: Ciencia y política en la lucha ambiental," *Pensamiento crítico* 8, no. 42 (January–February 1985): 18.

63. Neftalí García Martínez has also recorded other symptoms: eye, nose, and throat irritations; numbness of face, mouth, and limbs; skin irritations, depression, and fatigue. Ibid., 20–21.

64. Neftalí García Martínez, "El colonialismo, los recursos naturales y el ambiente," *Pensamiento crítico* 9, no. 51 (September–December 1986): 16–20.

65. Among the companies suspected of contaminating the Guanajibo-Castillo area were: Transworld Industries, a plastic-tubing manufacturer; Bristol Laboratories, one of the most important manufacturers of pharmaceuticals on the island; and Electronic Aids. Marya Muñoz-Vázquez, "La salud ocupacional y ambiental: Reto organizativo para el femenismo," *Pensamiento crítico* 11, no. 58 (March–April 1988), 6.

66. Linda Chávez, *Out of the Barrio: Toward a New Politics of Hispanic Assimilation* (New York: Basic Books, 1991), 145, 159.

67. Ibid., 142, 144–45.

68. Diana Pearce asserts that 90 percent of mothers on welfare have worked before applying for public assistance. Diana Pearce, "Welfare is Not for Women: Why the War on Poverty Cannot Conquer the Feminization of Poverty," in *Women, the State, and Welfare*, ed. Linda Gordon (Madison: University of Wisconsin Press), 271.

69. This is also true for other women on welfare. See ibid., 271.

70. For a complete description of the literacy program, see Rosa Torruellas et al., "Affirming Cultural Citizenship in the Puerto Rican Community: Critical Literacy and the El Barrio Popular Education Program," in *Literacy as Praxis: Culture, Language and Pedagogy*, ed. Catherine E. Walsh (Norwood, N.J.: Ablex, 1991), 183–219.

71. On the history of work incentives and welfare, see Mimi Abramovitz, *Regulating the Lives of Women: Social Welfare Policy from Colonial Times to the Present* (Boston: South End Press, 1989), 332–63. For specific information on the struggles of Puerto Rican women welfare recipients to obtain a college education while on welfare, see Doris Correa Capello, "Stress and Coping Strategies of Puerto Rican Single Mothers" (Ph.D. diss., Fordham University, 1986).

72. For essays critical of "maternalist politics" at the begining of the twentieth century, see Seth Koven and Sonya Michel, *Mothers of a New World: Maternalist Politics and the Origins of Welfare States* (New York: Routledge, 1993).

73. An excellent sociodemographic profile of contemporary women in the service economy and the occupational segregation they experience there may be found in: Luz del Alba Acevedo, "El desarrollo capitalista y la nueva división del trabajo por género: La terciarización del empleo de la mujer en Puerto Rico" (Department of Sociology, Universidad de Puerto Rico, Río Piedras, 1995).

74. For further information on women and the informal economy in Puerto Rico, see

Janice Petrovich and Sandra Laureano, "Towards an Analysis of Puerto Rican Women and the Informal Economy," *Hómines* 10, no.2 (1986–87): 70–80.

75. In the United States, several scholars have observed the increasing labor force participation rate of Puerto Rican women in clerical or white-collar jobs; yet, to date there is no in-depth study of their history or work experiences in this important occupational sector. For brief references to Puerto Rican women clerical workers in the States, see Nathan Glazer and Daniel P. Moynihan, *Beyond the Melting Pot: The Negroes, Puerto Ricans, Jews, Italians and Irish of New York City* (Cambridge, Mass.: MIT Press and Harvard University, 1963), 115–16; Teresa L. Amott and Julie E. Matthaei, *Race, Gender, and Work: A Multicultural Economic History of Women in the United States* (Boston: South End Press, 1991), 276; Christine E. Bose, "Puerto Rican Women in the United States: An Overview," in Acosta-Belén *The Puerto Rican Woman*, 152–53; and María do Carnio Fonseca do Vale, "Labor Force Status of Puerto Rican Women in the New York Labor Market, 1985" (Ph.D. diss., Fordham University, 1990), 121.

76. Ester Boserup, *Women's Role in Economic Development* (New York: St. Martin's Press, 1970); Lourdes Benería and Gita Sen, "Women's Role in Economic Development: Practical and Theoretical Implications of Class and Gender Inequalities," in *Class, Race, and Sex: The Dynamics of Control*, ed. Amy Swerdlow and Hanna Lessinger (Boston: G. K. Hall, 1983), 242–59; Carmen Diana Deere and Magdalena León de Leal, "Peasant Production, Proletarianization, and the Sexual Division of Labor in the Andes," *Signs: Journal of Women in Culture and Society* 7, no. 2 (1981): 338–60; Carmen Diana Deere, Jane Humphries, and Magdalena León de Leal, "Class and Historical Analysis for the Study of Women and Economic Change," in *Women's Roles and Population Trends in the Third World*, ed. Richard Anker et al. (London: Croom Helm, 1982), 87–114; María Patricia Fernández-Kelly, "Development and the Sexual Division of Labor: An Introduction," *Signs: Journal of Women in Culture and Society* 7, no. 2 (1981): 268–78; June Nash and María Patricia Fernández-Kelly, eds., *Women, Men, and the International Division of Labor* (Albany: State University of New York Press, 1983); June Nash and Helen Safa, ed., *Women and Social Change in Latin America* (South Hadley, Mass.: Bergin and Garvey, 1986); and Susan Tiano, "Gender, Work and World Capitalism: Third World Women's Role in Development," *Analyzing Gender: A Handbook of Social Science*, ed. Bess Hess and Myra Marx Ferree (Beverly Hill: Sage Publications, 1987), 216–43; Edna Acosta-Belén and Christine E. Bose, "Women in the Development Process in Latin America and the Caribbean," in *Researching Women in Latin America and the Caribbean*, ed. Edna Acosta-Belén and Christine E. Bose (Boulder, Colo.: Westview Press, 1993), 55–76; Edna Acosta-Belén and Christine E. Bose, *Women in the Development Process in Latin America and the Caribbean* (Philadelphia: Temple University Press, forthcoming).

77. For a comparison of Puerto Rican and Dominican women's experiences in the new international division of labor, see Helen I. Safa, "Women and Industrialization in the Caribbean," *Women, Employment and the Family in the International Division of Labor*, ed. Sharon Stichter and Jane Parpart (New York: Macmillan, 1990), 72–97.

78. Annette Ramírez de Arellano and Conrad Scheipp, *Colonialism, Catholicism and Birth Control in Puerto Rico: The History of Sterilization in Puerto Rico* (Chapel Hill: University of North Carolina Press, 1983); Iris Ofelia López, "Sterilization among Puerto Rican Women: A Case Study in New York" (Ph.D. diss., Columbia University, 1985). See also Iris López, "Social Coercion and Sterilization among Puerto Rican Women," *Sage Race Relations Abstracts* 8, no. 3 (August 1983): 27–40; Iris López, "Sterilization among Puerto Rican

Women in New York City: Public Policy and Social Constraints," in *Cities of the United States: Studies in Urban Anthropology,* ed. Leith Mullings (New York: Columbia University Press, 1987), 269–90.

79. For a general discussion of these connections, see Edna Acosta-Belén and Christine E. Bose, "From Structural Subordination: Women and Development in Third World Contexts," *Gender and Society* 4, no. 3 (September 1990): 299–319.

80. Elsa M. Chaney, "Research on Migration and Women in Latin America and the Caribbean," in Acosta-Belén and Bose, *Researching Women in Latin America and the Caribbean,* 99–134.

ONE

Needlewomen under the New Deal in Puerto Rico, 1920–1945

EILEEN BORIS

uring the month of October 1935 Hijinia Cruz machine-sewed cotton underwear, as she had from the time of her first pregnancy five years earlier. She earned what amounted to fifty cents for thirty hours of work spread over a six-day week, or about one and a half cents an hour. Cruz resided in an extended household—with her twenty-four-year-old unemployed husband, three small children, widowed mother, and divorced brother—in Peñuelas, a *barriada* (neighborhood) of Ponce, in the southern part of Puerto Rico. She typifies one major group of Puerto Rican needleworkers—mothers of small children—whose homework proved a necessary, though hardly sufficient, part of the family economy. While her mother owned their three-room house and its lot, the family still had to travel a quarter of a kilometer for water and depend upon kerosene for lighting. Her wage augmented the $1.50 a week her brother earned as a street vendor. The family also relied upon their two pigs, cow, and four chickens, which probably supplied them with meat, milk, and eggs to trade than with food to eat. Sometimes she had to walk three kilometers to the home of the needlework subcontractor to receive additional work. Hijinia Cruz thought that needlework prices were "lower than ever" following the suspension of the New Deal's industrial codes under the National Recovery

Portions of this chapter appear in Eileen Boris, *Home to Work: Motherhood and the Politics of Industrial Homework in the United States* (New York: Cambridge University Press, 1994). Copyright 1994 Cambridge University Press. Reprinted with the permission of Cambridge University Press.

Administration (NRA). Like other needleworkers, she believed that homework should be regulated rather than transferred to the factory. "Every worker should be given a fixed quantity weekly for a fixed salary," she told a Spanish-speaking federal investigator.

Sara Agraciani earned sixty cents for her thirty-six-hour, six-day-week, working for the same subcontractor. But while Hijinia Cruz received five cents for a dozen garments, Agraciani earned a rate of twenty cents a dozen. She had to machine-sew, finish by hand, and embroider each piece of cotton underwear. She paid her sixteen-year-old sister sixteen cents a week to help her with the embroidering. As a daughter, rather than a mother, Agraciani represents the other major group of women needle-workers in Puerto Rico at this time. She lived with her fifty-six-year-old father, who earned a dollar a week working on a farm; her fifty-year-old mother; her thirty-six year-old widowed aunt; and her four siblings. Six members of this family read Spanish and three read and spoke English.

Sara Agraciani had to walk five kilometers to reach the Peñuelas home of Casilda Santiago, the thirty-six-year-old married mother of four who served as a subcontractor for R. M. Fernández Suez, a leading needlework contractor in Ponce. Santiago's husband earned six dollars a week as a chauffeur, and she earned one dollar for parceling out cotton underwear to five homeworkers. Generally, she received three times per dozen as much as the homeworkers. For each dozen pieces of needlework she distributed she would pay five cents for machine-sewing, ten cents for embroidery, and twenty cents for all other operations. Like her homework-ers Sara Agraciani and Hijinia Cruz, Santiago owned a sewing machine. Living in her own five-room house that was equipped with electric light and water, the owner of two horses, one automobile, and a radio, Santiago "works very little because she has to take care of the household," reported an interviewer. A subcontractor for a decade, she had witnessed the Great Depression's impact on prices in Puerto Rico, relieved by the NRA codes, which had regulated production, prices, wages, hours, and other conditions for only a short time. For the present, Santiago believed that "prices are so low that there is no margin for a living income no matter what size order you take." She paid her workers a consistent price, depending on how many operations they performed; but while the contractor, Fernández, gave out his work for a rate of sixty cents per dozen to his other subcontractors, Santiago, who had to travel thirty-two kilometers to pick up her work, earned considerably less for her efforts.[1]

These women were among the seventy thousand needleworkers who embroidered, sewed, and finished women's garments in Puerto Rico or served as subcontractors, distributing work to other women, during the early 1930s. Most of these workers lived in cramped and drafty shacks in outlying mountain regions, on sugar and tobacco haciendas, and along the swampy outskirts of towns. Receiving their bundles of work from subcontractors known on the island as *comisionistas,* homeworking needle women labored for piece rates equivalent to one or two cents an hour in order to eke out a cash income in an economy that offered them few other opportunities. In the 1930s they became the focus of concern of trade unionists, New Dealers, and women social reformers, who saw them "paying the price for the rest of the world that insists on finding exquisite hand work on the bargain tables."[2] Both to protect mainland jobs and to alleviate economic exploitation, these groups desired to put an end to the homework system and to substitute local workshop centers in the rural regions for this industry. But home needlework was central to the Puerto Rican economy of the 1930s and could not be prohibited without causing severe dislocations.[3]

At this time in Puerto Rico, homework signified not only the gendered division of industry but of social roles as well. Less than 40 percent of the homeworkers were mothers, and single daughters composed about the same percentage. Most subcontractors also were women. The division of labor within households facilitated women's availability for homework. As one observer explained, "During the day the mother will take care of the home—cooking, cleaning, and taking care of the smaller children, while the daughters between 12 and 16 years of age will sew on the garments." The presence of grandmothers or older female relatives in many families also freed the mother to sew. Yet homework existed in Puerto Rico not so much because women preferred such labor but because they had no other choice: employers had organized needlework on the island in that manner. Contributing to this organization was Puerto Rico's economic underdevelopment, especially its lack of roads, which made rural workers inaccessible, and the absence of alternative employment for women. The colonial status of the island also made it possible for U.S. firms to exploit these factors.[4]

This chapter examines the political and ideological battle over the labor of Puerto Rican women needleworkers under the New Deal. It presents these women as active agents in the construction of their lives and not as passive objects of government investigators. From the vantage point of Puerto Rican needlewomen, homework was a necessary, albeit exploitative, means of making an economic contribution to the family. Their desire to change the system rather than abolish it put some of them in opposition to island trade unionists who accepted mainland labor's call for prohibition of homework. This challenge to the right of *puertorriqueñas* to do homework in the context of their social role as homemakers reveals the construction of gender identities among women needleworkers in the 1930s under Puerto Rico's colonial economy.

Toward a Gendered Political Economy

The United States occupation of Puerto Rico in 1898 diverted whatever tendency had existed on the island toward nationalist capitalist development in the waning years of Spanish rule. A monocultural export economy, with sugar as the major crop, emerged under U.S. domination.[5] So did the absorption of peasant plots into large landholdings, a marked rise in absentee ownership, and the draining of profits from the island to the mainland. Export production of sugar, and to a lesser extent coffee and tobacco, removed land from the production of food so that by the early 1930s over 80 percent of food was imported. In addition, by 1930 basic necessities cost 8 to 14 percent more in Puerto Rico than in New York City, where wages were four to ten times higher. As families became increasingly dependent on wage labor, and as male employment suffered from the seasonal nature of sugar production while coffee and tobacco cultivation continued to decline, more women became incorporated into the paid labor force. And, as is typical of many Western economies, they entered a gender-segmented labor market, with needlework as its cornerstone.[6]

The origins of the needlework trade in Puerto Rico lay in the commercial crisis brought on by World War I, which forced a halt in the export of finely sewn and embroidered garments and linen from Europe. After the war, immigration restrictions compelled American manufacturers to seek alternative sources of skilled, low-wage labor, which they found in the colonies of the Philippines and Puerto Rico. Since the days of Spanish rule, Puerto Rican women—including those of the urban, more prosperous classes—had learned fine lace and drawn work, in conformity with the traditional European ideology that regarded needlework as an appropriate economic activity for women to undertake within the shelter of their homes.[7] Most girls and young women learned to do needlework from older female relatives, but others were trained in Catholic convents or public schools. Beginning in 1909, Puerto Rico's Department of Public Instruction organized classes in crochet, embroidery, and sewing in some of the island's school districts.[8] In 1918, the public schools in Mayagüez adopted a needlework curriculum for all of its schools. But one Chicago department store owner, anxious to increase the import of needlework to the United States, felt that not enough workers could be trained to produce fine work in the quantities and at the low prices needed for the mass market. He therefore relied upon hastily trained workers to produce large quantities of "stamped designs [of] wreaths and sprays of leaves, petals, and flowers." Thus, Puerto Rican women's traditional needlework came to be defined by these conventional designs, many of which were geared to the developing chain-store trade of the 1920s. Most manufacturers, using these designs, contracted Puerto Rican women to embroider women's and children's apparel, handkerchiefs, towels, and household linens.[9]

United States firms supplied garments, usually precut with designs already stamped onto them, to contractors to distribute to home sewers and embroiderers. Some contractors ran workshops as well. A few mainland firms set up operations in Puerto Rico, while some sent a representative to the island with cut garments, to act as a contractor until he retrieved finished goods from homeworkers. Mayagüez, with its thirty or forty contractors of "recognized standing," became the center of the industry, with Ponce and San Juan as the other distributional points. Because many of the homeworkers lived in isolated rural regions, the contractor would often hire subcontractors to distribute the piecework and collect the finished garments. Work was irregular and contractors preferred spreading it out in small batches. NRA investigators understood that "the industry in Puerto Rico dealt only in labor—it never owned the goods received and had no problem of selling the finished article." Moreover, as Caroline Manning discovered in her 1934 study for the Women's Bureau of the U.S. Department of Labor, "there was no standard agreement that controlled the agents' business arrangements with the home workers. Whatever they could make for themselves they did." With contractors and their agents keeping from 12.5 percent to 33.5 percent of the price given by the mainland firm, homeworkers could receive as little as 55 percent of the price per dozen. At an extreme, agents withheld pay or reimbursed laborers with food or other goods, sometimes even forcing homeworkers to buy items at a "company store."[10]

The organization of the needlework industry thus reflected the dependent status of Puerto Rico, its place as a nascent "off-shore" production facility for the mainland industry, and its position as a cheap colonial labor market for U.S. manufacturers. The nature of needlework production in Puerto Rico further developed out of the struggle between workers and employers in the context of growing socialist and feminist movements. During the first decades of the century, working-class women fought for universal suffrage, conducted strikes, and actively debated class concerns. The bourgeois suffragists of the Liga Feminea de Puerto Rico lobbied for restricted suffrage in part to keep the vote away from those, like many needlewomen, who were poor and potential Socialist Party supporters. The Socialist Party counteracted by founding the Popular Feminist Association in 1920. Meanwhile, although labor and reform supporters gained a minimum-wage law in 1919, this was a hollow victory for needleworkers for the law excluded tobacco strippers and homeworkers, the most oppressed of all women workers on the island. About 75 percent of needlework employers responded by closing factories and parceling out the work to homeworkers. Early struggles against economic exploitation increased the amount of homework as employers attempted to circumvent workers' demands.[11]

With the coming of the Great Depression, needlework prices in Puerto Rico declined further since manufacturers could get work produced on the mainland for two cents an hour and also avoid extra freight charges, delays, and the cumbersome contractor system on the island. The Puerto Rican Socialist Party, part of a coalition government with the Union Republicans, the employers' party, introduced legislation to regulate home needlework in 1933. But it backed down when its coalition partner objected that regulation would lead to greater unemployment and hurt families dependent on the labor of homeworking women.[12] Though the state failed to aid them, Puerto Rican needlewomen protested Depression-era cuts in pay. In August 1933 the needlewomen of Mayagüez, both home and factory workers, struck. "[The workers] have not accepted the wages paid by those that have become rich at the expense of the unfortunate proletariat who spent his life working day and night . . . to earn two dollars a week," the socialist paper, *Unión Obrera*, reported.[13] Police, called to protect employer property, ended up killing and wounding strikers who had stoned the workshop of Representative María Luisa Arcelay, the only female member of the Puerto Rican legislature and a contractor who would represent Puerto Rican business interests at the NRA code hearings the following year. Union organization mushroomed in reaction, with more than three-quarters of the factory and shop workers organized in 1933, and about three thousand home-workers creating nine unions of their own within a year. Workers received an increase of 15 to 25 percent when the Commissioner of Labor, a member of the rightward-drifting Socialist Party, mediated the strike. However, most agents broke the agreement, keeping the raise for themselves and never informing the homeworkers of the increase.[14]

A Collective Portrait of the Needlewomen

Such militancy becomes even more impressive when we know something of the personal lives of the needleworkers who were part of federal and private surveys taken in the winter of 1933–1934 and the early fall of 1935.[15] All of these surveys relied upon native Puerto Rican interviewers, who recorded workers' voices along with the demographic facts of their lives. Because of the incomplete figures in some categories, a quantitative analysis of the existing schedules cannot provide reliable statistics. But because the words of the homeworkers closely match the experiences measured by statistics, we can hear the voices of these workers and not just see their numerical representation.

As Table 1–1 demonstrates, homeworking families were only slightly larger than the average family of 5.6 persons. A little over 40 percent had children under sixteen; Manning, too, found 57 percent of the women in her study had children under seven. Nearly 80 percent of the home-workers were married, even though Manning had found 40 percent of the homeworkers to be daughters still living with their parents. Yet it was a rare homeworker who claimed, as did one mother of five, to have devoted "only 4 or 5 hours to needlework as she has to take care of her children and husband."[16] For these families, average weekly income was low, with males engaged in agriculture earning $3.60 a week, when employed, and needleworkers about $1.28. But about a third of families with more than one needleworker could earn $2.00 or more a week; most earned about the same as single homeworkers. Until the latter part

Table 1–1. *Characteristics of Homeworkers and Their Households*

	NRA Survey Oct. 1935	Ortiz-Hayes Survey March 1934
Avg. no. of persons in family	5.81	5.73
Family members under 16 years	2.3	2.4
Civil status		
married	na	79.9%
single	na	13.4%
widowed	na	5.9%
Avg. income per family per week		
Needlework	$1.28	$1.28
Other	3.09	3.60
Relief	.05	na
Total	4.38	4.16
Amt. spent weekly for food	na	$3.90
Households with gardens		
and animals	29%	67.8%
animals only	na	27%
Housing		
own	57%	59.3%
rent	28.9%	19.4%
pay no rent	12.5%	19.4%

Source: "Test Survey of Homeworkers in Needlework Industry," Box 63, RG 9, National Archives; "Ortiz-Hayes Survey of Homeworkers in Needlework Industry," San Juan, Puerto Rico, Box 65, RG 9, National Archives.

of 1935, the government relief agency supplied very little supplemental income or other services. These families, then, lived on a starvation diet, spending about $3.90 a week on food with very little left for other expenses. Over two-thirds kept both gardens and animals, while a little over a quarter had only animals.

Nearly 60 percent owned their houses, and almost 20 percent in one study reportedly paid no rent, perhaps because they lived on plantations as *agregados* or resident farm laborers. Manning estimated that two-fifths lived on sugar company property, some in their own homes and others renting. Over one-fifth of the same families depended on irrigation ditches and rivers for their water while others bought water from neighbors or relied upon roof drainage and cisterns. Sanitation consequently was bad: interviewers found that of the nearly four-fifths of the homes with privies, nearly half appeared "dirty." Even though modern conveniences were lacking, both in the rural areas and in towns, interviewers also noted many women successfully kept their "home and family clean."[17]

As for the needlewomen themselves, as Table 1–2 shows, there was an average of one and one-half per family. In one study, 75 percent were between the ages of sixteen and thirty-five, as were nearly 65 percent in another, which also showed nearly 21 percent between the ages of thirty-six and forty-five. Only 4.2 percent of families had workers over fifty-five. Years at their trade varied, with 19 percent of women working up to two years, about 70 percent from three to nine years, and nearly 30 percent over ten years. Over half of the women obtained their work from a subcontractor, while another quarter received it directly from a contractor. About half had to travel fewer than five kilometers to obtain their work bundles; most of the rest traveled farther—often on unpaved, hilly, and muddy roads, and sometimes in inclement weather. Some women workers paid for car rides, and subcontractors spent money to go to the contractors, who often lived at greater distances than the homeworkers did from the subcontractors. Toiling an average of twenty-seven and a half hours per week—with 81 percent working fewer than forty hours and 91 percent fewer than forty-eight—at average rates of two and three cents an hour, most women earned less than a dollar a week.

Manning, who sometimes reveals her prejudices toward the needleworkers through backhanded praise, observed, "many regarded home work in a businesslike way and were able to make consistent answers throughout the schedule." She estimated that a quarter of the homeworkers had experience inside factories, and this "may have had some effect in establishing their industrious habits." Indeed, many interviewed needleworkers exhibited a clear job consciousness. They took pride in the fact that they had never ruined any of their needlework. Most felt that subcontractors did not abuse "the spoiled work privilege," which required workers to pay for the cost of replacing the material or redoing the imperfect garment. Many in Coamo, a town in the Ponce district, complained in October 1935 that "there is very little work being distributed and workers often find themselves without work for a week or two." As one mother of two explained, in terms derived from the domestic role of women within the household economy, "[the] price[s] of food stuffs have

Table 1–2. *Characteristics of Workers in the Needlework Industry*

	NRA Survey Oct. 1935	Ortiz-Hayes Survey March 1934
Needleworkers per family	1.5	1.37
Ages		
10–16	6.5%	1.5%
16–35	75.8%	63.5%
36–45	12%	20.9%
over 45	4.5%	11.4%
Years of experience		
up to 2	13%	19%
under 10	72.6%	67.2%
over 10	17%	29.6%
Source of work		
contractor	26.5%	22.3%
subcontractor	57.8%	56.6%
not stated	.07%	20.9%
manufacturer	14.8%	
Distance traveled		
not stated	22.6%	4.3%
brought to home	na	16.7%
below 5 km	51.5%	45%
5 km or more	23.4%	31.3%
Hours		
under 40	na	81%
under 48	na	91.2%
Weekly earnings (U.S. dollars)	.89	.939
Rate per hour	.0285	.034

Source: "Test Survey of Homeworkers in Needlework Industry," Box 63, RG 9, National Archives; "Ortiz-Hayes Survey of Homeworkers in Needlework Industry," San Juan, Puerto Rico, Box 65, RG 9, National Archives.

gone up, but the prices paid for our work have gone down. Things do not balance [out]." Another revealed she was "not working because [her] husband [did] not want her to work at such low prices." Her husband earned five dollars a week as an employee of a sugar mill, but the general economic crisis meant that other families could not afford to forego any cash, however meager.[18]

Their subcontractors agreed. Most were better off than the home-workers, although their own prosperity was precarious. One woman who had worked as a subcontractor for twenty years, and whose husband had a small cigar factory in their house, emphasized that "it is impossible to work under actual rates. Besides there is very little work at Coamo and workers are earning nothing." Another, who distributed for some Mayagüez contractors, demonstrated the sense of collective consciousness that was developing among women workers during this period: "if s.c.'s [subcontractors] in Puerto Rico were organized in a society during the [period of NRA] codes," she told the interviewer, "this would have been very beneficial to all." An embroiderer of cotton garments, who lived on a farm with her parents and siblings, likewise argued, "workers should be organized as to be able to claim for better salaries." But if most homeworkers failed to consider their potential power as an organized group, they nevertheless clung to a common conception of justice in analyzing their work situation. Specifically, they had a sense of a fair wage. "Work should be paid so that a worker could make at least $1.50 weekly," declared the wife of an irrigation service employee. Still others evoked the concept of justice itself, sometimes relating it to a desire for U.S. government intervention. One nineteen-year-old single woman, who felt that complaining would just bring "no more work," contended that under the NRA, "prices were better . . . and workers could protest of any injustice done." Others called for government investigations, bringing back the NRA codes, or—as María de Colón, a young married English-speaking woman, put it—drafting "a code that will meet [the] Supreme Court's approval and place it in force."[19]

Bringing the NRA to Puerto Rico

María de Colón spoke to a government interviewer late in 1935, nearly six months after the U.S. Supreme Court declared the NRA unconstitutional on the grounds that it regulated intrastate commerce, which was beyond federal jurisdiction. As the New Deal's initial attempt to stimulate the economy, the NRA imposed rules of fair competition for individual industries through an elaborate process involving representatives from business, labor, government, and consumers, and it set up mechanisms to enforce legislated provisions. Section 7(a) not only encouraged collective bargaining, it also required industry codes that included minimum wage and maximum hour provisions. These codes also defined unfair practices. Nearly 120 codes either prohibited or regulated homework. In this manner, the New Deal hoped to raise prices and stimulate consumption at the same time.[20]

Puerto Rican needlework threatened to undermine the codes established for cotton garments, handkerchiefs, and infants' apparel. While in the United States the numbers of needleworkers fell during the early Depression, they continued to grow in Puerto Rico, as did the quantity of Puerto Rican goods exported to the mainland. Puerto Rican workers, factory and home alike, worked longer hours for wages lower than even U.S. workers in the South, who were considered the most exploited needleworkers on the mainland. American manufacturers, trade unionists, and reformers eagerly sought to curtail such advantages through the code-making process, although it was agreed that the magnitude of Puerto Rico's economic crisis warranted a separate code for the island. Business and government leaders there, including the Socialist Party, were ready to accept a differential wage schedule.[21]

Manufacturers on the mainland who did not send work to Puerto Rico feared the labor differentials proposed for the needlework code, which was to cover all women's garment–related industries on the island. As the Acreson Harden Company of New York telegraphed to former garment worker Rose Schneiderman—president of the National Women's Trade Union League, friend of Eleanor Roosevelt, and labor representative on the NRA commission holding hearings in San Juan: "unscrupulous American manufacturers are and have been exploiting cheap Puerto Rican labor in the needle trades to the detriment of our own American workers." Yet other mainland manufacturers recognized, as the chairperson of the Handkerchief Industry Code Authority wrote, "any attempt to bring labor conditions for home work in Porto Rico up to our standard would stop practically all business there and affect the livelihood of . . . workers." Those manufacturers who sent their goods to be made up by Puerto Rican homeworkers argued that a minimum wage of even eight dollars a week would force them to China and other cheap labor markets, thus hurting mainland workers as well.[22]

With homework, Puerto Rico could afford to compete with other countries. Tariffs, which would protect their industries from foreign competition and could be evoked under NRA procedures, became the means preferred by Puerto Rican businessmen to lead to raises for homeworkers, not mandated minimum wages that would apply to all workers, regardless of whether they worked at home or shops. Maintaining a wage differential for homeworkers actually lowered shop wages as well. The code prepared by the Puerto Rican Needlework Association, a group of leading contractors, assumed that homework would continue but attempted to safeguard the worker from the worst abuses of the system by including the subcontractor as a "member of the industry" and making her or him responsible for paying homeworkers their minimum wage.[23] This may have been a sincere attempt to protect homeworkers but could also have reflected a tendency to place the onus of exploitation onto the subcontractor.

Conscious of the island's position within the world economy, Puerto Rico's Commissioner of Agriculture and Commerce cautioned workers against undermining the source of their livelihoods. He spoke of the similarity of interests between capital and labor, arguing that "the continuance of our industrial development" would bring "the dual benefit of fair wages for the laborers and reasonable profits for the industrialists." This notion of the higher interests of the whole, coupled with an appeal to Puerto Rican nationalism, became a device through which insular officials chided organized labor and called for a "justice" that would reinforce a model of economic development that maintained class differentials.[24]

Homework, the Mayagüez Chamber of Commerce asserted, was "essential and indispensable for the welfare of the community." Its representative, Oscar Suffront, framed the issue in gendered terms. Questioning whether Puerto Rican labor leaders, the American Federation of Labor, or the Socialist Party spoke in the interest of such women, he championed the "inalienable right" of homeworkers to their work and argued that removing that right, would "lower the standard of living of a considerable part of the Puerto Rican proletariat." He portrayed the needlewomen as geographically isolated, unable to work in towns without either abandoning their families or migrating with them to the cities, where husbands and children would augment the ranks of the unemployed. Homework actually served as a boon to such families, for "it has assisted in sustaining a *modus vivendi.*" Suffront recognized the connection between male underemployment and female homework, and feared disrupting the existing captive labor supply from which coffee growers as well as garment contractors benefitted.[25] Others argued that the existence of homework generated factory employment, which in turn improved living conditions. Abolition of homework was depicted as a scheme on the part of the labor unions to "dominat[e] . . . the masses."

Yet this association of tyranny with the trade unions and freedom (and even women's liberation from drudgery and backwardness) with homework obscured actual power relations.[26]

Shop workers understood that their fate was linked to that of the homeworkers. Gloria Rivera, treasurer of Needleworkers Local Number 2 of San Juan, noted, "the workers outside of the shop are working so cheap, we in the shops are without work. The reverse will be true if the home work is eliminated, for [then] the home workers will be out of work and we will have work in the shops." Rivera called for regulation of homework, rather than its elimination, asserting a commonality of interests with homeworking women, an occupation she herself had once held. Defending homeworkers, Rivera declared:

> What we want is that they earn the same amount [of] money as we do. A woman who works at home does as good a job as the woman who works in the shop on the same kind of work, so I do not see why she is getting less money on it. . . . [W]e do not want women who do homework to be kept out of work, but we want them to be paid just and reasonable wages so that they can live decently. Their necessities are the same as ours. There is no reason at all to say that work can be done at home cheaper than in the shop. On the contrary, the working time on a piece of work at home is longer than in the shop because they have to do their best so as to be sure the work will be accepted.

Local union officials from Mayagüez and Cabo Rojo similarly grounded their arguments on concepts of justice and solidarity. They merged justice arguments with those based on a mother's duty. As one official exclaimed: "A worker should be well fed and our children also, because we are human beings, we need food and demand a decent living and at the same time some recreation." This speaker continued, "it is not possible for me to educate and clothe [my eight children] with only $8.00 weekly, pay rent and buy food, and I cannot bring them up properly and nourish them well." Denying the charge that they were all socialists—although some did condemn greedy "capitalists and millionaires"—these working-class women rejected business arguments that higher wages would destroy the industry. The home needleworkers of Cabo Rojo, through the president of the Needleworkers' Union of

Mayagüez, actually claimed, "if the employer cannot raise our salaries, we prefer the industry to disappear for it is impossible to live under present conditions on the wages we are getting now." This group considered homework "a sacrifice" rather than "a help," as the employers considered it. They maintained that "the value of such work is so small that we have to work the whole week, day and night disregarding our housekeeping obligations, in order to earn 50 cents or 60 cents a week." They clearly understood that, "our services are used in order to make competition among contractors." These workers pleaded before the NRA hearings for the codes to bring about a better working world and that the employers should not be permitted to pay them less.[27]

Thus, the needleworkers' unions strove to raise the pay of homeworkers as well as shopworkers, and they saw homeworkers as part of their constituency. Their attempt to represent homeworkers contrasted with the approach of garment industry organizers in the United States, who regarded homeworkers as unorganizable and sought the immediate elimination of homework. But in Puerto Rico, given the predominance of homeworkers, the mainland unions' strategy made little sense. The Insular Council of Unions of Needleworkers, therefore, called for the same minimum wage of (eight dollars) per week for all workers, no matter their location. Organized workers did not want to settle for anything less, arguing they would rather lose an "industry that cannot afford to pay decent wages," than suffer further exploitation and unfair competition.[28]

Yet Puerto Rican national union officials demanded the gradual abolition of homework. So did Rose Schneiderman. But because, in a maternalist way, Schneiderman saw herself as a "labor adviser for these girls," she felt "a great responsibility" not "to chase the industry out of Puerto Rico." Until homework could be eliminated, she would agree to equalize wages and conditions between the home and shop. Nevertheless, she maintained that the eventual abolition of the industry would aid the employer as much as the workers because homework was inefficient, with unstandardized work, irregular hours, and slow turnover of goods. She also held that needlework in Puerto Rico was produced by those suffering from tuberculosis and other forms of ill health, and therefore that customers on the mainland should be leery of Puerto Rican goods. Here, Schneiderman was drawing upon the argument that women reformers had deployed on the mainland during the previous twenty-five years—that is, that offshore homework brought dirt and disease. Thus, she reiterated the views of her political ally, Eleanor Roosevelt, who had traveled to Puerto Rico herself and upon her return warned mainland women "to boil" Puerto Rican embroideries "before putting them on or using them"—displaying the decades-old strategy of the National Consumers' League to end homework by appealing to the consumer. Finally, Schneiderman argued that homework increased the burdens for women already suffering from a double day of waged and family labor without compensating them with a living wage.[29]

Teresa Anglero, president of the Insular Council of Unions of Needleworkers, argued in more abstract terms. Drawing upon a discourse of freedom and slavery that long shaped union arguments about homework, she proclaimed: "There had to be a cry for liberty to abolish slavery, and this is another kind of slavery, and the cry for liberty must be raised to free us from this slavery also. . . . [T]he home work is prejudicial to the health, the life and comfort of the worker, not only in the home but in the factory, and it merely works to the discredit of our workers." While some local trade unionists called for intensive organizing to end homework, Anglero promoted the community workshop plan as a first step. Proposed in Manning's report on women workers, embraced by Schneiderman and other members of the NRA and the Puerto Rican Department of Labor, the idea was to establish local shops for women in rural districts. Women would labor from two to six hours a day in these branch factories, where they could work more efficiently than at home, become more proficient in their work, and enjoy cleaner and healthier conditions, which would benefit both the worker and the consumer of hand-embroidered items. Anglero further called for a commission to study homework and develop a plan for its termination.[30]

Anglero labeled homeworkers who defended the existing system as "slaves" who needed "to be set free by those at liberty to clamor for human freedom." In contrast, homeworkers defended the system as the only "honest means" by which they could provide their children with bread. Thus they relied upon the same image—the mother breadgiver as breadwinner—that local trade union women had evoked to demand a higher minimum wage for all women, a wage that ironically would make homework unprofitable for employers (since the advantage of cheapness would no longer compensate for inefficiency and delay). From Camuy, women wrote officials not to end the homework "from which Puerto Rican mothers earn a living working in their independent homes, during spare hours in a useful occupation." Undoubtedly, these telegrams in support of homework were organized by contractors, but this fact hardly negates the language in which the women argued. While economic discourse dominated the hearings (with only the Commissioner of Labor condemning homework for undermining the "home"), these women emphasized their role as mothers, which included providing for their families. As one working mother from Mayagüez asserted, "each mother would miss it, for it is a help for their children and for the husband." Some women argued that the children in their households also could do needlework since they needed so many things that the family was unable to provide. Needlewomen also invoked the issue of justice in their defense of needlework. "It would be inhuman that a large part of the district of Mayagüez, 50 percent of which has contributed so that we can come here to defend them, should be left without work, merely because they cannot go the factories. This would not be human, and I think the Department of Labor is just," another homeworker declared. A widow from the rural district of Rosario contended that the horrible roads made it impossible to establish branch factories in her area and without homework she and her family would starve. She believed, "the country women need it and [by keeping it] there must be justice for all."[31]

The NRA operated in Puerto Rico for less than a year. Imposed on July 19, 1934, the needlework code became operational about a month later, after a commission established piece rates for the myriad processes performed in the various needlework trades. Many operations such as embroidery were better paid; they were to yield minimum wages of five dollars per week for factory workers and two dollars for homeworkers. The Needleworkers Union insisted, "no workers should draw another stitch until they receive the increase that they are to get," and unionists should "instruct the homeworkers to do no work in the homes . . . unless they get the corresponding increase." The Mayagüez union published a public notice in local newspapers, "to help us enforce the law," informing homeworkers of the increase and asking "all the organized workers [on] the island" to instruct the homeworkers to stop work until their piece rate increased. Inside workers took the lead, educating their home-working kin and neighbors.[32]

However, work was scarce as economic conditions on the island continued to deteriorate. Subcontractors were not getting enough work, and, according to the NRA, they "did not pay the workers the proper code rates, in an effort to meet their expenses. The workers, perhaps knowingly, allowed the subcontractors to do it because there was no work and they needed to work even if for only one or two cents an hour." As on the mainland, compliance officers were lacking, and so, with workers not complaining, subcontractors constantly violated NRA provisions. Furthermore, community workrooms never materialized. These conditions led Schneiderman to proclaim at another NRA meeting that "the Puerto Rican Code is the worst Code we have."[33]

The NRA in Puerto Rico upgraded standards for the needlewomen on paper, but for the most part it failed to improve them in actuality. When the Women's Bureau surveyed the island in 1935, it discovered new homework industries developing in the manufacture of gloves and women's linen suits amid the decline of some of the other needlework trades. Additionally, competition from lower-wage labor in the Philippines, Japan, Mexico, and the southern United States also decreased the quantity of cheap cotton underclothes and children's dresses embroidered in Puerto Rico. Still, by 1940 home needlework continued to account for more than 44 percent of all manufacturing on the island. That year the U.S. Congress amended the Fair Labor Standards Act of 1938 (which established labor standards for interstate commerce) to allow lower-wage minimums in Puerto Rico. By 1949 homeworkers still predominated on the island, but they earned only fifteen cents an hour—a rate that scarcely kept up with the cost of living. During the next decade, homeworkers remained among the lowest paid workers, earning no more than one-third of the median wage of other women working in industry on the island. But with the insular government committed to higher wages to meet Puerto Rico's high cost of living, needlework manufacturers took their work to other countries. In contrast with the 31 percent of all women who worked at home in 1940, fewer than 1 percent of women sewed and embroidered at home for wages in 1979. Economic transformation, guided by state policy and union watchfulness, finally ended most homework in Puerto Rico.[34]

What was the final legacy of the NRA in Puerto Rico? Many needleworkers thought conditions improved with government regulation of the industry under the NRA, despite the loss of work as manufacturers sought to undermine the code by withholding their goods. Women were unable to move to community workrooms, and none wanted the work transferred to factories.[35] They preferred to remain homeworkers; homework was part of their household economies. Yet, their preference for remaining with their families as they performed wage labor did not negate their wish for a reasonable, living wage. That the two desires were contradictory reminds us that gender roles shaped women's work in the home as well as in the marketplace in 1935, as they do today. If the tenacity with which they held onto the home as a workplace suggests that we cannot dismiss homeworkers' consciousness as a product of employer threats, the solidarity of local trade union women with their homeworking counterparts reminds us that the division between home and factory was very permeable among working-class women in Puerto Rico, where kinship and community united, rather than divided, such laborers.

The significance of women's home needlework activities during the first three decades of the twentieth century has been noted by many scholars. As María del Carmen Baerga has contended, needlewomen on the island during the 1920s and 1930s engaged not only in needlework production but in the social reproduction of the Puerto Rican working class. That is, their labor made it possible for working-class families to survive and create new workers. Furthermore, while they may have engaged in ongoing direct action, their labor made it possible for others within their households to sustain organizing and militant action.[36] Still, these workers were at the bottom of the economic structure; they were the most vulnerable of all workers.

NOTES

Acknowledgments: A Little-Griswold Grant in Legal History from the American Historical Association and a fellowship from the Woodrow Wilson Center facilitated the research for this paper. I also would like to thank Altagracia Ortiz for her editorial assistance; Herbert "Tico" Braun for his translations; and research assistants Paul Frymer, at the Woodrow Wilson Center, and Florence Woodward, at Howard University, for their efforts. Parts of this essay appear in different form in chapter 7 of my book *Home to Work: Motherhood and the Politics of Industrial Homework in the United States* (New York: Cambridge University Press, 1994).

1. These life experiences are recorded in National Recovery Administration, San Juan, Puerto Rico, Reverse Needlework Survey, Case B-2, Ponce, Box 67, Record Group (RG) 9, National Recovery Administration (NRA) Papers, National Archives (NA), Washington, D.C.

2. Government of Puerto Rico, Department of Labor, Bureau of Women and Children in Industry, San Juan, untitled report, Records of the Homework Committee, Box 8389, RG 9, NA, 9.

3. For further information on needleworkers during the 1930s, see Blanca Silvestrini, "Women as Workers: The Experience of Puerto Rican Women in the 1930s," in *The Puerto Rican Woman: Perspectives on Culture, History, and Society*, ed. Edna Acosta-Belén (New York: Praeger, 1986), 59–74.

4. Walter M. Barrow, "Report on Homework Conditions in the Island of Puerto Rico; Part One: Conditions Prior to Codification," NRA, San Juan Office, July 12, 1935, Box 63, RG 9, NA, 16; Caroline Manning, "The Employment of Women in Puerto Rico," United States Department of Labor, Women's Bureau, *Bulletin of the Women's Bureau* 118 (Washington, D.C.: Government Printing Office, 1934), 2. For a superb analysis of the gendered implications of homework, see María del Carmen Baerga, "Women's Labor and the Domestic Unit: Industrial Homework in Puerto Rico during the 1930s," *Centro de Estudios Puertorriqueños Bulletin* 2, no. 7 (Winter 1989–90): 33–39.

5. James L. Dietz, *Economic History of Puerto Rico: Institutional Change and Capitalist Development* (Princeton: Princeton University Press, 1986), 98–124; Angel G. Quintero Rivera, "Background to the Emergence of Imperialist Capitalism in Puerto Rico," in *The Puerto Ricans: Their History, Culture, and Society*, ed. Adalberto López (Cambridge, Mass.: Schenkman, 1980), 97–127.

6. Dietz, *Economic History of Puerto Rico*, 127–28, 130–31. See also Barrow, "Report on Homework Conditions," 2–5; Victor S. Clark et al., *Porto Rico and Its Problems* (Washington, D.C.: Brookings Institution, 1930). On women's work, see Nina Lane McBride, "Women Workers of Porto Rico," *International Socialist Review* 17, no. 12 (June 1917): 717–19.

7. Lydia Milagros González, *Una puntada en el tiempo: La industria de la aguja en Puerto Rico (1900–1929)* (Santo Domingo, D.R.: Editorial Taller, 1990), 13.

8. Ibid., 20.

9. "Memorandum on Homework in Puerto Rico," Records of the Homework Committee, Box 8389, NA, 23–24; Special Report No. 14, "The Needlework Industry of Porto Rico," October 29, 1929, Box 97, folder 8, Papers of the Amalgamated Clothing Workers of America (ACWA), Labor-Management Documentation Center, Cornell University, 1–3.

10. Manning, "The Employment of Women in Puerto Rico," 7–12; "The Needlework Industry of Porto Rico," 4–7; Barrow, "Report on Homework Conditions," 17–18.

11. On the early working-class struggles of Puerto Rican women, see Yamila Azize, *Luchas de la mujer en Puerto Rico, 1898–1919* (Puerto Rico: Litografía Metropolitana, 1979); on the early labor movement on the island in general, see Angel Quintero Rivera, *Workers' Struggles in Puerto Rico: A Documentary History* (New York: Monthly Review Press, 1976).

12. For a full account of the politics of the Socialist Party, see Blanca Silvestrini-Pacheco, *Los trabajadores puertorriqueños y el Partido Socialista (1932–40)* (Río Piedras: Editorial Universitaria, 1979).

13. As quoted in Silvestrini, "Women as Workers," 67.

14. Ibid., 66–69; Manning, "The Employment of Women," 11–12. For a comparison with mainland wages, see Dietz, *Economic History of Puerto Rico*, 175.

15. These were: Caroline Manning's study for the Women's Bureau; the Ortiz-Hayes survey under the NRA, compiled by students at the University of Puerto Rico under Julio B. Ortiz, dean of the College of Business Administration, and by attachés of St. Andrew's Craft Shop of Mayagüez under the direction of superintendent Mildred Hayes; and the 1935 test survey of homeworkers in the needlework industry conducted by the NRA after the codes were no longer in effect. Manning, "The Employment of Women"; "Ortiz-Hayes Survey of Homeworkers in Needlework Industry," San Juan, October 4, 1935, Box 65, RG 9, NA; "Test Survey of Homeworkers in Needlework Industry in Puerto Rico" (Test Survey), Box 63, RG 9, NA; Needlework Case Files by Contractor, Sub-contractors, and Homeworkers, Boxes 66, 67, RG 9, NA.

16. Reverse Needlework Survey, interview schedule: A. Pérez, B-2–4, Box 67, RG 9, NA. For a comparison of percentages of mothers and single daughters, see Manning, "The Employment of Women," 2.

17. Manning, "The Employment of Women," 17–18.

18. Ibid., 3; Carole Manning, "Hearing on Code of Fair Practices and Competition for Puerto Rico Presented by Needlework Industry Code," NRA, San Juan, February 18 and March 1, 1934 [known as Puerto Rico Hearings], 106, Box 7117, RG 9, NA; Reverse Needlework Survey interview schedules: A. Corcore, B-7–2; J. Colón, B-7–3; O. Alvarado, B-7–4; Galarza, C-13, Box 67, RG 9, NA. For women's consciousness as derived from the domestic economy, see Temma Kaplan, "Female Consciousness and Collective Action: The Case of Barcelona, 1910–1918," Signs 7 (Spring 1982): 545–66.

19. Reverse Needlework Survey interview schedules: M. Rodríguez, B-7–1; E. Rodríguez, B-9–1; A. Santiago, B-2–3; de Jesús, B-2–1; V. M. Burgos, B-7–3; M. de Colón, B-7–3, Boxes 66 and 67, RG 9, NA.

20. On the NRA see Donald R. Brand, Corporatism and the Rule of Law: A Study of the National Recovery Administration (Ithaca, N.Y.: Cornell University Press, 1988); Eileen Boris, "Regulating Industrial Homework: The Triumph of 'Sacred Motherhood,'" Journal of American History 71 (March 1985): 745–63.

21. "Rise in Imports of Puerto Rican Cotton Wear Cited," Daily News Record, March 20, 1934; H. O. Stanbury Co. to Beatrice McConnell, August 20, 1934, both in "Homework Committee," Box 8389, RG 9, NA, 23.

22. NRA Puerto Rico Hearings, Box 7117, RG 9, NA, 269, 13, 254; see also 267–68, 76, 245, 183–84, 211–12. Complaints by New York manufacturers were more pronounced at the National Industrial Recovery Administration, Washington D.C., "Hearing on the Cotton Garment Industry and the Needlework Industry in Puerto Rico: Modification Proposal," held March 28, 1934, Box 7117, RG 9, NA.

23. Puerto Rico Hearings, 41, 187–88, 220–22.

24. Ibid., 44–45, 238–39, 234–37.

25. Ibid., 41, 46–49, 194–96.

26. Ibid., 256–66.

27. Ibid., testimony of Gloria Rivera, 197–99; Catalina Otero, 199–202; Pilar Llanos, 203–4; Nereida Basora, 204–6; Angela Padilla, 219; Pasuala Figueroa, 213–17.

28. On trade unions' relation to homeworkers, see Eileen Boris, "Organization or Prohibition? A Historical Perspective on Trade Unions and Homework," Women and Unions:

Forging a Partnership, ed. Sue Cobble (Ithaca, N.Y.: Industrial and Labor Relations Press, 1993), 207–25; Puerto Rico Hearings, 82–89.

29. Puerto Rico Hearings, 66, 227–33; Eleanor Roosevelt, *This I Remember* (New York: Scribner's, 1949), 138–40. For the arguments of women reformers, see Boris, *Home to Work,* 214–17, 245–62.

30. Puerto Rico Hearings, 223–26, 151–52, 145, 166–70, 159; Manning, "The Employment of Women," 14.

31. Puerto Rico Hearings, 85, 154, 253, 270–72, 147–50.

32. "Ningún trabajador ni del taller ni de la casa," *El Imparcial* (San Juan), July 21, 1934, translated clipping, RG 9, Box 48, NA; in folder titled "Correspondence No. 2," Manuel Serra, Jr., "Report on Homework: Conditions in the Island of Puerto Rico; Part Two: Conditions during and after Codification," NRA, San Juan Office, July 12, 1935, Box 48, RG 9, NA, 37–66.

33. NRA, "Code of Fair Competition for the Needlework Industry in Puerto Rico," as approved on June 28, 1934, by President Franklin Roosevelt (Washington: Government Printing Office, 1934); Serra, "Report on Homework," 37–66; Rose Schneiderman, "Hearing on the Novelty Curtains, Draperies, Bedspreads and Novelty Pillows Industry," November 2, 1934, RG 9, NRA Transcripts of Hearings, NA, 130.

34. Mary Anderson to Frances Perkins, January 29, 1935, Box 81, RG 174, "File: Women's Bureau," NA; Dietz, *Economic History of Puerto Rico,* 224–26. There was a drop in the female labor force from 1950 to 1960 when the number of homeworkers fell from fifty thousand to ten thousand, and these women did not reenter the labor force in any significant numbers. See Lloyd G. Reynolds and Peter Gregory, *Wages, Productivity, and Industrialization in Puerto Rico* (Homewood, Ill.: Richard D. Irwin, 1965), 33.

35. Test Survey of Homeworkers, Table 27, Box 63, RG 9, NA.

36. María del Carmen Baerga, "Wages, Consumption, and Survival: Working-Class Households in Puerto Rico in the 1930s," in *Households and the World Economy,* ed. Joan Smith, Immanuel Wallerstein, and Hans Dieter Evers (Beverly Hills, Calif.: Sage Publications, 1984), 233–51.

TWO

"En la aguja y el pedal eché la hiel": Puerto Rican Women in the Garment Industry of New York City, 1920–1980

ALTAGRACIA ORTIZ

Whenever my mother, Matilde Rodríguez Torres, was asked about her work as a seamstress in the garment factories of Manhattan, she would sigh and say: "¡En la aguja y el pedal, eché la hiel!" Literally this means that over her sewing-machine needle and pedal, she poured her "bile"; but as an idiomatic expression these words also mean that she worked very hard at home and in various workplaces using her needlework skills to help my father support a family of eight children. My earliest memories of this gifted seamstress recall a slim young woman bending over a small manual sewing machine, making dresses for some of the women of El Polvorín, a poor *barriada* (neighborhood) in the town of Cayey in Puerto Rico. She was a modest but accomplished couturier, suggesting to her clients beautiful and creative designs or copying fashionable 1940s styles straight out of Sears catalogs; precisely measuring and cutting the dresses by following a sample brought in by the customer; and then sewing and decorating the garments with great care. In Puerto Rico Doña Matí, as her friends and customers called her, did other kinds of needlework—intricate crochet, elegant embroideries, fine tatting and silk stitching. For my mother this fine needlework was not work, and the articles she made soon became the art work that adorned the homes she lived in, or they became precious gifts to friends and relatives. But after Matilde Rodríguez Torres came to New York City in 1951, she rarely did sewing at home, either for pay or for art's sake. All of her sewing energies were now consumed by work in the garment factories, and she had little time for other kinds of sewing.

The story of my mother is one of many stories that make up the history of Puerto Rican garment workers in America in the twentieth century. This is the history of countless women who migrated from the island of Puerto Rico to this country in search of a better life, only to become absorbed by an industry that bought their labor cheaply and gave them few opportunities for advancement. Like women workers before them, Puerto Rican women experienced many problems in the garment trades; additionally, *puertorriqueñas* were seen and labeled as "non-white" by white bosses, co-workers, and union members. Therefore, my essay focuses for the most part on the racial and ethnic issues that set Puerto Rican garment workers' struggles apart from those of white European workers in the clothing trades. In order to understand the depth of the struggle Puerto Rican garment workers experienced in New York City between 1920 and 1980, I also have examined the technological and market changes that have transformed clothing manufacturing in the twentieth century. It is my hope that this history of Puerto Rican needleworkers will lead to greater recognition of their contributions to this industry and of the significant role *puertorriqueñas* played in the survival of their community through their work in the garment trades.[1]

Puerto Rican Garment Workers in New York City, 1920–1945

Puerto Rican women needleworkers first became a discernible part of New York City's garment labor force in the 1920s. Initially a large majority of these workers were concentrated in the home needlework industry making handkerchiefs, blouses, skirts, dresses, and other items for extremely low wages.[2] In the 1930s home needleworkers usually earned no more than six to eight dollars per week.[3] According to one researcher, who interviewed Puerto Rican women working in this industry during the 1920s and 1930s, some migrant women from Puerto Rico dedicated themselves exclusively to home needlework despite low wages because it allowed them to supplement their husbands' incomes while they cared for their families.[4] The exact number of *puertorriqueñas* in the home needle trades during these early years remains unknown. However, even when the anti-homework campaign of the New York State Department of Labor and the International Ladies' Garment Workers' Union (ILGWU) caused an overall decline in garment homework in New York City in the 1930s, Puerto Rican women continued to work in this industry. Labor Department figures indicated that in 1933 there were 402 *puertorriqueñas* working at home; by 1936 their numbers had fallen to 327.[5] In succeeding decades Puerto Rican seamstresses continued to sew in the privacy of their homes—for employers, for independent subcontractors, or for personal clients—thereby contributing to the support of their families and thus to the very survival of the Puerto Rican community in New York City.

Puerto Rican garment workers also entered the city's garment factories in the 1920s and 1930s, but, as in the case of homeworkers, we lack precise records of their numbers. An informal count of Hispanics living in four assembly districts (16, 17, 18, 19) in south central Harlem in 1925 lists some six hundred women working in production jobs. Presumably this number included Puerto Rican dressmakers and seamstresses; unfortunately, the count did not isolate the numbers of *puertorriqueñas*.[6] The only evidence for their presence in garment factories consists of scattered historical accounts and a few oral histories of elderly Puerto Rican seamstresses who have shared memories of their work experience with us.[7] Through their stories we have learned much about the problems these women encountered in the garment industry during these early years. Finding employment was not always easy, although a few had jobs when they arrived in New York. The latter often were recruited in Puerto Rico by employers in nonunion shops who promised them jobs upon their arrival in the city as part of a campaign to undermine the unionization efforts of the ILGWU. Others found employment through friends and relatives, or simply by walking through the garment district or looking in the pages of the few Spanish-language newspapers in search of want ads that announced: "Se necesitan operadoras" ("Sewing-machine operators needed"). Many did not speak or understand the English language well; most did not know how to travel throughout a city that was new and strange to them; and for working mothers there was always the problem of child care. To help find solutions to these individual problems, these workers developed an informal system of networking, consisting of relatives, friends, and *comadres* (godmothers of their children) who found them employment, guided them to distant factories, eased communication with English-speaking employers and coworkers, and cared at times for their children.[8]

Puertorriqueñas were not able to resolve the problems they encountered in the garment factories and in the locals of the ILGWU as easily. If they got past signs reading: "No Negroes or Porto Ricans," they usually had to work extremely long hours at jobs that had been downgraded from skilled work to the semiskilled category of "section work."[9] Many of these jobs had traditionally been held by young Jewish and Italian women, but during the 1920s and 1930s Puerto Rican women slowly began to replace these workers in certain trades—particularly dressmaking, accessories, and children's clothing. The initial integration of Puerto Rican women into the garment industry after World War I was short-lived because the Depression of the 1930s forced many factories to close or to relocate to New England or other mid-Atlantic states, leaving many *puertorriqueñas* without jobs or earning meager wages in the establishments that remained in the city.[10] Moreover, those sectors of the garment industry that were still hiring workers resorted more and more to deskilling or to using subcontractors (small factory owners) to avoid paying higher wages—both to the detriment of Puerto Rican workers. The personal accounts of some of these workers reveal a period of immense struggle to survive not only in the garment industry but in the city's small Spanish-speaking communities as well.[11]

The economic crisis of the 1930s forced many *puertorriqueñas* to realize that they could not resolve the problems in their workplaces as individuals, and they soon sought admission into the ILGWU. The union, in turn, had begun a drive to organize them at the beginning of the decade, but only in the locals of those trades where they had begun to pose a threat to white organized labor. In job categories where Puerto Rican women already predominated and where few white workers remained—such as pinking (garment edging), floor work (cleaning and distributing work), and packing—the union made no effort at organization. Efforts to include Puerto Ricans in some of the locals during these years could also arouse the opposition of the rank and file. One Puerto Rican dressmaker remembers that in Dressmakers' Local 22 the Italian women workers opposed granting membership to *puertorriqueñas* and sought to keep them out of union shops altogether.[12] The Italian workers failed to exclude Puerto Rican women from this local, but they effectively blocked their entrance into the Italian Dressmakers' Local 89 and the Italian Cloakmakers' Local 48.

In response to this and other kinds of discrimination in Dressmakers' Local 22, a radical group of Hispanic seamstresses (which probably included *puertorriqueñas*) petitioned ILGWU president David Dubinsky in 1933, and again in 1934, for the right to organize their own local and select their own leaders.[13] Dubinsky received their petition cordially but refused to recognize Hispanic workers as a separate unit of the union in spite of the fact that the ILGWU had allowed Italian workers to create two locals of their own (48 and 89). To appease Hispanic union members, Dubinsky instructed Saby Nehama, a Sephardic Jewish organizer in Local 22, to bring together all the Spanish-speaking women into a "special department" (but not a local), and at the ILGWU's 1934 annual convention Nehama and Charles Zimmerman, head of Local 22 at the time, arranged to have two Puerto Rican women recognized as delegates.[14] Although this appears to be an egalitarian treatment of *puertorriqueñas* and other Latinas, in reality the ILGWU leadership, having purged the union of its most radical members in the late 1920s, was no longer willing to grant the rank and file (or for that matter even white women organizers) a more powerful role in the organization.[15] Puerto Rican women could expect to be accepted as members of the union, but they could not look forward to its protection or expect full participation within its ranks.

With the onset of World War II *puertorriqueñas* found renewed employment opportunities in the garment industry. The military demands of the war caused a decline in the production of consumer durable goods, releasing more money for garment purchases. Encouraged by this, and by a shift in women's clothing styles, manufacturers increased their production of such popular items as informal dresses, separates (skirts and blouses), and sportswear. In the meantime, the establishment of defense plants in the New York area, which drew away white women workers, created job openings in the garment factories.[16] Northern factories that had been converted to the production of war-related apparel and materiel likewise were in need of new workers. Because Puerto Rican women still formed one of the most available and skilled groups of needleworkers in the area, they were recalled into the clothing factories of the city.[17] They were most noticeable in the skirt trade, where section work had greatly increased the need for semiskilled workers. Some Puerto Rican women, however, remember earning their livelihoods during the war years making life preservers and shirts for soldiers in the service.[18]

Puerto Rican Garment Workers in New York City, 1945–1965

The two decades following World War II were profoundly important years in the history of Puerto Rican garment workers in New York City. By the early 1950s a new migration wave from the island tremendously increased their numbers throughout all the garment factories in the city, and in some trades, such as dressmaking, skirts, and blouses, they became the predominant ethnic group. Yet the absorption of large numbers of Puerto Rican women into the city's garment-manufacturing establishments, and into their corresponding ILGWU locals, did not significantly improve factory conditions for these workers nor change their subordinate status in the union. An important reason for this was that as *puertorriqueñas* were entering the garment industry in greater numbers, the industry itself was threatened by new technologies, the comparatively higher labor and overhead costs in the city, and by growing foreign imports, challenges to which it had begun to respond by relocating its factories to other parts of the country. The incorporation of *puertorriqueñas* into the garment industry of New York City during these two decades therefore occurred during a period of slow decline characterized by reductions in the number of workplaces in the city, increased competition between New York City and other regions of the country for low-wage labor, and decentralization of the industry, a process whereby production was relocated while designing and merchandising remained in Manhattan's garment district. These industrial trends had extremely negative consequences for Puerto Rican women workers during these years. Their problems were further aggravated by persistent discrimination in the factories and in the locals during the height of their participation in this industry.

In the meantime, various sectors of the garment industry had come to rely quite heavily on the labor of *puertorriqueñas* for their survival during this critical period. The skirtmaking, blouse, sweater, casual dress, and underwear trades particularly profited from their labor. For example, Puerto Rican skirtmakers contributed to the production of some 83 million items in 1955 alone.[19] While Puerto Ricans were conspicuously absent from the better-paid shops and the men's coat and suit industry (the latter being exclusively a white male domain), they could be counted among workers in sectors of the industry making neckwear (scarfs and ties), children's apparel, rainwear, belts, and embroidery. Although there are no accounts of their total numbers in these trades, we can safely assume that they were a significant portion of the 72 percent of all *puertorriqueñas* employed as "operatives" in the 1950 census, and of the 65.3 percent employed as "operatives" in the 1960 census.[20] Incomplete numbers notwithstanding, a few contemporary sources claimed that without the labor of Puerto Rican women, the garment industry of New York City would not have survived the economic crisis of the 1950s and early 1960s.[21]

However, by the mid-1960s even the poorly paid labor of hard-working Puerto Rican women could not prevent the decline of the city's garment industry: its problems were too vast and of too long duration. Starting in the late 1940s, for example, the entire industry had suffered as a result of shifts in consumer spending. People began to buy less clothing and more of the durable goods (cars, refrigerators, televisions) that had been unavailable during the war years. The decline of the industry, especially of the women's and children's clothing trades, was also directly connected by some observers to the comparatively high cost of labor and rents in the city.[22] Others maintained that employers in these particular trades had been unable to remain competitive because of union opposition to increased use of section work.[23] The small physical size of factories producing such items as knit goods also meant that employers were prevented from taking advantage of the newer technologies (automated looms or faster and larger sewing machines), while photomarking machines (later called laser copiers) initially threatened the cutting craft in almost all trades. Finally, competition from garments imported from India, South Korea, Japan, and other Southeast Asian countries drastically cut into American clothing manufacturers' profits.[24] The reactions of New York employers to these problems were to standardize production further (mainly through the increased use of section work); to decentralize their operations; or to relocate their factories to other parts of the Northeast region—at first to upstate New York, New Jersey, Pennsylvania, Massachusetts—and later to the South and even Puerto Rico, where labor costs were lower.

Before the end of this first phase (1950–65) of a decline that by 1980 had engulfed the entire garment industry in the mid-Atlantic region, New York City's Puerto Rican garment workers had begun to feel the impact of these economic transformations. Many seamstresses continued to work not only in organized shops but in sweatshops in Harlem, the Bronx, and Brooklyn, where they earned extremely low wages. Dan Wakefield, a reporter who investigated the illegal shops in East Harlem in the late 1950s, observed:

The shops unknown or unorganized by unions have a whole world of devices to hold their workers at the lowest and cheapest conditions. These methods of course are much easier to use on workers who don't know the language and laws of the city, and the managers press that advantage to the hilt. A shop that opened on 106 Street promised new workers a guaranteed wage of $42.00 a week and paid them all $29.00 each at the end of the week. When the "girls" asked where the other thirteen dollars was, the boss said that had been "taken out for taxes."[25]

Since this was an illegal sweatshop, it was highly unlikely these deductions were for tax purposes. In general wages did not rise above fifty dollars per week, though on occasion a fast section worker could make up to seventy dollars in a week. Sweatshop employers also attempted to bribe discontented workers by offering to raise their wages, lend them money, or give them credit references. If these tactics failed, bosses threatened to fire women workers and report them to lenders or store owners who had extended them credit.[26]

Although Puerto Rican women could readily find employment in these low-wage shops, the work conditions they encountered there resembled those that had characterized the industry in earlier years. Some of the shops were dark and dingy places with no windows or fire escapes, unsanitary bathrooms, and unreliable heating systems.[27] In many shops there were insufficient workloads, so that bundles of work were given to those who arrived at the factories at the crack of dawn, and even then workers were allowed to take only one bundle at a time. In order to make ends meet, some *puertorriqueñas* were forced to sew at home for "fly-by-night" shops in their neighborhoods.[28] One Puerto Rican seamstress, Rosie Flores, recalled making belts and blouses as a child of eleven for her mother, who brought the work home from a local factory in East Harlem; another home needleworker, Eugenia Feliciano Bermuda, a widow, supported herself and her five children by knitting scarves and finishing skirts.[29] *Puertorriqueñas* in the garment industry during these years also remember frequent job changes because of the seasonal layoffs that were common in the industry, or because of factory closings or relocations.[30] One source estimates that, "Between 1947 and 1958 total apparel employment declined by 54,000 jobs; in the succeeding decade, yet another 72,000 jobs were lost."[31] Many of these were jobs lost to

Puerto Rican women, who in the 1960s were still the largest source of available needleworkers in the area.

On top of these adverse economic conditions Puerto Rican garment workers continued to experience discrimination and isolation in their workplaces and in the ILGWU during the post–World War II decades.[32] In factories throughout the city, *puertorriqueñas* complained of unequal treatment and antagonistic behavior on the part of other workers and their employers. In 1984 Lucila Padrón, who had worked in one of the city's factories in the late 1940s, described a situation that was fairly common in her day and one that illustrates how openly discrimination operated in the workplace. She was often sent home early, supposedly because there was no work for her; yet she had observed that her "chairlady" (or foreman) allowed Italian women in the shop to get up and take extra bundles as soon as the cloth was cut. She tried to do the same, but the chairlady objected. Incensed, Padrón quit her job.[33] Other women's testimonies confirm this kind of discriminatory treatment in the garment factories of the city during the postwar period. One woman recalled in the late 1970s the insulting behavior of a foreman in a factory she worked in the 1950s:

We were almost all Puerto Rican women in that factory, and that was why he was so insulting. It was before the time of the civil rights movement, and he had no respect for us. I finally went to the union to complain about him, but the union took his side, not mine, and I lost my job. I decided at that point not to work ever again in union shops.[34]

Among employers, attitudes toward Puerto Ricans varied, as Roy Helfgott indicates in his research on discrimination in the skirt industry in the late 1950s. He found that while one employer considered Puerto Ricans "too clannish, sloppy in their workmanship, and generally undependable" and only "hires them because there is no other help available," another found Puerto Ricans to be good workers and "when in need of additional workers, depends upon his present employees to bring in their friends."[35] In spite of some of the negative views expressed by employers, Helfgott argues in his study that firms did not report any disputes over work distribution and that none of the cases brought before the skirt local (Local 23) dealt with issues of discrimination.[36] The presence in this industry of many Spanish-speaking Sephardic Jewish employers and business agents, who perhaps were able to communicate with and understand Hispanic workers better than their colleagues in the rest of the industry could, may have accounted for the apparent equanimity that existed among skirt makers, manufacturers, and union representatives. Helfgott's observations regarding the abundance of work and good pay in the skirt industry and the efforts of dedicated union officers to integrate all skirt workers into its local also may have contributed to smoother interethnic group relations in this trade and local.[37]

This was not the case in many of the other union locals. In some locals, such as the Italian Seamstresses' Local 89, which controlled some of the highest-paid jobs in the industry, *puertorriqueñas* continued to be excluded altogether. In 1947 the ILGWU leadership publicly agreed before the New York Commission against Discrimination to open up the Italian locals to all workers, yet there is no evidence that it ever enforced this decision.[38] And while Puerto Rican women continued to be admitted into Seamstresses' Local 22 in the next two decades, they were not completely accepted by the other workers here either. Will Herberg's 1953 study of this local revealed that Jewish and Italian "old-timers" resented the "newcomers" and "grumbled" at the prospects of the union being "flooded" with "non-union elements." They thought these "aliens" were "selfish," "lazy," and "irresponsible" and refused to help them learn the skills they needed to move into the better-paid shops.[39] Almost ten years later, during the 1962 congressional hearings on discrimination, Herbert Hill, the labor advocate for the National Association for the Advancement of Colored People, testified that discrimination against people of color was rampant throughout all the locals, particularly those that had organized the better-paid shops, and that the top leadership of the union did little to prevent this by following a "non-policy" against discrimination.[40]

The impact on Puerto Ricans of the ILGWU leadership "nonpolicy" concerning ethnic prejudice in the garment industry has been carefully scrutinized by Hill and other critics of the union.[41] For Hill, the most serious effect was that throughout the 1950s and 1960s *puertorriqueñas* entered the lowest-paid and least-skilled locals and were forced to remain in them with few chances for advancement either in the union or in the shops. Throughout the 1960s he bitterly criticized the union leaders for this situation and challenged them to democratize their union.[42] Writing almost twenty years later, Robert Laurentz similarly chastised the leaders of the ILGWU for their tacit acceptance of discrimination in the locals and for their own undemocratic practices as heads of the union, although he recognized, "the onus here did not completely lie with the ILGWU. The union was not the motive force for social relations within the industry, the employers were." For Laurentz, "the employers were essentially responsible for the racial stratification system that developed within the industry;" yet he acknowledged that "the union had its realm of responsibility and within this realm it may have acted in ways that could be seen by some as 'racist.'" [43]

One of the ways in which the top leaders of the union acted if not in a "racist" manner at least undemocratically was by perpetuating a political hierarchy that assured Jewish and Italian males control over the entire union.[44] This was made possible by an election process that rested on rigid eligibility rules for the offices of president and secretary-treasurer and for membership on the General Executive Board. These rules severely limited the number of challengers for elective office, especially among newcomers to the union. Since political groups or caucuses were not allowed to convene until three months before the annual convention, it was difficult for contending candidates to meet with the rank and file to present their platforms. Those in office, however, could meet with members as often as they wished. Exclusiveness in appointment methods also prevented Puerto Rican women from becoming local managers or agents in the lower ranks of the ILGWU. Vacancies, transfers, or new appointments were systematically given to Jewish or Italian members of the union.[45] Even in areas such as East Harlem, where Puerto Rican female garment workers were clearly in the majority, the union maintained an Italian male representative, Joseph Piscatello, as the ILGWU organizer during these years.[46] Thus, the Puerto Rican rank and file was excluded from full participation in union activities while its Jewish and Italian male members retained control.

One obvious outcome of Puerto Rican women's powerlessness in the union locals and in the ILGWU leadership was their complete exclusion from the decision-making processes that determined issues of great concern to them as workers. A key issue was the union's decision to accept the low wage schedules that bosses and job contractors offered garment workers during the years when Puerto Ricans constituted the bulk of the industry's labor force. Throughout these years the contracts that were negotiated by the ILGWU called for wages that were far below those of other manufacturing jobs. In 1956, for example, the average weekly wage for a garment worker in New York City was $55.60 as compared to an average manufacturing wage of $74.60.[47] By 1961, in the areas of Harlem, the Bronx, and Brooklyn where the majority of Puerto Rican garment workers were found, average weekly wages had risen to only $62.54.[48] In addition, the wage schedules prevalent in some locals—including Locals 32, 40, 62, 91, and 98, which contained large numbers of Puerto Rican members—did not distinguish between jobs in a particular trade. As a result, until 1963 all operators, cleaners, examiners, floor workers, and shipping clerks in most of these locals were offered a basic pay scale of $1.15 per hour.[49] Not only did the union accept the low wages set by manufacturers for its own, predominantly Hispanic, rank and file, but in the early 1960s it staunchly rejected proposals seeking to increase the minimum wage from $1.25 to $1.50 for city workers.[50]

The reasons why the ILGWU instituted a wage policy that obviously was contrary to the best interests of the majority of its labor constituency are controversial. One theory is that the union's preoccupation with the expansion of communism after World War II led Dubinsky and other labor leaders to forge an alliance with American entrepreneurs to safeguard the capitalist world from the Soviet "red plague." The suppression of wage levels, therefore, was simply one manifestation of the ILGWU's leadership's long-standing anticommunist ideology.[51] Viewed within the historical context of the union's earlier battles against its own radical and communist members, this explanation is quite plausible. The union's acceptance of low wages has also been linked to the garment industry's struggle for survival in New York City, and directly related to increasing competition from foreign imports and to the relocation of jobs to other parts of the country during the 1950s and 1960s. This argument maintains that because union leaders feared garment employers would abandon New York City if they asked for "too much," they quietly accepted lower wages for their members in their contract negotiations with employers.[52] But the low-wage policy of the ILGWU has also been defined as a deliberate effort on the part of Jewish union leaders to "artificially" restrain the wages of people of color in the garment industry.[53] One supporter of this thesis believes that, "By refusing to endorse the $1.50 minimum wage during this period, the ILGWU, in effect, helped keep Blacks and Puerto Ricans as low-wage labor for garment employers" while its leadership continued to profit.[54] Regardless of one's interpretation of the policy, its overall effect was to create distrust between union leaders and Puerto Rican workers. This is evident in the job actions taken by Puerto Rican workers in two New York City factories in 1957 and 1958. On these two occasions workers criticized a negotiation process that produced what they called "sweetheart" contracts, and they demanded that the courts replace the ILGWU as their bargaining agent.[55] Interviews with Puerto Rican women workers also indicate that these women did not think the union had handled their requests for higher wages fairly during these years.[56]

The exclusion of Puerto Ricans from powerful positions in the ILGWU likewise meant that they could not effectively oppose the union's decision to prevent the establishment of federally sponsored training programs in the garment industry during the early 1960s. By the late 1950s visible shortages in the high-skilled industries had become apparent. While it encouraged workers to improve their skills in the city's High School of Fashion Industries and the Harlem Institute for Fashion, or in some of the locals, the ILGWU refused to sanction the establishment of training programs in the garment industry.[57] Union leaders claimed that the garment business did not need a trained labor force and that the application of the Manpower Development and Training legislation of the early 1960s to the garment industry would be detrimental to the "stability" of this industry.[58] The stability they referred to depended, of course, on the low-wage, unskilled labor that Puerto Rican women provided for the industry at this time. The vehement opposition of the ILGWU to the creation of training programs and the unwillingness of white skilled workers in shops and in the locals to teach Puerto Rican women the more advanced skills they needed for work in the better-paid shops thus prevented these women from advancing in the trades and perhaps from using the garment industry as a vehicle for upward mobility, as had been possible for earlier ethnic groups.[59] We should remember, however, that unlike the white European workers who entered the garment industry at a time of expansion, *puertorriqueñas* also were generally disadvantaged by the contractions that the industry experienced in the region during the post–World War II decades.

Last, because Puerto Rican women were never represented on the union's executive board, they were not in a position to influence the distribution of union funds. A careful analysis of ILGWU assets during the 1950–64 period shows that union resources were quite vast. Most of these funds went into benefit programs for the workers, but some were specially reserved by ILGWU leaders for political propaganda or for pet national or international causes. An examination of disbursements from the union's 1952 reserve fund, for example, shows contributions of $100,000 to the United Jewish Appeal, $75,000 for the Jewish Labor Committee, $25,000 and $10,000 respectively for orphans and flood victims in Italy, $5,000 for a Jewish school in Paris, $3,000 for the United Negro College Fund, and $3,000 for the National Association for the Advancement of Colored People.[60] Budgetary reports published in *Justice* from 1950 to 1959 reveal the same pattern of distribution of union funds. In 1956 *Justice* did report that the ILGWU donated monies for the purchase of a bus that was later converted to a healthmobile and given to the people of Puerto Rico, and in 1960 the union made a contribution to the victims of a hurricane that swept the island.[61] But there is no evidence to indicate that the ILGWU leadership ever granted any other aid to Puerto Rico or to other Latin American countries during the decade. Although Hispanic workers objected to the insensitivity of union leaders, who allocated vast sums of money for projects that reflected their own personal interests rather than those of the rank and file, they did not succeed in creating a more equitable distribution of funds in the ILGWU during these years.[62]

Puerto Rican Garment Workers in New York City, 1965–1980

By the late 1960s the garment industry in New York City had entered an accelerated period of decline that deeply affected the lives of Puerto Rican garment workers throughout the city. The reasons for the decline were not significantly different from those of the preceding decade. Increasing competition from lower-wage areas and the rise of foreign imports simply caused larger numbers of the city's garment businesses to shut down or relocate to new sites. However, the expansion of multiunit firms (those operating more than one plant) in other parts of the country, and the establishment of U.S. multinational corporations abroad, threatened to decimate the entire industry during this period.[63] Yet because these large-scale, concentrated forms of production focused on the more standardized items of the trade, such as children's clothing, women's underwear, and sportswear, and avoided the more fashion-sensitive women's dress and outerwear industries—sectors of the industry historically based in New York City—the city retained its position as an important center of clothing manufacture.[64] An influx of new immigrant women workers predominantly from Cuba, Haiti, the Dominican Republic, and Southeast Asia—workers who were forced by a variety of circumstances to accept wages far below those set by federal law or union contracts—also contributed to the survival of the garment industry in the city. For *puertorriqueñas* continuing to work in the garment trades during these years, this meant increased job competition, deteriorating work conditions, and declining wages. Meanwhile, constricted by an unchanging labor relations ideology, the ILGWU was not effective in addressing the problems that continued to plague the industry in the next two decades.

Most of these problems, researchers agree, stemmed from the failure of New York's garment manufacturers to remain competitive in the midst of mounting pressures brought on by new consumer market shifts, increases in foreign imports and relocations, and the takeover of the apparel industry by big business. During the 1960s and 1970s intensification of consumer demands for more casual wear—now manifested by a craze for blue jeans and T-shirts, and for women's paid-work clothes—dealt a heavy blow to the city's garment industry. As the demand for more informal wear increased, many more of the city's manufacturers lost ground because they were unable to transform their limited workplaces into factories of mass production. In contrast, producers such as Levi Strauss, Blue Bell, Warnaco, and Evan Picone expanded their operations across the country. Using economies of scale (huge plants, bulk buying, and shipping), modern technology, highly standardized production, and the labor of women in lower-wage areas—particularly throughout the South, Southwest, and California—these large firms came to dominate important sectors of the U.S. consumer market by the early 1980s. But the threat of increased imports from Japan, South Korea, Hong Kong, and Taiwan, among other areas, and the attraction of a still-lower-wage workforce abroad also impelled American-owned multiunits to expand as multinational corporations during these years. Multinational garment employers usually set up their plants in countries such as Mexico, Haiti, the Dominican Republic, and the Philippines, whose governments offered lucrative tax exemptions and guaranteed a fairly "stable" (nonstriking) labor force.[65] Whether controlled by American entrepreneurs or by foreign investors, multinational corporations undermined vital sectors of the city's garment industry by flooding the consumer market with garments made with the poorly-paid labor of women workers abroad and imported almost duty-free under existing tariff laws.

These transformations in the garment industry spelled doom for Puerto Rican needleworkers in New York City, especially those who worked in the trades most affected by the rise in low-cost imports— namely, skirts, casual dresses, sportswear, children's clothing, and underwear. Their oral histories, recorded by so many scholars, tell of an ever greater difficulty in finding jobs, more frequent layoffs, increasingly adverse working conditions, and wages that in many instances were far lower than what garment workers had earned in the 1950s.[66] Because jobs were so hard to come by, *puertorriqueñas* who had been employed as highly paid, skilled (or semiskilled) seamstresses in the 1950s were at times reduced to unskilled low-wage labor in the 1960s and 1970s. Often these women were forced to work off the books in run-down shops without health and pension benefits or paid vacations and holidays. Elderly migrants especially had difficulty getting jobs when they were laid off or their factory had closed. To survive many employed factory workers supplemented their meager earnings through garment work at home, a second job, or government programs.[67] And for all of them there was the constant threat of job loss. In 1969 alone the city lost some twenty thousand apparel jobs, and many of these were jobs traditionally held by Puerto Rican needle and garment workers.[68] It is not surprising, therefore, that the 1970 census should record a sizable decline (27 percent) in the labor-force participation rate of Puerto Rican women in the area, as compared to the 40 percent present in the workforce in 1950 and the 38 percent in 1960).[69] A systematic comparative analysis of the labor-force participation rate of *puertorriqueñas* in fifty-six cities across the nation, based on this census, suggests that the decline in the labor-force participation rate of working Puerto Rican women in New York City during these years was directly related to reduced demand for "nondurable" operatives—among these sewing-machine operators.[70] This study estimated that only about 40 percent of all employed *puertorriqueñas* were still working as operatives in 1970. By 1980 this figure had dropped to 25.5 percent (as compared to 73 percent in 1950).[71]

The decline of Puerto Rican needleworkers in New York City during the 1960s and 1970s was also related to ILGWU policies that did not effectively challenge the deteriorating conditions *puertorriqueñas* encountered in their workplaces. Indeed, the ILGWU seemed paralyzed during this period by the magnitude of the problems that beset the industry. Its campaign to prevent clothing manufacturing companies, such as Vanity Fair, Judy Bond, and Kellwood, from relocating by seeking a court injunction, failed miserably.[72] Although the union succeeded in increasing federal minimum wages for American workers, it was powerless to affect the international labor market, and it was only partially successful in halting imports, the exploitation of undocumented workers, and the spread of homework throughout the city. Moreover, in spite of the obvious reality that the ILGWU's wage-restraint and nonstrike policies had not contained relocations, the union still maintained these as the cornerstone of its bargaining philosophy of no strikes or other job actions.[73] This perennial conservatism on the part of the ILGWU, and its continuing pro-business attitude during these critical years, therefore, made some labor-conscious *puertorriqueñas* feel this union was no longer a workers' organization. One woman summed up these feelings in a late 1970s interview by commenting, "The basic problems with the union is that the union is very tight with the bosses. In terms of workers' rights, the union will intervene only if there is a big problem, and even then, one must go directly to the union office and make a big fuss in order for them to do anything."[74] In addition, Puerto Rican women were dissatisfied with the fact that the ILGWU leadership continued to ignore them for important posts while Jewish males held tight to the reins of power.[75] Still others complained of the union's neglect of workers' benefits, especially medical care, which did not cover major medical expenses or members' dependents until 1979.[76] Unable to air these criticisms publicly, because of the strength and persistence of union repression, most *puertorriqueñas* withdrew from the garment industry and gave way to a new immigrant labor force consisting mainly of Haitian, Central American, Chinese, and Dominican women whose experiences in the industry and in the ILGWU have been similar to their own.[77]

Conclusion

The case of *puertorriqueñas* in the garment industry of New York City is a significant chapter in the history of Puerto Rican women workers in the twentieth century. The arrival of migrant women from the island presented New York garment employers with a vast new "reserve army of labor" for their factories and sweatshops, especially after severe shortages in European immigrant labor developed in the late 1940s and 1950s. Because of the important role Puerto Rican women played in the preservation of critical sectors of the city's garment industry, some researchers argue that if it were not for:

the Puerto Rican migration, New York City would not have been able to hold on to this very important industry. Puerto Ricans have, in a sense, provided a 'positive tipping point'. Without this source of cheap labor many more firms would have had to reduce their production. In this sense, New York's claim to be the garment capital of the world rests upon Puerto Rican shoulders.[78]

Additionally, the fact that Puerto Rican needleworkers were among the first U.S. colonial subjects forced to migrate to the mainland during this century in search of work allows us to explore the nature of modern colonial labor migrations within the context of capitalist configurations. *Puertorriqueñas* readily came to this country because Puerto Rico was an American territorial possession; hence, their migration was unencumbered by obstructive immigration laws. Yet Puerto Rican women workers also flocked to the United States in response to employment opportunities in the domestic labor market; but during periods of economic crisis many women workers returned to Puerto Rico.[79] These labor-migration trends have been carefully documented by demographic studies indicating that in the 1940s more women than men emigrated from Puerto Rico to the United States; in the 1950s there were still more women than men (though only in the forty-to-seventy age bracket) as revealed by the island's emigration counts.[80] Conversely, studies on return migration in the early 1960s noted that over half (58.8 percent) of migrants returning to Puerto Rico were women workers in the operatives category.[81] In sum, what these statistics indicate is that the migration of *puertorriqueñas* has been greatly influenced by the economic needs of New York's garment industry, but also that the movements of needleworkers specifically have strongly shaped Puerto Rican patterns of labor migration to and from the United States in the twentieth century.

The history of Puerto Rican garment workers in New York City also sheds light on the persistence of exclusionary sexist patterns in a patriarchal work setting that have denied women an equal share in the economic gains of this country. Further, it suggests the evolution of concomitant patterns of discrimination based on cultural and racial differ-

ences that embittered the lives of women of color in the garment factories
and union locals. As was the case with earlier needleworkers, Puerto Rican
women were incorporated into the garment trades as semiskilled, low-
wage laborers because of employers' (and union leaders') expectations
concerning the work women were best suited to do. Thus, like Jewish, Italian, and African American women before them, *puertorriqueñas* worked in
a sex-segregated environment controlled by male bosses who exploited
their labor to maximize profits, while male union leaders ignored their
concerns. But, unlike the white European immigrants who predominated
in the garment labor force in earlier years, *puertorriqueñas*—along with
the African American needleworkers who were present but in smaller
numbers—were also handicapped by racist and ethnocentric attitudes and
practices that gave white workers a preferential status in the trades and in
the union locals. The deliberate exclusion of Puerto Rican women from
the better-paid jobs and from important posts in the locals eventually denied these workers their potential for advancement as skilled tailors and
labor leaders in the clothing industry. Since they were the forerunners of
other workers from the Caribbean, the rest of Latin America, and Asia,
puertorriqueñas in the garment industry had much to share with other
"Third World" women about economic exploitation and racial hostility in
an American workplace.

Moreover, Puerto Rican women garment workers were the first in the
area to experience on a large scale the negative consequences of the production and labor market changes that resulted from the globalization
of the industry after the 1960s.[82] Increasing domestic and foreign competition forced many of the city's garment businesses to relocate to other
parts of the country and abroad, thus taking jobs that women traditionally performed in the industry. Yet, in spite of the severe contractions the
industry experienced during these hard times, various sectors of the garment trades survived the 1950s and 1960s as Puerto Rican migrant
women steadily supplied the low-wage labor the industry required during these years. But by the 1970s conditions in the industry had deteriorated so badly that Puerto Rican garment workers were forced either to
withdraw from the industry or to submit to extremely stressful work conditions: heavy increases in section work, sharp declines in wages, constant layoffs, loss of jobs. Since many Puerto Rican garment workers were
migrant women with few other occupational skills, and little education
or English-speaking ability, they were not able to shift easily to other

kinds of jobs. Eventually, many were forced to join the ranks of the permanently unemployed—forever abandoning the hope of using work in the garment industry as a stepping-stone to a better life in America. With their wages in this industry, however, some *puertorriqueñas* were able to support and educate children, who are now part of a new generation of Puerto Rican workers in America.[83]

NOTES

Acknowledgments: I wish to give my very special thanks to Myra Armstead, Eddie González, Dorothy O. Helly, Steve Krueger, Ruth Milkman, and David Sternberg for commenting on earlier versions of this essay. I am grateful for their probing questions and valuable suggestions.

1. For a detailed account of the contributions of other women workers to the construction of Puerto Rican communities in New York City, see Altagracia Ortiz, "Historical Vignettes of Puerto Rican Women Workers in New York City, 1895–1990," in *Handbook of Hispanic Cultures in the United States*, ed. Felix M. Padilla (Houston, Tex.: Arte Público Press, 1994), 219–38.

2. Virginia Sánchez Korrol, "Survival of Puerto Rican Women in New York before World War II," in *The Puerto Rican Struggle: Essays on Survival in the U.S.*, ed. Clara E. Rodríguez, Virginia Sánchez Korrol, and José Oscar Alers (New York: Puerto Rican Migration Research Consortium, 1980), 49.

3. Lawrence Chenault, *The Puerto Rican Migrant in New York* (New York: Columbia University, 1938; New York: Russell and Russell, 1970), 72.

4. Virginia Sánchez Korrol, "On the Other Side of the Ocean: The Work Experiences of Early Puerto Rican Migrant Women," *Caribbean Review* 8, no. 1 (March 1979): 22–23.

5. Chenault, *The Puerto Rican Migrant in New York*, 72.

6. Virginia Sánchez Korrol, *From Colonia to Community: The History of Puerto Ricans in New York City, 1917–1948* (Westport, Conn.: Greenwood Press, 1983), 89.

7. Between 1984 and 1985 the Oral History Task Force of the Centro de Estudios Puertorriqueños of Hunter College of the City University of New York conducted a series of interviews of Puerto Rican migrant women who worked in the garment industry during these years. These interviews became the basis for a radio documentary entitled "Nosotras trabajamos en la costura: Puerto Rican Women in the Garment Industry" (a program that won the 1985 Community Program Award from the National Federation of Community Broadcasters) and for a number of publications by Centro scholars.

8. Sánchez Korrol, "Survival of Puerto Rican Women," 47, 51. *Comadres* were either relatives or very close friends of a family who in the Catholic religious ceremony of baptism agreed to accept the responsibilities of coparenting a child or children in a given family. As *comadres* these women were not only godmothers to the children but became part of the tight kinship system that helped these early Puerto Rican migrant households to survive.

9. Chenault, *The Puerto Rican Migrant,* 79. Interestingly, Rosalyn Terborg-Penn notes that some West Indian women were able to obtain employment in the garment industry by passing as "Spanish." See Rosalyn Terborg-Penn, "Survival Strategies among African-American Women Workers: A Continuing Process," in *Women, Work and Protest: A Century of U.S. Women's Labor History,* ed. Ruth Milkman (Boston: Routledge and Kegan Paul, 1985), 139–55. In addition, studies conducted by Edward B. Shils and Elaine G. Wrong on African American and Puerto Rican participation in the garment industry indicate that by the 1960s and 1970s, although both groups suffered as a result of industry declines, Puerto Ricans were the preferred labor force. This was probably because economic and political conditions in Puerto Rico permitted the needlework tradition to continue among women on the island to a greater degree than sewing and quilting did among African American women on the mainland, leading employers to believe that "blacks do not make good needle workers." Elaine Gale Wrong, *The Negro in the Apparel Industry* (Philadelphia: University of Pennsylvania Press, 1974), 97. The funneling of African American women into service and laundry jobs that Mary Romero demonstrates so well may also have contributed to their exclusion from other occupations. Mary Romero, *Maid in the U.S.A* (New York: Routledge, 1992), 73–74, 78–79, 83.

10. Robert Laurentz, "Racial/Ethnic Conflict in the New York City Garment Industry, 1933–1900" (Ph.D. diss., State University of New York at Binghamton, 1980), 104–5, 135–39.

11. See, for example, Centro de Estudios Puertorriqueños, Oral History Task Force, interviews with Santos Pí by Celia Alvarez, Brooklyn, N.Y., August 30 and September 20, 1983. Transcriptions of interviews conducted under the auspices of the Centro de Estudios Puertorriqueños are on file at the Centro.

12. Centro de Estudios Puertorriqueños, Oral History Task Force, interview with Lucila Padrón by Ana Juarbe, New York City, January 24, 1984. African American workers also received the same treatment in the ILGWU: most locals did not organize them and if one or two African Americans joined a local, members boasted it was integrated. Jacqueline Jones, *Labor of Love, Labor of Sorrow: Black Women, Work, and the Family from Slavery to the Present* (New York: Basic Books, 1985), 168.

13. Transcript from article in *La Prensa* (New York) (December 23, 1933) and strike leaflet of 1934 in the International Ladies' Garment Workers' Union Archives, Charles S. Zimmerman Collection Records, Box 33, File 11, Cornell University, Ithaca, N.Y.

14. Laurentz, "Racial/Ethnic Conflict in the New York City Garment Industry," 123–24, 167.

15. Robert Asher, "Jewish Unions and the American Federation of Labor Power Structure, 1903–1935," *American Jewish Historical Quarterly* 40, no. 3 (March 1976): 222. On the struggles of white women in the ILGWU, see Alice Kessler-Harris, "Organizing the Unorganizable: Three Jewish Women and their Union," in *Class, Sex, and the Woman Worker,* ed. Milton Cantor and Bruce Laurie (Westport, Conn.: Greenwood Press, 1977), 144–65; Alice Kessler-Harris, "Problems of Coalition-Building: Women and Trade Unions in the 1920s," in Milkman, *Women, Work, and Protest,* 110–38. See also Rose Pesotta, *Bread upon the Waters* (Ithaca, N.Y.: New York State School of Industrial and Labor Relations, ILR Press, 1987).

16. Laurentz, "Racial/Ethnic Conflict in the New York City Garment Industry," 454.

17. African American women also entered the industry in large numbers during this

period. A 1943 survey reported some four thousand new hires (presumably mostly women) among African Americans in the eighteen months before the survey. Herbert R. Northrup, *Organized Labor and the Negro* (New York: Kraus Reprint Co., 1971), 121.

18. Centro de Estudios Puertorriqueños, Oral History Task Force, interview with Gregoria Lausell by Suzana García and Ana Juarbe, Brooklyn, New York, April 2, 1984; interviews with Santos Pí by Celia Alvarez, August 30 and September 20, 1983; interviews with Louise Delgado by Rina Benmayor and Blanca Vázquez, New York City, February 19 and 22, 1985. In her interview Delgado noted that in 1941 the factory she worked in had closed, but that the owner immediately set up five factories in Puerto Rico, illustrating the trend toward relocation to lower-wage areas by New York City clothing employers even during this early period.

19. Roy B. Helfgott, "Puerto Rican Integration in a Garment Union Local," *Proceedings of the Tenth Annual Meeting (1957), Industrial Relations Research Association* (New York: Industrial Relations Research Association, 1958), 1.

20. Rosemary Santana Cooney, "Intercity Variations in Puerto Rican Female Participation," *Journal of Human Resources* 14, no. 2 (Spring 1979): 225; Clarence Senior, *The Puerto Ricans: Strangers—Then Neighbors* (Chicago: Quadrangle Press, 1965), 93.

21. Christopher Rand, *The Puerto Ricans* (New York: Oxford University Press, 1958), 10; Roy B. Helfgott, "Women's and Children's Apparel," in *Made in New York: Case Studies in Metropolitan Manufacturing*, ed. Max Hall (Cambridge, Mass.: Harvard University Press, 1959), 94–95; Raymond Vernon and Edgar Malone Hoover, *Anatomy of a Metropolis: The Changing Distribution of People and Jobs within the New York Metropolitan Region* (Cambridge, Mass.: Harvard University Press, 1959), 220; Nathan Glazer and Daniel P. Moynihan, *Beyond the Melting Pot: The Negroes, Puerto Ricans, Jews, Italians and Irish of New York City* (Cambridge, Mass.: MIT Press and Harvard University, 1963), 131.

22. Helfgott, "Women's and Children's Apparel," 80–81; Vernon and Hoover, *Anatomy of a Metropolis*, 65.

23. Helfgott, "Women's and Children's Apparel," 82.

24. Laurentz, "Racial/Ethnic Conflict in the New York City Garment Industry," 263–69.

25. Dan Wakefield, *Island in the City: The World of Spanish Harlem* (Boston: Houghton Mifflin, 1959), 201.

26. Ibid., 202–3.

27. Ibid., 199–201; Dan Wakefield, "Worker from Puerto Rico: The Vulnerable Stranger," *The Nation*, April 13, 1957, 321.

28. Wakefield, *Island in the City*, 198.

29. Ibid., 199; Author's interview with Julia Bermuda Rodríguez, Brentwood, New York, November 17, 1984.

30. Oral History Task Force, interview with Lucila Padrón by Ana Juarbe, January, 24, 1984; interview with Santos Pí by Celia Alvarez and Blanca Vázquez, August 30 and September 20, 1983.

31. Roger Waldinger, *Through the Eye of the Needle: Immigrants and Enterprise in New York's Garment Trades* (New York: New York University Press, 1986), 56.

32. For more general discussion of the experiences of Puerto Rican men and women in the garment industry, see Altagracia Ortiz, "Puerto Rican Workers in the Garment Industry of New York City, 1960–1980," in *Labor Divided: Race and Ethnicity in United States La-*

bor Struggles, 1835–1960, ed. Robert Asher and Charles Stephenson (Albany: State University of New York Press, 1990), 105–25.

33. Oral History Task Force, interview with Lucila Padrón by Ana Juarbe, January 24, 1984.

34. Carol J. Smith, "Immigrant Women, Work and Use of Government Benefits: A Case Study of Hispanic Women Workers in New York's Garment Industry" (Ph.D. diss., Adelphi University School of Social Welfare, 1980), 91. See also Oral History Task Force, interview with Louise Delgado by Rina Benmayor and Blanca Vázquez, New York City, February 22, 1985.

35. Helfgott, "Puerto Rican Integration in a Garment Union Local," 2–3.

36. Ibid., 3.

37. Roy B. Helfgott, "Puerto Rican Integration in the Skirt Industry in New York City," in *Discrimination and Low Incomes: Social and Economic Discrimination against Minority Groups in Relation to Low Incomes in New York State,* ed. New School for Social Research (New York: Studies of New York State Commission against Discrimination 1959), 252–53.

38. Laurentz, "Racial/Ethnic Conflict in the New York City Garment Industry," 295.

39. Will Herberg, "The Old-Timers and the Newcomers: Ethnic Group Relations in a Needle Trades' Union," *Journal of Social Issues* (Summer 1953): 15, 17.

40. Labor Subcommittee of the House Committee on Education and Labor, testimony of Herbert Hill, August 17, 1962, 88th Cong., 1st sess., *Congressional Record* 109, part 2 (January 31, 1963); 1569–72. Florence Rice, an African American garment factory chairlady from 1957 to 1961 who also testified before the House Committee on Labor, Education and Welfare in 1962, was very critical of the absence of black representation in the top positions of the ILGWU and the blatant discrimination that prevailed in the shops. (For example, she charged that white women were the last fired when jobs were slow and the first recalled when work became available.) Rice was convinced that her difficulties in obtaining good jobs in the industry following the congressional hearings were due to an ILGWU campaign to blacklist her. Florence Rice, "It Takes a While to Realize That It Is Discrimination," in *Black Women in White America: A Documentary History,* ed. Gerda Lerner (New York: Random House, 1973), 275–81.

41. The focus of Hill's work, however, was on the impact on African Americans of discriminatory practices in the ILGWU and in the industry. Elaine Gale Wrong in her 1974 study on African Americans in the industry and the ILGWU also points out that although African Americans (like Puerto Ricans) had been present in the industry since World War I, by the 1960s they were still mainly found in shops "producing less expensive items" and in pressing jobs; they were rarely found as cutters and were not represented in top leadership positions in the union. Wrong, *The Negro in the Apparel Industry,* 31, 54–55, 60.

42. Herbert Hill, "Guardians of the Sweatshops: The Trade Unions, Racism, and the Garment Industry," in *Puerto Rico and Puerto Ricans: Studies in History and Society,* ed. Adalberto López and James Petras (New York: John Wiley and Sons, 1974), 393–94.

43. Laurentz, "Racial/Ethnic Conflict in the New York City Garment Industry," 306.

44. The exclusion of women from top leadership positions in organized labor was not unique to the ILGWU. A 1978 study by the Coalition of Labor Union Women indicated that while there were only two women officers and board members in the ILGWU and in the United Food and Commercial Workers' Union, there was only one in the American

Federation of State, County and Municipal Employees and none in the International Brotherhood of Teamsters (which had one of the largest female memberships), the International Brotherhood of Electrical Workers, and in the Communication Workers of America. The largest numbers of women in leadership positions were found in the National Education Association (five), Amalgamated Clothing and Textile Workers' Union (six), Service Employees International Union (seven), and the American Federation of Teachers (eight). Ruth Milkman, "Women Workers, Feminism and the Labor Movement since the 1960s," in *Women, Work and Protest,* 306.

45. Ibid., 286–88, 367, 445; Hill, "Guardians of the Sweatshops," 386–87; Herberg, "The Old-Timers and the Newcomers," 17–19.

46. Wakefield, *Island in the City,* 211.

47. Hill, "Guardians of the Sweatshops," 404.

48. Laurentz, "Racial/Ethnic Conflict in the New York City Garment Industry," 256–57.

49. In Local 91 all operators, ironers, cleaners, and finishers were paid $1.20 per hour. In Local 98 all operators, shipping clerks, and plastic-material cutters were likewise paid $1.20 per hour. "Floor-girls" in the latter local were paid $1.15 per hour. Hill, "Guardians of the Sweatshops," 405.

50. Michael Meyerson, "ILGWU: Fighting for Lower Wages," *Ramparts,* October 1969, 53.

51. Ibid., 55.

52. Ibid., 51; Hill, "Guardians of the Sweatshops," 388; Laurentz, "Racial/Ethnic Conflict in the New York City Garment Industry," 264, 250–57.

53. Hill, "Guardians of the Sweatshops," 388, 390; Laurentz, "Racial/Ethnic Conflict in the New York City Garment Industry," 444–45.

54. Laurentz, "Racial/Ethnic Conflict in the New York City Garment Industry," 308.

55. Hill, "Guardians of the Sweatshops," 392.

56. Centro de Estudios Puertorriqueños, Oral History Task Force, interview with Lucila Padrón by Ana Juarbe and Rina Benmayor, New York City, July 6, 1984. Distrust also marked African American and ILGWU relations. Florence Rice believed: "Many of the black workers never felt that the union really represented them. What you always found out was that the union man would say something in front of your face and he would go back to the boss and it would be completely different. So the union members began to learn that it was always a sweet-heart arrangement with the manufacturers." Rice, "It Takes a While," 278.

57. Even the training at the High School of Fashion Industries (HSFI) had its limitations. A study conducted by Sally Hillsman and Bernard Levenson in the mid-1970s suggested that race rather than potential or skills determined the placement of students at HSFI: white students were usually assigned to the elite fashion design program; black and Puerto Rican students were placed in the lower-status, less-skilled trade programs. In a 1982 update of their research Hillsman and Levenson tracked the placement of HSFI graduates, observing that 40 percent of all black and Puerto Rican women were placed in apparel jobs while only 25 percent of whites were placed in these jobs; 76 percent of blacks and Puerto Ricans, as opposed to 47 percent of white students, were placed in dressmaking; and 73 percent of blacks and Puerto Ricans were placed as sewing-machine operators, while only 40 percent of these students were white.

Hillsman and Levenson conclude that because of school administrators' and employers' racial stereotypes, African American and Puerto Rican young women were systematically discriminated against in the vocational programs of this high school, thus limiting their opportunities in the garment industry and in non-industry-related employment. Sally T. Hillsman and Bernard Levenson, "Job Opportunities of Black and White Working-Class Women," in *Women and Work: Problems and Perspectives,* ed. Rachel Kahn-Hut, Arlene Kaplan Daniels, and Richard Covard (New York: Oxford University Press, 1982), 218–33.

58. Hill, "Guardians of the Sweatshops," 396. According to Wrong the real reason was the fear that funds would be used in other areas of the country to gain an advantage over New York City where the union was strong, but this ploy failed. The South, for example, was able to expand its garment sector in despite the lack of federally funded programs. In light of this, Wrong finds it surprising that the ILGWU did not develop more job opportunities and an affirmative action plan to incorporate more African Americans and other minorities into leadership positions, thus increasing its strength in areas where it already had a base. Wrong, *The Negro in the Apparel Industry,* 107–8.

59. Waldinger, *Through the Eye of the Needle,* 53. See also Altagracia Ortiz, "The Labor Struggles of Puerto Rican Women in the Garment Industry of New York City, 1920–1960," *Cimarrón* (City University of New York Caribbean Studies Journal) 1, no. 2 (Spring 1988): 51–52.

60. *Justice,* February 1952, 3.

61. *Justice,* July 15, 1956, 3; *Justice,* October 1, 1960, 5.

62. Laurentz, "Racial/Ethnic Conflict in the New York City Garment Industry," 285.

63. For a discussion of the factors that precipitated the evolution and growth of multinational firms and the consequences of this for the garment industry, see Waldinger, *Through the Eye of the Needle,* 57–63. For a discussion of the impact of multinational corporations on women workers abroad, see Helen I. Safa, "Runaway Shops and Female Employment: The Search for Cheap Labor," *Signs* 7, no. 2 (1981): 418–33. See also Barbara Ehrenreich and Annette Fuentes, *Women in the Global Factory* (Boston: South End Press, 1984).

64. Clothing manufacturing in New York City continued in small shops, most with fewer than fifty employees.

65. Jorge A. Bustamante, "Maquiladoras: A New Face of International Capitalism on Mexico's Northern Frontier," in *Women, Men, and the International Division of Labor,* ed. June Nash and María P. Fernández-Kelly (Albany: State University of New York Press, 1983), 224–56; Helen I. Safa, "Women and Industrialization in the Caribbean," in *Women, Employment and the Family in the International Division of Labor,* ed. Sharon Stichter and Jane Parpart (New York: Macmillan, 1990), 72–97; André Corten and Isís Duarte, "Proceso de proletarización de mujeres: Las trabajadoras de industrias de ensamblaje en la República Dominicana," *Revista de ciencias sociales* 22, no. 3–4 (July–December 1981): 528–67; Cynthia H. Enloe, "Women Textile Workers in the Militarization of Southeast Asia," in Nash and Fernández-Kelly, *Women, Men, and the International Division of Labor,* 407–25; Cynthia H. Enloe, *Bananas, Beaches and Bases: Making Feminist Sense of International Politics* (Berkeley: University of California Press, 1989), 151–76.

66. Smith, "Immigrant Women, Work and Use of Government Benefits," 65–66, 85–90, 99, 164–65; Centro de Estudios Puertorriqueños, Oral History Task Force, interview with

Gloria Maldonado by Rina Benmayor and Blanca Vázquez, New York City, February 14, 1985.

67. Hill, "Guardians of the Sweatshops," 407; Smith, "Immigrant Women, Work and Use of Government Benefits," 127–57, 162, 165; Elizabeth Weiner and Hardy Green, "A Stitch in Our Time: New York's Hispanic Garment Workers in the 1980s," in *A Needle, A Bobbin, A Strike: Women Needleworkers in America* ed. Joan M. Jensen and Sue Davidson (Philadelphia: Temple University Press, 1984), 280.

68. Waldinger, *Through the Eye of the Needle*, 56.

69. Andrés Torres, "Human Capital, Labor Segmentation and Inter-Minority Relative Status: Black and Puerto Rican Labor in New York City, 1960–1980" (Ph.D. diss., New School for Social Research, 1988), 46.

70. Cooney, "Intercity Variations in Puerto Rican Female Participation," 222–35.

71. Ibid., 225; Palmira Ríos, "Puerto Rican Women in the U.S. Labor Force" (paper presented at Nosotras trabajamos en la costura: Puerto Rican Women in the Garment Industry, conference sponsored by the Centro de Estudios Puertorriqueños, New York City, September 30, 1984).

72. Laurentz, "Racial/Ethnic Conflict in the New York City Garment Industry," 259, 348–49.

73. For the origins of this philosophy, see Jesse Thomas Carpenter, *Competition and Collective Bargaining in the Needle Trades, 1910–1967* (Ithaca, N.Y.: New York State School of Industrial and Labor Relations, 1972), 38.

74. Smith, "Immigrant Women, Work and Use of Government Benefits," 92.

75. See for example Oral History Task Force, interview with Gloria Maldonado by Rina Benmayor and Blanca Vázquez, February 14, 1985.

76. It was not until 1979 that the ILGWU began to provide Blue Cross and Blue Shield benefits to its members and their dependents. But in the same year the ILGWU terminated its supplementary unemployment benefits program, designed to aid those unemployed by factory closings. Smith, "Immigrant Women, Work and Use of Government Benefits," 171.

77. Roger Waldinger, "Immigration and Industrial Change in the New York City Apparel Industry," in *Hispanics in the U.S. Economy*, ed. George J. Borjas and Marta Tienda (New York: Academic Press, 1985), 323–49; Patricia R. Pessar, "The Dominicans: Women in the Household and the Garment Industry," in *New Immigrants in New York*, ed. Nancy Foner (New York: Columbia University Press, 1987), 103–29; Weiner and Green, "A Stitch in Our Time," 278–79; Peter Kwong, *The New Chinatown* (New York: Hill and Wang, 1987), 25–42.

78. Clara Rodríguez, "The Economic Factors Affecting Puerto Ricans in New York," in *Labor Migration under Capitalism: The Puerto Rican Experience*, ed. Centro de Estudios Puertorriqueños, History Task Force (New York: Monthly Review Press, 1979), 213, 229 n. 29.

79. José L. Vázquez Calzada, "Demographic Aspects of Migration," in Centro de Estudios Puertorriqueños, *Labor Migration under Capitalism*, 223–24, 235.

80. José Hernández-Alvarez, *Return Migration to Puerto Rico* (Berkeley: Institute of International Studies, University of California, 1967), 60.

81. José Hernández-Alvarez, "Migration, Return, and Development in Puerto Rico," *Economic Development and Cultural Change* 16, no. 4 (July 1968): 579–80.

82. By the 1960s African American women had begun to leave operative positions for

clerical and other better-paid jobs that became available as a result of civil rights legislation and affirmative action programs. Wrong, *The Negro in the Apparel Industry*, 47–49, 73.

83. My mother's work in the garment industry made it possible for my brother and my sisters to get a high-school education and for me to go to college. The life stories of other children of garment workers in the United States also reaffirm these women's legacy of hard work and commitment to family. See, for example, Rina Benmayor et al., "Stories to Live By: Continuity and Change in Three Generations of Puerto Rican Women," *Oral History Review* 16, no. 2 (Fall 1988): 1–46 and Pereta Rodríguez, "Growing up in the International Ladies' Garment Workers' Union," *Visión (El periódico del barrio)* 5, no. 4 (May–June 1993): 6–7.

THREE

Toward Bilingual Education: Puerto Rican Women Teachers in New York City Schools, 1947–1967

VIRGINIA SÁNCHEZ KORROL

T he last thirty years, and particularly the decades of the 1970s and 1980s, have set the stage for a proliferation of scholarly investigations that both extend and challenge the interpretations of the Puerto Rican experience of earlier researchers. More recent studies have begun to focus on the intersections of gender, race, class, and ethnicity. Among them are critical representations of the transformations forged by Puerto Rican women in several arenas, including the pedagogical. Utilizing the methodology of oral history, archival materials, and the testimonials of Puerto Rican women themselves, such studies aim to reconstruct this historical legacy, providing a more balanced interpretation of the group's experiences and placing it within broader societal perspectives.

Scholarly sources now document the history, gender roles, labor force participation, political and sociological developments, and cultural legacies of Puerto Ricans in the United States prior to the mid-twentieth century. But while urgent and overarching themes such as migration, colonialism, race, and intergroup relations inform the study of the community in current research, less has been written about those specific historical moments when Puerto Ricans have both challenged and collaborated with the dominant society to bring about important and mutually beneficial social change for the community. Such a dynamic process characterized the activities of Puerto Rican educators in their attempts to bring quality education to the Spanish-speaking children of the New York City public schools in the decades following World War II.

This chapter documents the particular struggles of Puerto Rican teachers, predominantly middle- and working-class women, to provide alternative modes of instruction for the increasing numbers of Spanish-speaking youngsters arriving in this city during the late 1940s and throughout the 1950s. Specifically, my study examines the historical role these educators played in the development of bilingual and English as a Second Language (ESL) educational practices and the events that institutionalized bilingual education in New York. The essay will show that, contrary to popular opinion, the education of children has long been a primary objective in continental Puerto Rican communities.

Educational Issues between World Wars

The educational concerns of Puerto Rican communities in the United States are of long standing. For the leaders of the small pre–World War II community in New York City, education rapidly became a principal concern, as was apparent in the organized activities of the fledgling migrant community. Such evidence appears as early as 1913, when a tobacco worker residing in New York alludes to the educational committees and study groups pledged to generating and disseminating intellectual and cultural information. These early workers' organizations varied in ideology and purpose, as this worker observed:

> The educational circles [of the mutual aid societies] were always of anarchist ideology with the exception of the Círculo de Trabajadores [Workers' Circle] in Brooklyn, which admitted workers of diverse ideologies. . . . In my neighborhood there was a club called El Tropical, which sponsored dances and held conferences from time to time.[1]

But maintaining the community's language and culture, along with an awareness of Puerto Rican and Latin American history and politics became important goals for numerous community organizations, such as the Alianza Obrera and the Puerto Rican Brotherhood of America.[2] Other groups, fearful that migrant children would lose their fluency in Spanish, offered language and culture classes after the regular school day, while others placed more emphasis on organizing religious festivals, such as events for Three Kings' Day and Easter, specifically geared for young audiences. At the next level, the Liga Puertorriqueña e Hispana, formed in 1926 in order to advocate for the welfare of the Puerto Rican community, represented a confederation of community associations. Among its guiding principles were: "obtaining civic defense and promoting the general welfare of United States citizens of Porto Rican and Spanish birth." One of its immediate objectives was to promote an education center.[3] League activities often combined social action with a political consciousness bent on protecting the civil rights of Puerto Ricans as American citizens.

Another grassroots association, Madres y Padres Pro-Niños Hispanos (Mothers and Fathers in Support of Hispanic Children) openly petitioned local school officials to recognize their children's Spanish-language proficiencies and academic skills. Active in the late 1930s and early 1940s, the group consisted of community parents who felt their children's education in city schools was substandard. A major concern of these parents was the common practice in New York schools of placing migrant children in grades below their age levels because they lacked proficiency in English, even when they had already completed that grade in Puerto Rico. Such children were also often placed in remedial or other special classes. The parents went so far as to volunteer their services as interpreters or liaisons between the school and the *barrio latino*, suggesting the placement of a parent in every classroom.[4] By bridging the language gap, this group intended to demonstrate the intelligence and capabilities of their children under more favorable conditions.

As early as 1937 the Catholic settlement house, Casita María, offered English instruction in partnership with the Board of Education. During the 1930s, the Puerto Rican Department of Labor also prided itself on creating programs in New York aimed at increasing the numbers of English-speakers among Puerto Rican migrants. The difference between these efforts and the projects of earlier community groups seemed to be that the more formal programs sought to Americanize the student, while the grassroots groups recognized the importance of maintaining native language fluency and cultural identity. While some groups ascribed to the theory that fluency in Spanish would facilitate English-language acquisition, others simply saw no conflict in learning both, and in fostering bilingualism and biculturalism.

Along with weekly and daily presses, magazines like *Artes y Letras,* published in New York City between 1933 and 1945, frequently editorialized about educational issues, citing the importance of nurturing the child's heritage in primary education. Local newspapers and community groups often interpreted their roles as defenders of cultural ties and tradition, leading them to challenge the dominant Anglo society on the education of barrio children. One example was the *Artes y Letras* editorial of March 1936, which denounced as harassment the intelligence testing of Harlem's Spanish-speaking youth. With the support of influential community groups, the journal launched a crusade against the New York City Chamber of Commerce, the group responsible for the testing, which had found Puerto Rican children to be genetically impaired slow learners. These obviously biased results so angered the Puerto Rican and Latino community that it rejected the conclusions of the testing service in an open forum, not only for stigmatizing Puerto Rican children but also for failing to involve Spanish-speaking professionals, who might have been more sensitive to the community's reality, in the testing.[5] This incident became a rallying cry for Harlem congressman Vito Marcantonio, long considered a champion of Puerto Rican causes. The politician contended that Puerto Rican children were unjustly served by the report precisely because the exams failed to take into account such factors as social, economic, linguistic, and environmental barriers.

In 1938 American social scientist Lawrence Chenault, in his classic study, *The Puerto Rican Migrant in New York City,* described common attitudes of teachers and other professionals toward Puerto Rican children:

Many Puerto Rican children who enter the public schools in New York City speak or understand little English. The children who are transferred from schools in Puerto Rico to those in New York are usually put back in their classes so that they are with children who are two or three years younger than they are. Americans who are teaching Puerto Rican children express the opinion that these children have had less training in discipline and in group cooperation than American children. . . . One large agency in the settlement, which has dealt with Puerto Rican children for many years, reported that under proper conditions Puerto Rican children are responsive, easily managed and affectionate. In contrast to this, another large institution said that for some reason which they could not explain the Puerto Rican children were more destructive than any group of children with whom they have had contact. All the evidence obtainable shows the relation of unsatisfactory home conditions to difficulties at school.[6]

Thus Chenault reiterated opinions held by many educators who typically were not Hispanic themselves and knew very little about Puerto Ricans. They were committed to promote Americanization by policies that failed to consider the cultural and linguistic heritage of Puerto Rican students, and these educators generally misunderstood the positive impact that could come from engaging parents and the community in the educational process. Faced with the need to accommodate growing numbers of children who, although American citizens by birth, nevertheless represented a foreign culture and language, the educational establishment responded with English-only instructional programs steeped in convention and inflexibility. But as a steady stream of these newcomers continued to pour into the city's school corridors, particularly in the years immediately following World War II, new strategies had to be formulated. This was, in general, the situation to which Puerto Rican educators would respond.

Puerto Ricans and the Post–World War II Public School System

Following the Second World War, thousands of Puerto Rican men and women, "excess" laborers dislocated by the industrialization program known as Operation Bootstrap, migrated to the United States. Lured by the promise of jobs, Puerto Rican laborers became essential to New York City's thriving industrial productivity, particularly in the garment industry and other kinds of manufacturing, and in restaurants, laundries, and hospitals. This "Great Migration," as the massive exodus was called, also meant sharp increases in the numbers of school-age Puerto Rican children, who would soon overcrowd the city's institutions, agencies, and support services. So pervasive was the situation that the arrival of a flight from San Juan on Sunday invariably meant Spanish-speaking newcomers would be registered in the school system on Monday.[7]

In 1948 a Committee of the Association of Assistant Superintendents attempted to address the situation by recommending the appointment of Spanish-speaking teachers as liaisons between the migrant population and the schools. This recommendation was contained in a report that is considered the first systematic study of Puerto Rican children in the

United States.[8] Highlighting the migration, assimilation, acculturation, and instruction of Puerto Rican children arriving in New York City, the report noted that some 13,914 Spanish-speaking students were enrolled in the city's public schools, many of whom needed instruction in their native language before they could progress into the regular school curriculum. Thus

> the Elementary Division of the Board of Education has appointed a group of 10 Puerto Rican teachers (Substitute Auxiliary Teachers) to schools having the greatest concentration of Puerto Ricans . . . to assist in the orientation of these children [and to] serve as liaison between the school and the community.[9]

From 1949 to 1953, another group—the Mayor's Committee on Puerto Rican Affairs—also assessed the condition of the community and issued a series of reports that essentially endorsed the superintendents' recommendations and the actions of the Board of Education. The Mayor's Committee called for a more comprehensive plan that included appointing Spanish-speaking teachers, expediting licensing procedures and examination schedules, disseminating information about Puerto Ricans, and creating curricular materials for the instruction of Spanish-speaking students.[10] However, the implementation of this plan depended on an adequate supply of bilingual teachers and except for those who taught the language at the secondary level, Spanish-speaking teachers were virtually nonexistent.

Up until this time, the methods and staff for teaching English to speakers of foreign languages had been woefully limited. There was no established curriculum for teaching English as a second language. The New York public schools favored a policy of total immersion, whereby English was the only language used in the classroom. But language was not the sole issue affecting the education of Puerto Rican children, according to authorities in the field: "Some have never attended school; others lack fundamental abilities in the communication arts; some lack basic concepts in many curricular areas."[11] And all confronted the inherent problems of the uprooted. Meanwhile, as these issues were being debated, the Board of Education continued to place migrant children in regular classes, where they were paired in a "buddy system" with an older or more experienced Spanish-speaking child who would help them negotiate the complexities of the language and the new school experience. Students unable to function in mainstream classrooms were relegated to classes especially designed to focus on English-language instruction.

Within the assimilationist paradigm, it was considered important to teach the concept of the American melting pot. However, the Great Migration coincided with a growing tolerance for cultural pluralism in schools, at least in principle. In response, pedagogical theories became focused on the whole child in what was described as a "total educational and social philosophy."[12] Educators of Puerto Rican children in New York City believed that many of their adjustment problems stemmed from their prior schooling in the homeland, where an inappropriate curriculum structured along the lines of mainland educational goals and using English as the language of instruction had been autocratically imposed upon the island. Mandated by acts of Congress—first the Foraker Act in 1900, and later the Jones Act of 1917—the island's educational system came under the supervision of appointed United States commissioners. The medium of instruction shifted between English and Spanish, depending on the philosophy of the particular government appointee. Such vacillation rendered students academically ill equipped in both languages.

In retrospect, the Mayor's Committee on Puerto Rican Affairs was progressive in its mid-century deliberations because it recommended an educational policy that met a constellation of mainland Puerto Rican needs. It gave attention to the delivery of social programs including health services, housing, foster care, and recreation. Moreover, the committee legitimized bilingualism and biculturalism in New York City classrooms when it stated:

> There is no doubt that a Spanish-speaking person on the staff will facilitate this initial contact with the schools. Many questions that arise in the minds of the parents concerning the school program, routines and special services offered by the school as well as many questions that arise in the minds of the school personnel concerning important aspects of the child's previous schooling and background will be resolved through the medium of the foreign language.[13]

The rationale for encouraging the use of Spanish by the classroom teacher, that it was "important that he [the student] communicate with others in Spanish until he is able to express himself somewhat adequately in English," was logical.[14] But the utilization of the students' language, even as a temporary medium for instruction, did indeed signal a radical shift from conventional methods couched in assimilationist theories and a move toward a more pluralistic, multilingual and multicultural paradigm. Whether of its own volition or not, the Board of Education embraced this new direction and proposed policies over the next two decades designed for its implementation.

What transpired to bring about such changes in the Board's policies, if not in its daily practices, from total immersion to consideration of bilingual methods? Several factors may be considered as catalysts for this ideological transition. First, around this time pedagogical theories emerged that emphasized the education of the complete child. This approach entailed sensitivity to the child's home and community, environment, the experiences he or she brought into the classroom, and the language and culture of the individual student. Second, the Puerto Rican community itself brought pressure to bear on city agencies, especially over the difficulties the Board of Education had in providing for the needs of Spanish-speaking youth. Third, since the turn-of-the-century European immigration, there had not been such a massive infusion of non-English speakers in New York City schools. Teachers and staff were totally unprepared to deal with this influx. To complicate the situation further, the Board could not lose sight of the fact that Puerto Ricans were U.S. citizens, educated under American policies in their native land. Finally, within the political context of the Cold War, the early 1960s witnessed the creation of viable bilingual programs for Cuban refugees in Miami. These represented concrete pedagogical models that would ultimately be adopted in the education of Puerto Ricans in New York.

The Substitute Auxiliary Teacher: A Profile

One of the earliest efforts at addressing the problems of educating Puerto Rican youngsters came about in New York City in the late 1940s. This occurred when a principal in Public School (P.S.) 25, a Bronx elementary school with a significant Spanish-speaking population, assigned a bilingual teacher to serve as an intermediary between the school and the community. This opened the door to the hiring of Spanish-speaking teachers as substitute auxiliary teachers (SATs), the title given to the new position. The first such teacher was Ana Peñaranda Marcial. Before her appointment, and the employment of the ten SATs who followed her into the system, the few Puerto Rican educators found in the schools were teachers of Spanish at the secondary level. Their relative scarcity in the schools had less to do with their academic preparation than with the fact that Puerto Rican teachers typically had pronounced accents and seldom passed the speech test required of all teachers by the city's Board of Examiners. Indeed, many teachers trained in Puerto Rico probably left the profession in New York to become bilingual case workers with the Department of Welfare or with Catholic Charities because of such bureaucratic obstacles. Many of these individuals made their careers by providing bilingual and bicultural social services to the Spanish-speaking community and founding impressive organizations of their own.[15]

Because she was the first of the educators hired as substitute auxiliary teachers, it is important to note the experiences and qualifications that Peñaranda Marcial brought to the profession. She was born Ana Peñaranda in Arecibo, Puerto Rico, just three years after the United States invaded and occupied the island. Thus, Peñaranda Marcial grew to adulthood under a colonial system that essentially denied her any legal status until 1917, when American citizenship was bestowed on Puerto Ricans. As part of a process of fostering Americanization, compulsory education had been extended throughout the island since 1900, as a way to prepare Puerto Rican youth to function in the political-economic system of the new order. This objective necessitated an increase in teacher-training programs. Although these programs were designed to attract men, they mostly drew women into the teaching profession. Peñaranda Marcial was one who took advantage of a seven-week program that offered a temporary teaching certificate providing one continued to study toward the baccalaureate degree.

From 1921 until 1943, when she earned her baccalaureate degree as a teacher (*maestra graduada*) from the University of Puerto Rico, Peñaranda Marcial accumulated knowledge and experience that would subsequently serve her well in the New York barrios. On the island she taught all levels of elementary school. From a heterogeneous one-room schoolhouse where all the grades mixed together to village schools where students rotated according to grade level, Ana Peñaranda Marcial weathered it all. As a novice rural teacher, she learned to ride horseback in order to travel the circuitous mountain routes between village and countryside. Resources and teaching salaries were woefully inadequate. Peñaranda Marcial earned $60.20 per month, a sum that would rise to $70 only in her final years of teaching. In the early years of her career, she was expected to spend the entire week, from Sunday to Friday, in the village where her school was located. Expenses for room and board, although modest, came out of her salary.

Committed to earning the baccalaureate degree, Peñaranda Marcial, and others like her, took courses on Saturdays at the University of Puerto Rico. Some lucky ones, who could travel to San Juan on Fridays, matriculated for classes on that day too. In time, the university instituted off-campus sites to which college professors traveled to offer the requisite courses. One of the university centers was located in the city of Arecibo, where Peñaranda Marcial lived. She attended classes there with teachers from neighboring towns like Quebradillas, Camuy, Hatillo, and Barceloneta. For many, Peñaranda Marcial included, this routine became a life-long habit. By the time she completed her degree in 1943, it had taken over twenty years to accomplish that goal.

In Puerto Rico her reputation as a teacher was solid. She believed in the highest ideals of her profession and had the common sense to cultivate her students' parents as her friends and allies. Peñaranda Marcial remembers:

I always tried to involve the children's parents in school affairs. Some teachers had the pupils in the morning and that was it. Not me, I would call the parents in for after-school conferences and before I knew it, I had gathered three or four parents and I began to gain their confidence. That helped me a lot. When I changed to the Barrio San Luis, to the Roosevelt School . . . and my assignment was to teach English to grades four and five . . . it was an unruly group. They were terrible. Oh, my God! But I said, "I have to earn a living so I am going to work with them." Slowly, the rumor had spread . . . that [Ana] Peñaranda was going to be the teacher for this class. Many mothers already knew about me, that I was strong and they knew that the child who entered my classroom was there to work, not to waste his time. The child has to be supported between two pillars, the parents and the teacher. . . . [This way] he would not fall to one side or the other, and would grow up straight.[16]

Her honest approach toward teaching and no-nonsense philosophy promoted classroom efficiency with little wasted time. In one class, she recalled:

When the students arrived on the first day one had his books tied together and from mid-way into the room, flung the books [on] the desk. One by one they all did the same, so that their books banged onto their desks. Then, one would push another, the other would shove a third, and so on. Then some of them sat in their seats, but others put their feet on their desks. . . . I stood still and watched them. When they were all in the room, I went to the door and slammed that door in such a manner that the room trembled . . . but I still did not say a word, and they continued [their destructive behavior], thinking they could destroy that classroom. I slammed the door again, and looked at my watch. . . . When they calmed down, then I began, not the lesson, but to talk to them. . . . [I said] you come in here to learn; I come to earn an honest living by teaching you, and what I teach is not lost. It is to remain in your heads one way or another. Then I began my lesson. When the bell rang to change classes, I said to them: "I waited twenty minutes to start the class. When the 3 P.M. bell rings, I want all of you, *all of you,* to return for the twenty minutes you owe me." . . . They came back. Next day you could hear a pin drop.[17]

During the summer of 1945, as the United States moved closer to victory in Europe, Peñaranda Marcial made the first of three visits to New York City. The recent death of her mother, followed by her daughter's migration to the city, kindled a desire for change that would lead Peñaranda Marcial to new opportunities. Although she only worked for a brief period in a Brooklyn pocketbook factory, she came to realize that better economic prospects existed in New York City than in Puerto Rico, and by 1947, with her husband and youngest son, she made the visit permanent. A chance meeting with an old school friend, now pastor of Christ Church in Brooklyn, led her to join his church. The quintessential organizer, Peñaranda Marcial promptly founded two associations, the Sociedad de Damas and the Sociedad de Jóvenes (the societies for women and for youth) for Christ Church. She continued her graduate education by taking courses at New York University, and at the Hunter and City Colleges of the City University of New York. Before long, Peñaranda Marcial was instructing the members of the two societies she organized for Christ Church in the English language. Her teaching and language skills quickly came to the attention of her archdeacon who encouraged her to seek employment with the Board of Education.

The appointment of Peñaranda Marcial as the first SAT in 1949 was soon followed by the institutionalization of the position by the Board of Education. With the expansion of the Spanish-speaking student population, the number of SAT appointments also increased, as shown in Table 3–1.

Examining employment questionnaires completed by 155 of these teachers between 1950 and 1957 and now on file at the commonwealth of Puerto Rico Office of the Migration Division, one begins to understand just who these educators were. The qualifications of Puerto Rican SATs living in the city, together with their ages, gender, marital status, English language proficiency, academic backgrounds, experience, and

Table 3–1. *Substitute Auxiliary Teachers' Professional Development*

Year	Number of SATs	Professional Milestones
1949	10	Position is created.
1949–55	20	
1957–58	70	
1958–59	90	
1960–61	100	
1963–64	109	Regular license is established for auxiliary teachers.
1964–65	117	License for supervisors of SATs is established. Five are appointed in 1967.
1965–66	142	License for Chinese auxiliary teacher is established.
1968–70	189	The designation of auxiliary teacher is changed to Bilingual Teacher in School and Community Relations.
1970–71	234	

Source: Informational bulletin circa 1971, "Historical Background of the Bilingual Program in School and Community Relations." Board of Education of the City of New York, Office of Instructional Services.

length of residency in the city, appear on their employment applications. As expected, males accounted for a minority (39) of the applicants, while 116 were women. One hundred and fifty-two held university degrees. Of these, 132 earned baccalaureates and 20 held degrees at the master's level. Eighty-eight were fluent in English, while 58 felt their proficiency was only moderate. Twenty-nine received their degrees from colleges or universities in the States. With the exception of 11 applicants, all had some prior experience in the classroom; 138 were licensed teachers in Puerto Rico and 3 held licenses from the United States. Most of the teachers were in the prime years of their productivity, between the ages of thirty and thirty-five.[18]

The Work of the Auxiliary Teachers

In 1953 the Board of Education reported 40,000 non-English speaking students in attendance in New York City's public and parochial schools, a sharp increase compared to the 8,828 counted in 1948.[19] This same year the Board initiated the Puerto Rican Study, a four-year inquiry into the education and adjustment of Puerto Rican students in the city schools.[20] Its objectives were to assess the most effective methods for teaching English to nonspeakers of the language, evaluate their progress, encourage a more rapid adjustment to school and community life, and create a model for educating the Puerto Rican child. With respect to the first task, the study recommended an integration of the several methods of language instruction then in existence. In addition, resource units and language guides were to be developed, along with special and orientation classes for migrant students.[21] The study also deemed essential the continued use of substitute auxiliary teachers, Puerto Rican coordinators (the junior high school equivalent of the SAT), school-community coordinators, and other teaching positions (OTPs), both at the elementary and junior high school levels. In the senior high schools, teachers of English as a Second Language and Spanish-speaking counselors were also viewed as necessary.[22]

Once again a major educational study had endorsed measures consistent with current pedagogical and community concerns and suggested a bilingual and bicultural approach to the education of Puerto Rican students. The strategies it recommended were not unlike the informal practices utilized by Spanish-speaking SATs in the years since the hiring of Peñaranda Marcial. Although the recommendations of the 1953–57 study were only partially implemented, the report's endorsement of bilingual staffing throughout the system helped to strengthen the position and programs of the SATs.[23] By the time the Puerto Rican Study report was published in 1958, their numbers had substantially increased. In a poem, "Pioneros Maestros Bilingües," written in 1984, Rafael Vega, himself among the first educators and supervisors in the system, pays homage to his colleagues. In one of its stanzas he succinctly summarized their contributions:

> Hubo cambio de ideas, se creció de talento,
> se abrieron horizontes, y se ampliaron avenidas;
> Y, seguros de que el niño era el factor potente,
> se peleó por programas hasta ser conseguidos.[24]

The educational functions of the auxiliary teacher varied. In many instances he or she became the specialist who bridged the gap between the schools and the community. In addition to teaching abilities the bilingual educator was also expected to have skills in guidance, to be knowledgeable about social and educational services in New York City, and to understand the cultural backgrounds of the Spanish-speaking students they taught. Throughout their careers, they fostered positive community relations by developing close communication and rapport between the school and the neighborhood. They also offered themselves as cultural resources throughout the educational system, provided sensitivity training to teachers and staff, and implemented programs that enhanced the "cultural heritage and self concept of the children."[25] Believing that their work as bilingual teachers furthered the educational experience of all children, and not simply native Spanish speakers, they supported 1950s initiatives designed to expose all school children to Hispanic culture and history, such as this directive from the Board of Education to all city schools:

> As in the past years *all* public schools at *all* levels are asked to join with the New York Puerto Rican community and the Commonwealth of Puerto Rico in observing the commemoration of the discovery of Puerto Rico by Christopher Columbus on his second voyage to the New World in 1493. This celebration should

be used to direct the attention of *all* children to the distinct contribution of Puerto Ricans and other Spanish-speaking peoples to their own society and to the American cultural mosaic in the fields of art, literature, music and the dance, science, technology and family living. This special focus on Discovery Day should be part of an on-going school effort to further the goals of multiculturalism and multi-lingualism. It is particularly important that children who do not have a Puerto Rican or Spanish background be afforded an opportunity to learn some of the significant facts about Puerto Rico.[26]

The decade of the sixties witnessed the continuing development of the SAT program and the advancement of its bilingual educators. These gains occurred in the midst of a highly charged atmosphere in New York City, where battles for racial integration were underway, and proponents of the neighborhood school had to contend with pressures toward more centralized control. The nation's leading scholars debated vigorously about the function of public education. Were American schools oppressive instruments for the transmission of middle-class mores, agencies for social change, or community support systems—providers of jobs, sources of leadership and cohesion?[27] These issues assumed more urgency in New York City's minority communities as African American and Puerto Rican students became the majority in 1967. Of 639 schools, some 42 at the elementary level and 9 junior high schools were disproportionately composed of African American and Puerto Rican students.[28]

A school population of roughly 190,000 children of Puerto Rican background, many of whom needed to learn English as a second language, motivated the activities of the SAT program.[29] As members of a tightly knit professional community, substitute auxiliary teachers met regularly to share ideas and evaluate their experiences. These close interactions, reinforced by a strong sense of commitment and mission, contributed to defining their goals and led the teachers to develop the theories and practices that lay the foundation for bilingual education as we understand it today. Among these were the belief that Spanish-speaking children were more receptive to instruction when they were taught initially in their native language, and that a person with bilingual skills and abilities was better educated than someone only able to function in one language.

What transpired in the professional life of an SAT over the course of an ordinary school year? Peñaranda Marcial offers us one perspective:

> We started as special teachers in this program. That is how I began. . . . My group was composed of fourteen or fifteen students recommended by their teachers . . . the most recent arrivals. They posed problems in their classes because they didn't understand anything. . . . Basically, my class was conversational English . . . so I began to work with my children and since I was already a teacher, I had worked twenty-five years in Puerto Rico, . . . I began to teach them English. Then I started to teach them to read, to speak. When I read the word, I would immediately write it, and I had to use both languages, which was what the American teacher could not do. But once I was able to teach them a phrase, I would translate it [from the Spanish], and they had to use it in English from then on. . . . By the end of the semester the youngsters were learning to read, write and speak English.[30]

As Peñaranda Marcial points out, the class consisted of children recommended by their teachers and drawn from grades throughout the school. She customarily spent an hour with each grade in the mornings, but the afternoons were reserved for the community aspect of her responsibilities.

Pioneers in the field, Peñaranda Marcial and the other SATs were obliged to develop their own curriculum and create the materials for its implementation. They formed study groups and participated in academic retreats for their own intellectual growth; wrote pamphlets and booklets and suggested activities for classroom use; published materials on the history and geography of Puerto Rico; and created filmstrips like *Puerto Rico Today, Children of Puerto Rico,* and *The Bilingual Teacher in School and Community Relations,* with accompanying teacher guides.[31]

Their professional organization, the Society of Puerto Rican Auxiliary Teachers (SPRAT), paved the way for numerous Puerto Rican educators' associations. It served as an institutional vehicle for solidarity and support while advocating for the members' professional and political advancement.[32] SPRAT held academic conferences that provided a forum for the dissemination of new scholarship in what was rapidly becoming the field of bilingual education. The group assessed the status of the profession and lobbied for recognition and permanency, not merely under substitute licensure but as regular teachers in the system. They argued for increased visibility of Spanish-speaking professionals at all levels. SPRAT was at the forefront of the movement for licensure that ultimately resulted in institutionalizing the position of regular Bilingual Teacher in School and Community Relations. By 1960, the School Board had drafted the resolution for the license, and the first competitive examinations were held in February 1962. All of the bilingual teachers in the School and Community Relations program were active members of SPRAT. Many of them also pursued their professional interests in the Puerto Rican Educators' Association (PREA), an organization they helped to create, and by establishing the first SAT chapter of the United Federation of Teachers.

Many bilingual educator-activists who began their careers as SATs rose to prominent positions in the schools and in the community. Nilda Maldonado Koenig, appointed an SAT among the first group of ten to follow Peñaranda Marcial, became assistant to the director of substitute auxiliary teachers and non-English coordinators at the Board. When she retired, it was not from the school system but after an impressive career with New York City's Office of Civil Rights. María E. Sánchez became an SAT in 1958, rose to supervisor in District 14, and later became a licensed principal. Leaving the public schools, she accepted a position at Brooklyn College to develop the bilingual-education major at both the undergraduate and graduate levels. Appointed chairperson of the Department of Puerto Rican Studies in 1974, Professor Sánchez guided the department through an early struggle with the college over autonomy issues.[33] She retired as professor emerita in 1990. Dolores Nazario began her career with the Department of Welfare before becoming a substitute auxiliary teacher. She rose to supervisor and then director of bilingual programs for District 4. Carmen Rodríguez and Laura Maldonado became district superintendents. María Power and Pura Bonilla began as SATs; both ultimately became principals in the system.[34]

These educators now joined the ranks of earlier Puerto Rican principals and supervisors, among them Carmen Rivera, assistant principal at Intermediate School (I.S.) 201; Hernán La Fontaine, acting assistant principal at I.S. 201; Irma Fuentes, chair of foreign languages at Evander Childs; and Alfredo Mathew, assistant principal in charge of the auxiliary teachers program.[35] By the mid-sixties, Puerto Rican educators were also employed at the Board of Education, among them Aida Legazpy, who aided in establishing the Board's bilingual office, and Carmen Miranda and Beatrice López-Pritchard.

Auxiliary Teachers and the Puerto Rican Community

The activities of the SATs in the community generated intensive parental involvement that went far beyond a basic orientation to school policies and surroundings. SATs groomed parents for leadership roles in the Parent-Teacher Association and encouraged them to avail themselves of English-language and other practical instruction. Within the schools, parents formed support and informational networks that fostered the development of valuable coping and occupational skills.[36] Because they were themselves part of the community, the SATs gained the confidence of the parents. They found ways to enhance the educational experiences of their students by involving parents in the schools and also to empower the community by increasing parents' understanding of the dominant society. Once knowledgeable about the system, SATs and the parents set about honing their advocacy skills. The parents were given access to decision making through active participation at board meetings, political rallies, conferences, and lectures. They were politicized on a variety of issues that affected not only their children's educations but their own survival as well. Instructed about health, nutrition, housing, and even their rights in the workplace, they became a strong and self-reliant base of support for educational reform, including the bilingual movement.

Peñaranda Marcial, for example, mobilized barrio parents to serve as corridor monitors, crossing guards, playground assistants, and chaperons for class trips. She organized a group of some eighteen or twenty parents, who were bilingual themselves, to teach English to the parents who wished to learn the language. At her insistence, English language classes were soon offered to adults in the evenings. As she recalls:

> The afternoon was dedicated to the community, to the parents, to the problems. . . . On Mondays, for example, meetings were scheduled for all our parents, not just the parents of my students. There we talked and discussed issues and problems that really presented obstacles to them . . . so that they would become informed of the role of the school. That's when I began to find that avalanche of parents who pledged themselves to do this or that and that was all [accomplished] during those meetings.

She adds:

> Then I organized a sewing class. The school provided the parents with sewing machines. In the afternoon the parents would get together in the library . . . I had scissors, material, patterns and everything that was needed. . . . In the sewing class, we made dresses for the girls for when we gave the graduation activities. The moment came when we would dress the girls in uniforms and they would speak and recite . . . The mothers worked with me in everything. I think I got the support from those mothers that had never been gotten before. . . . It was for me a real triumph. The work we accomplished with the parents meant a great deal to me.[37]

Peñaranda Marcial taught an additional twenty years in the New York schools as a substitute auxiliary teacher. During that period the number of SATs increased minimally in proportion to the numbers of children who required their pedagogical expertise.

Conclusion

As the decade of the 1960s came to a close, the SATs had become part of an extensive network committed to educational equity and excellence for Puerto Rican children as well as to bilingual education. The formation of grassroots minority and Puerto Rican coalitions, like the People's Board of Education, and community groupings such as ASPIRA and United Bronx Parents, lent strong support to their goals.[38] ASPIRA in particular, ably led by of community activist and educator Antonia Pantoja, was intended to provide much-needed Puerto Rican representation in policy making in both the private and the public sector. Utilizing education as its agent for change, ASPIRA advocated on countless issues and sought to "guide Puerto Rican youth towards professional, business and artistic fields, to direct them towards fields with promise and employment opportunities."[39]

In 1968, reacting to the limitations of American institutions to adequately educate Puerto Rican youth, ASPIRA called a conference in New York City. This historic gathering coincided with the tumultuous struggle for community control of the schools and served notice to the American educational establishment that Puerto Ricans were defining their own agenda and prepared to work toward meaningful gains. The conference was attended by leaders and students representing the Puerto Rican communities in Buffalo, Boston, Chicago, Rochester, and cities in Connecticut and New Jersey. Joined by Mexican Americans, the other major Spanish-speaking group in the United States, and key members of the non-Hispanic community, the participants pledged to renew the campaign for bilingual education and assert the rights of Puerto Ricans in the political and economic agenda of urban America. Toward this end, AS-PIRA and the Puerto Rican Legal Defense and Education Fund initiated a class-action suit against the city's Board of Education that later culminated in the ASPIRA Consent Decree (1974), which guaranteed bilingual education to all who needed it.[40] *ASPIRA vs. the Board of Education,* a landmark case in bilingual education, was predicated on evidence that Puerto Rican youth were being denied equal educational opportunities. By the late 1960s this was apparent in their frequent classification as slow-learners and underachievers, and in the low numbers of high school graduates among Puerto Rican students. All of this attested to the need for specific educational and language policies for Spanish-speaking pupils.

Although the Board of Education during the late 1940s and 1950s had enacted a series of measures to provide for the educational needs of Puerto Rican and other students with limited English-speaking abilities, the results were uneven. One reason was the fact that the basic operational policy continued to be English only, and many students lacked a complete command of the language. As the numbers of Puerto Rican students steadily increased, resistance among teachers to methods perceived as foreign or compensatory also increased. Thus in 1967 the Congress of the United States enacted legislation that was designed to meet the needs of children aged three to eighteen who had limited English-speaking ability and who came from environments where the dominant language was not English (the Bilingual Education Act, Title VII).[41] In essence, the act mandated equality of educational opportunity for non-English speakers, promoted bilingualism, and reaffirmed the ideas of Puerto Rican SATs in bilingual education. It supported many of the recommendations of former New York City educational studies and declared pluralistic, multilingual, and multicultural education to be the law of the land.

Four years later, during the course of the ASPIRA case, approximately 450 full- and part-time teachers of English as a Second Language, specially licensed English teachers, and newly designated bilingual (Spanish-speaking) teachers in school-community relations and bilingual elementary teachers prepared to teach some 260,000 children from Spanish-speaking backgrounds in New York City.[42] The student-teacher ratio remained alarmingly inadequate. Nevertheless, the recognition that specialized methods of instruction were legitimate and necessary for teaching students lacking English-language proficiency, and the adoption of professional licensure in the field, marked the culmination of a twenty-year campaign led, initially, by SATs and other Puerto Rican educators in New York City. And this was only the beginning.

NOTES

Acknowledgments: This essay is dedicated to María E. Sánchez, Rafael Vega, and Aida Legazpy, pioneers in bilingual education who gave me the opportunity to understand our history from their perspective. I also want to thank Sonia Nieto, Marco Hernández, and Luis Fuentes for reading and commenting on the manuscript for this chapter.

1. César Andreu Iglesias, ed., *Memorias de Bernardo Vega* (Río Piedras: Ediciones Huracán, 1977), 123. The author is responsible for all translations from Spanish to English.

2. Virginia Sánchez Korrol, *From Colonia to Community: The History of Puerto Ricans in New York City, 1917–1948* (Westport, Conn.: Greenwood Press, 1983), chapter 5.

3. Ibid., 154.

4. Ibid., 75–76.

5. Ibid., 76. See also C. P. Armstrong, *Reactions of Puerto Rican Children in New York City to Psychological Tests: A Report of the Special Committee on Immigration and Naturalization* (New York: Chamber of Commerce, 1935).

6. Lawrence R. Chenault, *The Puerto Rican Migrant in New York City* (1938; New York: Russell and Russell, 1970), 146.

7. Author's interview with María E. Sánchez, Professor Emerita, Brooklyn College, New York City, January 29, 1992. Tapes are in the author's private archives.

8. J. Cayce Morrison, ed., *The Puerto Rican Study, 1953–1957, A Report on the Education and Adjustment of Puerto Rican Pupils in the Public Schools of the City of New York* (New York: Board of Education, 1958), 2.

9. Isaura Santiago Santiago, *A Community's Struggle for Equal Education Opportunity: ASPIRA vs. the Board of Education* (Princeton, N.J.: Educational Testing Service, 1978), 14.

10. "The strength and effectiveness of the Committee has been due to the nature of its membership, comprising as it does practically all heads of governmental departments whose responsibilities touch and are affected by the newly-arrived Puerto Ricans, and embracing also civic leaders of the whole city, including a large and distinguished group of

Puerto Rican leaders." Office of the Mayor, *Interim Report of the Mayor's Committee on Puerto Rican Affairs in New York City, 1949–1953* (New York: City of New York, 1949–53), 4.

11. Mary Finocchiaro, "Puerto Rican Newcomers in Our Schools," *Journal of Educational Sociology* (December 1954): 157.

12. Ibid.

13. *Interim Report of the Mayor's Committee on Puerto Rican Affairs*, 42.

14. Ibid., 43.

15. Among the teachers who subsequently became social workers was Antonia Pantoja. With the help of other community leaders, Pantoja went on to found numerous organizations (e.g., ASPIRA) for the social and educational advancement of the Puerto Rican people.

16. Author's interview with Ana Peñaranda Marcial, retired New York City teacher, New York City, September 10, 1987. Tapes are in author's private archives.

17. Ibid.

18. Tordis Ilg and the Education Section of the New York Office of the Migration Division, "A Brief Study of Questionnaires Submitted by Puerto Rican Teachers Available for Elementary and Secondary School Positions in the New Metropolitan Area" (New York: Commonwealth of Puerto Rico, Department of Labor, Migration Division, 1957).

19. Morrison, *The Puerto Rican Study, 1953–1957,* See also Santiago, *A Community's Struggle*, 14.

20. In 1953 the Board of Education also issued a brief report, "Teaching Children of Puerto Rican Background in New York City Schools." The report indicated awareness of the importance of Spanish usage in the classroom, bilingual teachers, and fully developed instructional programs for the non-English speaker.

21. Isaura Santiago Santiago, "ASPIRA vs. the Board of Education of the City of New York: A History and Policy Analysis" (Ph.D. diss., Fordham University, 1987), 42–44. See also, Morrison *The Puerto Rican Study*, part 1.

22. Morrison, *The Puerto Rican Study*, part 3, chapter 16.

23. See the proceedings of the first city-wide conference of the Puerto Rican community, Office of the Mayor of New York City, *Puerto Ricans Confront Problems of the Complex Urban Society: A Design for Change: Proceedings of the Puerto Rican Community Conference* (New York: Office of the Mayor, April 1967).

24. Rafael Vega, "*Los Pioneros Maestros Bilingües,*" July 20, 1984. Unpublished poem in author's archival collection. My translation:

There was an exchange of ideas, a flowering of talent,
horizons opened, and avenues expanded;
And, certain that the child was the all-important factor,
we fought for programs until we got them.

25. Office of the Superintendent of Schools, Board of Education of New York City, "Special Circular No. 64, 1967–1968;" February 21, 1948; ed., Rafael Vega, *The Bilingual Teacher in School and Community Relations* (New York: Board of Education, Multimedia Production Unit of the Bureau of Audio Visual Instruction, 1968).

26. Office of the Superintendent of Schools, Board of Education of New York City, "Special Circular No. 27, 1967–1968" (addressed to all superintendents, heads of bureaus, directors, and principals of all schools).

27. Diane Ravitch, *The Great School Wars: A History of the New York City Public Schools* (New York: Basic Books, 1974), 329.

28. The figures Ravitch gives are 90 percent at the elementary level and 85 percent in the junior high schools. Ibid., 253.

29. New York City Board of Education, press release, November 12, 1965.

30. Author's interview with Peñaranda Marcial, September 10, 1987.

31. Ibid.; Vega, *The Bilingual Teacher in School and Community Relations.* By this time teachers like Carmen Sanguinetti were already creating bilingual curriculum materials for classroom use. See Arnold D. Raisner, Philip A. Bolger, and Carmen Sanguinetti, *Science Instruction in Spanish for Pupils of Spanish-Speaking Background: An Experiment in Bilingualism* (New York: Board of Education, Bureau of Educational Research, 1967).

32. María E. Sánchez's, private collection of papers on SAT activities and SPRAT communications, author's private archival collection.

33. María E. Sánchez exemplifies the commitment of Puerto Rican educators to qualify education at all levels. She was at the core of the struggle to determine the autonomy of the Department of Puerto Rican Studies at Brooklyn College of the City of New York, which she headed from 1974 to 1989.

34. Author's interview with María E. Sánchez, January 29, 1992.

35. By the early sixties, a cadre of United States–born, college-educated Puerto Ricans, including individuals like Hernán La Fontaine, Marco Hernández, Frank Bonilla, Alfredo Mathew, as well as the author, were increasingly incorporated into the teaching profession. While many entered the schools as specialists in discrete disciplines, they also began to play key roles in advancing the educational concerns of the Puerto Rican community. The arena in which they came together with the island-born educator was in the professional organizations. Little has been documented about their joint efforts.

36. A number of key community activists, including figures like Evelina Antonetty and Amalia Betanzos, were among the first parents involved with reforming schools. Little has been written about this phase of our community history.

37. Interview with Peñaranda Marcial.

38. For a discussion of the Ocean Hill–Brownsville and I.S. 201 struggle and the conditions that resulted, see Ravitch, *The Great School Wars,* 251–399. See also Luis Fuentes, "The Struggle for Local Political Control," in *The Puerto Rican Struggle: Essays on Survival in the U.S.,* ed. Clara C. Rodríguez, Virginia Sánchez Korrol, and José Oscar Alers (Maplewood, N.J.: Waterfront Press, 1984), 111–120.

39. ASPIRA, Inc., *Hemos trabajo bien: A Report on the First National Conference of Puerto Ricans, Mexican Americans, and Educators on the Special Needs of Urban Puerto Rican Youth* (New York: ASPIRA of New York, 1968), 34.

40. Santiago, *A Community's Struggle,* 6.

41. For information about the Bilingual Education Act, see Francesco Cordasco and Eugene Bucchioni, *The Puerto Rican Experience: A Sociological Sourcebook* (Totowa, N.J.: Littlefield, Adams, 1973), 337, 349–54.

42. Cordasco and Bucchioni, *The Puerto Ricans,* 113.

FOUR

The Impact of Job Losses on Puerto Rican Women in the Middle Atlantic Region, 1970–1980

ALICE COLÓN-WARREN

I f one group can represent the forces that have been related to the "feminization of poverty" in the United States, it is Puerto Rican women living in the Middle Atlantic region.[1] As capital has displaced workers and employed new groups that permitted greater accumulation, few groups have suffered as intensely the effects of the ongoing economic crisis that has placed women and men of different skill levels and national origins in unequal positions in the labor market. In this process, Puerto Rican families have become stratified with an increased proportion of women in these families living in poverty and economic dependency. Although this chapter will not analyze these issues completely, I would like to suggest some theoretical considerations and hypotheses that relate the historical labor force participation of migrant Puerto Rican women to the labor market dynamics in which they were involved from 1970 to 1980. Specifically, I will consider how these may have affected the labor force participation of Puerto Rican female heads of family. This analysis will describe some of the factors governing the economic status of Puerto Rican women in the Middle Atlantic region during this period, and relate them to those in previous decades. The chapter will also compare the status of Puerto Rican women to that of other ethnic and racial groups in the region's labor market in 1980. Thus, it attempts to contribute to the development of a historical and theoretical exploration of labor market dynamics that considers the intersection of national origin, class, and gender, an exploration that may contribute to the discussion of the feminization of poverty. As has been suggested by other authors, poverty is not only an issue of gender or of female-headed households. It is also conditioned by national and regional economic structures and the class status that these structures allocate to men and women, as well as by the ways these factors are mediated by changes in family composition.[2]

My study focuses on the Middle Atlantic states of New York, New Jersey, and Pennsylvania because these are the states where Puerto Ricans have been most highly concentrated. Moreover, these states are part of a region that reflects most acutely the tendencies characterizing advanced capitalism in the United States. In this country unequal development has perpetuated regional differences in industrial structure, ways of organizing production, and levels of employment and earnings. Regional differences sometimes are affected by the militancy, skill levels, and other characteristics of the workers in these areas as well. These regional characteristics represent differences in the conditions of labor supply and demand and in the pressure on earnings of competing labor reserves, differences that are obscured by analyses that look solely at the national level. One of these differences is, precisely, the unequal concentration of distinct population groups by race, ethnicity, and national origin among regions. The incorporation of these various groups into the U.S. labor market, therefore, must be analyzed in relation to the particular economic structure in which they are located.

Growing Poverty among Puerto Rican Women

The plight of the majority of Puerto Rican women in the Middle Atlantic states shows that migration to the mainland has not been a solution for their economic distress. On the contrary, the economic status of Puerto Rican families in the Middle Atlantic states continued to deteriorate during the 1960s relative to the totality of families in the area. Moreover, this deterioration must be explained in terms of the increasingly difficult conditions faced by Puerto Rican female heads of families.[3] As Table 4–1 shows, the median income of Puerto Rican families with both a husband and wife present improved in percentage terms relative to the economic status of all such families in New York and New Jersey from 1970 to 1980. However, the median incomes of all Puerto Rican families deteriorated relative to the median income of all families in the area. This decline was explained by the worsening income status of Puerto Rican families headed by women relative to that of total and

Table 4–1. *Median Family Income in the Puerto Rican Population in New York and New Jersey, 1970 and 1980*

Median Family Income	Total 1970	Total 1980	Puerto Rican 1970	Puerto Rican 1980
	NEW YORK			
Total	10,719	20,180	5,697	9,654
Husband/wife	11,517	22,466	6,781	14,557
Female head	5,668	9,543	3,191	4,913
Female head income as percent of husband/ wife income	49	42	47	34
Puerto Rican family income as percent of total husband/wife family income				
Husband/wife			59	65
Female head			28	22
Total Puerto Rican family income as percent of total family income			53	47
	NEW JERSEY			
Total	11,589	22,906	6,458	10,510
Husband/wife	12,235	25,264	7,284	15,699
Female head	7,301	11,098	3,380	4,631
Female head income as percent of husband/wife income	60	44	46	29
Puerto Rican family income as percent of total husband/wife family income				
Husband/wife			60	62
Female head			28	18
Total Puerto Rican family income as percent of total family income			56	46

Source: Bureau of the Census, *1970 Census of Population,* vol. 1, *Characteristics of the Population,* chapter D, "Detailed Characteristics," part 34, New York; part 32, New Jersey (Washington, D.C., 1973); Bureau of the Census, *1980 Census of Population,* vol.1, *Characteristics of the Population,* chapter C, "General Social and Economic Characteristics," part 34, New York; part 32, New Jersey (Washington, D.C., 1984).

Puerto Rican husband-wife families. The particular conditions experienced by Puerto Rican female heads of families, therefore, represent an important case of what has been called the "feminization of poverty."[4]

The feminization of poverty has been described as the growing incidence of female-headed families among households below the poverty level, both throughout the world and in the United States. These families are more likely to be poor than those, that—given and assuming patriarchal family relations—are reported as male headed. Tables 4–2 and 4–3 show this to be the case among groups in the Middle Atlantic region in 1980. Thus, it has been suggested that even if female-headed families remained equally likely to be poor, their increase as a proportion of all families may explain their greater representation among families in poverty.[5] It is not surprising, then, that poverty among Puerto Ricans in the United States has been attributed mainly to the impressive increase of female-headed families among this group. Table 4–3 shows that while the total proportion of female-headed families in the region increased from 12 to 16 percent from 1970 to 1980, it increased from 27 to 40 percent among Puerto Rican families, a proportion similar to that found in the black population.[6]

One must emphasize, however, that Puerto Ricans were by far the most likely to be poor among all the groups of female-headed families. Puerto Rican and black female-headed families were also the most highly represented among the groups' total families below poverty. Furthermore, Table 4–3 indicates that while the probability of poverty among total female-headed families slightly increased from 27 to 31 percent from 1970 to 1980, it increased even more, from 58 to 68 percent among Puerto Rican female-headed families. Among Puerto Ricans, the increase in poverty has been intensified, not only by the expanding proportion of all families headed by women but by the growing likelihood of that these families will fall below the poverty line. But attributing to female headship the incidence of poverty among Puerto Rican families, first of all, begs the question of why poverty should be the disproportionate burden of female-headed families. It should also raise questions as to why Puerto Rican female heads of families have been even more likely to be poor than in previous decades and why the extent of their poverty has been greater than that of other female family heads.

Among the stereotypes that have been elaborated regarding Puerto Rican women in poverty is that their lack of a work ethic is the reason

Table 4-2. *Family and Poverty Status in 1980 as Related to Employment Status of Householder in 1979 (percentage)*

Family Characteristics	Puerto Rican	Mexican	Cuban	Other Latino	White	Black
Proportion of families in which householder worked (1979)	57	74	81	77	79	68
Female-headed families as proportion of all families	40	23	17	26	12	42
Female-headed families with working householder (1979)	25	48	60	51	57	54
Families below poverty as a proportion of all families	39	21	12	21	6	25
Families below poverty with working householder (1979)	21	42	37	39	48	31
Female-headed families below poverty level	68	50	30	48	19	44
Female-headed families below poverty level with working householder (1979)	11	27	28	25	37	27
Families below poverty level that were female headed	70	54	41	58	40	74
Working-poor householders that were female headed	37	35	31	38	31	63
Total families (n)	319,087	14,641	46,679	177,667	7,867,758	995,592

Source: Bureau of the Census, *Census of Population*, vol. 1, *Characteristics of the Population*, chapter C, "General Social and Economic Characteristics," part 34, New York; part 32, New Jersey; part 40, Pennsylvania (Washington, D.C., 1984).

Table 4–3. *Family and Poverty Status in 1969 and 1979 as Related to Employment Status of Householder in 1970 and 1980 (percentage)*

Family Characteristics	1970		1980	
	All Families	Puerto Rican Families	All Families	Puerto Rican Families
Families in which householder worked in 1960 and 1979	85	71	77	57
Male-headed families in which householder worked	89	87	81	78
Female-headed families as proportion of all families	12	27	16	40
Female-headed families in which householder worked in 1969 and 1979	56	27	54	25
Families below poverty line as proportion of all families	8	29	9	39
Households below poverty line in which householder worked in 1969 and 1979	41	33	39	21
Female-headed households below poverty line	27	58	31	68
Female-headed households below poverty line in which householder worked in 1969 and 1979	27	9	28	11
Percentage of families below poverty that were female headed	41	53	55	70
Total families (*n*)	9,421,659	251,439	9,557,948	319,097

Source: Bureau of the Census, *1970 Census of Population,* vol. 1, *Characteristics of the Population,* chapter D, "Detailed Characteristics," part 34, New York; part 32, New Jersey; part 40, Pennsylvania (Washington, D.C., 1973); Bureau of the Census, *1980 Census of Population,* vol. 1, *Characteristics of the Population,* chapter C, "General Social and Economic Characteristics," part 34, New York; part 32, New Jersey; part 40, Pennsylvania (Washington, D.C., 1984).

they have become welfare dependents—a dependency that allows for, if not reproduces, increases in female-headed households. Female family headship, poverty, and welfare, then, have been linked to the view that unmarried men are less likely to be employed, while entitlements reinforce women's economic inactivity and their becoming family heads.[7] The feminization of poverty, however, must not be referred mainly to personal and sociocultural traits or changes in family structure. We also must analyze poverty, inequality, and joblessness in relation to the conditions of production and distribution in the prevalent economic structures that frame these social and cultural characteristics. These determine the range and configuration of opportunities in a given society and thus provide the framework in which to analyze the allocation and responses of particular groups and individuals. In capitalist societies, economic benefits are distributed on the basis of class allocation, which among workers is mediated by their relation to the labor market and other forms of economic activity. In the United States these are intersected by sexual, racial, ethnic, and other social and political segmentations, including the subordinate status of work in the domestic sphere and the hierarchical sexual division of labor.

In capitalist economies, any examination of inequality must include reference to competition for greater shares of accumulation among enterprises and their tendency to displace workers through technological development, reorganization of the labor process, the flight of industries to more profitable areas, and the incorporation of additional groups such as minorities and women as labor reserves. These must be seen as mechanisms that have expanded poverty as they have maintained a permanent oversupply of workers whose competition exerts a downward pressure on earnings. In the labor market, therefore, we must consider the impact of declining numbers of jobs and increasing competition among workers, who are segregated along sexual, racial, ethnic, national, and other sociodemographic characteristics and are played against each other in different segments of the industrial and occupational structure in a process that tends to lower earnings at all levels. Group and individual characteristics or circumstances may mediate who occupies particular positions in relation to these labor market dynamics, but they do not explain the structure of inequality itself. Hence, moving the analysis to group and personal characteristics without considering the structural framework in which they are played out assumes such a structure of inequality to be acceptable.

Minorities, women, and other oppressed groups with reduced bargaining power are more likely to act as reserves, positioned either out of the labor market or in the lowest-paid positions.[8] Historically, this reserve labor force has seldom been used to displace employed workers or downgrade their wage levels directly. Rather, it has been used to fill demand in jobs requiring lower-paid labor, either because these have been expanding or because other workers have been unavailable to fill these positions. This segregation in the labor market concentrates subordinate groups in low-paid job spheres where they compete as labor reserves mainly among themselves while at the same time it maintains other workers who compete for higher-paid jobs.

We, therefore, have a labor market that, through this unequal concentration of groups at different levels of earnings, appears to be segmented by sex, race, national origin or other sociodemographic characteristics. This process of segregating labor into different groups not only creates employment for some and joblessness for others but also leads to the succession of workers into particular job spheres, thus maintaining an available labor reserve for positions of different ranks and income levels. The resulting competition for jobs, even if it does not displace workers, limits the possibility of employment of all workers and drives down earnings throughout the total employment structure. Not only may the availability of a reserve segregated to the lowest ranks of the job structure push workers who are able to do so to move to other jobs, but it may also constrain wage levels at higher-paying positions. The low wages at the bottom of the earnings structure, and the goods and services that can be provided more cheaply because of these reduced labor costs, could mean that workers in other job sectors are less demanding of higher earnings. This may be a process whereby the downward pressure on wages exerted by reserves at lower levels "trickles up" to depress wages at higher levels as well. Work done in the domestic sphere and the informal economy, such as food and clothing sales or production—that is, unpaid work or work paid at lower prices than the formal market provides—may also allow families and individuals to survive on lower earnings. Subsistence through such work, and other means like welfare benefits, may directly or indirectly provide the conditions for workers to become the labor supply of peripheral jobs and industries. For employed workers and reserves positioned at different spheres of the job market the alternatives of work and subsistence may become linked and their impact transferred through the whole earnings structure. Under these conditions, by providing workers with a minimum subsistence, welfare benefits may provide the means for workers to resist worsening employment conditions. Welfare benefits must be considered, as well, as a response where by the state legitimizes itself and the system and maintains social stability under deteriorating economic conditions. Thus, welfare may ultimately provide a subsidy for employers in lower-paying job spheres, who may not be pressured to provide higher earnings for workers who instead supplement their income through public benefits.

Poverty, therefore, must first be analyzed in terms of capitalism's inherent tendencies toward joblessness and competition, forces that restrain the earnings of both men and women. Analyses of the feminization of poverty must also focus on segregation in women's employment and the discriminatory wage structures that maintain women in conditions of poverty as forces impelling family instability make them main family supporters. What has been described as the feminization of poverty highlights the fact that, given this discrimination against women and the changes in household structure in our societies, women with children represent an increasing proportion of families in the lower strata of the working class. It is through this relegation of women to the lower strata of the working class that poverty is related to gender.

In this context, it must be recalled that not all women are equally likely to be poor as they become heads of families. The probability of poverty among female-headed families is also related to their class status, race, national origin, and ethnicity, factors that bear on our observation that Puerto Rican female heads of families have shown the highest poverty rates among the different ethnic groups analyzed in this chapter.

The feminization of poverty finally must be related to the class and economic status of men and male-headed families, as well as to the extent to which men remain family heads. In the United States, economic instability and male unemployment have been linked to changing family structures and to the declining incidence of male-headed families, while this is less apparent for example, in Puerto Rico.[9] Thus it is necessary to disentangle the complex relationships between poverty and female-headed households that are expressed in the tendency toward the feminization of poverty. We must also remember that, even when female-headed families remain the poorest among the poor, poverty among women may not be limited to female heads and their families. It also affects women living in households headed by poor men, where they may also share the fewest resources.

My main focus here is to consider that while female family headship and family structure may mediate poverty and economic status, the roots of economic inequality must ultimately be sought in the unequal distribution of productive resources and the labor market dynamics imposed by the prevalent economic system on all workers, as well as in the institutionalized segregation by sex, race, and national origin that the system reproduces. It is these dynamics that this chapter will analyze. I have been cautious, therefore, in using the concept of the feminization of poverty for it is important not to suggest that female heads of families of all groups, classes, and strata are equally likely to be poor. Neither do I wish to suggest that poverty is mainly a function of gender as an isolated category, which would obscure labor market dynamics that also explain male poverty.

As part of this analysis, the discussion will initially refer to the unequal incorporation of men and women, of different groups into the employment structure. It appears that the industrial restructuring and sociodemographic shifts between 1970 and 1980 in the Middle Atlantic region left Puerto Rican women, and particularly Puerto Rican female family heads, disproportionately marginalized from the labor market and locked in conditions of poverty. Further research would be necessary to offer a fuller explanation of why Puerto Rican women, and particularly Puerto Rican female family heads in the United States, have been most affected by these structural tendencies. In this essay I focus mainly on the labor market dynamics of competition, segregation, and succession among groups of workers as part of the economic structures that underlie their marginalization. This may offer a framework to analyze the historical trajectory of labor force participation among Puerto Rican women in the Middle Atlantic region and of the variables that have been identified in previous research as being related to their economic activity.

Puerto Rican Women's Employment and Joblessness, 1960–1980

The history of the Middle Atlantic region can be considered in many ways as prototypical of industrial trends leading to the integration of migrants, minorities, and women into the labor market. Until the 1950s the Northeast was the unquestioned industrial and commercial center of capital in the United States. Manufacturing employment was centered in this region, and it was geographically linked to the commercial, financial, and service jobs that were generated by the economic development of the area. Even as their economic power was being contested by the movement of capital out of the region in the following decades, the Middle Atlantic states, and particularly the New York metropolitan region, remained the site of the largest corporate headquarters and evolved into a financial-commercial-financial economy.[10] This economic development was, in many ways, impelled by the work of immigrants uprooted from Europe in the initial stages of monopoly capitalism, and it continued to be impelled by migrants until the present time. The restrictions imposed on European immigration in the 1920s were counterbalanced by the increased migrations of southern blacks and Puerto Ricans. These latter migrations were interrupted by the Depression and World War II, then peaked in the postwar decades. By the 1960s, they were followed by waves of additional Latino groups.[11] Women have been an integral part of all these migratory movements, not only in their role as workers in the home but as workers active in the labor market.[12] As Table 4–4 shows, by 1980 there were 23,350,250 whites, 3,004,760 blacks, 839,742 Puerto Ricans, and 720,367 non-Puerto Rican Latinos sixteen years and over in the region. Women represented 53 percent of the whites, 56 percent of the blacks, 55 percent of Puerto Ricans, and 54 percent of non-Puerto Rican Latinos.

The economic transformations characteristic of monopoly capitalism after World War II were dramatically felt in the Northeast and the Middle Atlantic region. The period was characterized by a tendency to increased automation and the industrialization of all sectors of the economy, including agriculture, fuel production, marketing, and social services. These transformations reduced the demand for labor, particularly that for unskilled and semiskilled workers in manufacturing industries. The tendencies were reinforced by the regional and international displacement of industries that could not be fully automated into the southern United States and peripheral countries, areas where cheaper labor was more abundant.[13] As economic stagnation accelerated by the end of the 1960s, the loss of manufacturing jobs had reached even the higher paid positions.[14] It has been projected that increased automation and the relocation of manufacturing employment will continue to be used by corporations as mechanisms to restructure production and restore higher capital accumulation in order to survive global economic instability.[15]

Table 4-4. *Labor Force Status among Ethnic Groups in the Middle Atlantic Region, 1980 (percentage)*

Labor Force Status	Puerto Rican		Mexican		Cuban		Other Latino		White		Black	
	Total	Female	Total	Female	Total	Female	Total	Female	Total	Female	Total	Female
Labor/force participation*	51	37	59	47	66	56	65	53	60	47	58	52
Unemployment†	12	14	10	10	8	10	9	11	6	6	12	11
Employment‡	45	32	53	42	61	51	59	48	56	44	51	46
Total Population	839,742	458,043	49,150	24,836	140,150	74,338	531,067	286,847	23,350,250	12,360,828	3,004,760	1,682,741

*Proportion of population employed or looking for work 16 years old or over

†Proportion of the labor force that is not employed

‡Proportion of the labor force employed 16 years old and over

Source: Bureau of the Census, *1980 Census of Population*, vol. 1, *Characteristics of the Population*, chapter C, "General Social and Economic Characteristics," part 34, New York; part 32, New Jersey; part 40, Pennsylvania (Washington, D.C. 1984).

Ironically, the capitalist economic crisis may have provided the conditions for the limited survival of lower-paid manufacturing and the revival of the sweatshops.[16]

This industrial restructuring has created new employment tendencies under monopoly capitalism. With advances in technology and the increased geographic dispersion of production and marketing, there arose a demand for workers in scientific and technical production, in bureaucratic control and coordination, and in the clerical and sales functions that accelerate commercial activity. Labor demand also increased in other services as capital accumulation increasingly transferred from the family to the market and the state activities such as education, child care, entertainment, and the consumption of food. This shift to a technologically advanced and service economy meant an increased demand in professional, technical, clerical, and sales workers. Yet, while employers required better educated workers, the jobs themselves had become routinized, and tasks subdivided. Menial services, on the other hand, still generated a demand for unskilled labor.[17] The expansion of low-level, low-paid sales and service jobs is, in fact, the other side of restructuring that accompanies the contraction of manufacturing jobs. There exists, therefore, a polarization between unemployed, underemployed, and low-paid workers at one extreme and, at the other, a much smaller group in economic and bureaucratic control.[18]

A cause and consequence of these trends has been the change in the sociodemographic composition of the labor force. The lowering of labor costs required to increase accumulation and to face the ongoing economic crisis has been achieved by employment cuts as well as by the continuing employment of women, minorities, and migrants as additional contingents. The decline of manufacturing jobs, on the other hand, implied a loss of higher-paid positions that were disproportionately occupied by men. This tendency underscores the unity of labor market dynamics, in which no group of workers is totally protected from the competition of available labor reserves or from poverty. Women's labor, meanwhile, has allowed a containment of the costs imposed by the expansion of clerical and sales jobs, which are generally unproductive in capitalist terms but nevertheless necessary for accumulation. Their labor has also provided for the expansion of professional, social, and personal services—the new spheres of accumulation based on the extensive use of low-paid workers—as well as for the survival of low-paid manufacturing.[19] As Table 4–5 shows, the slight increase in the labor force from 1970 to

Table 4-5. *Labor Force Status in the Puerto Rican Population in the Middle Atlantic Region, 1970 and 1980 (percentage)*

Labor Force Status	1970				1980			
	Total		Puerto Rican		Total		Puerto Rican	
	Total	Female	Total	Female	Total	Female	Total	Female
Labor force participation*	58	41	50	30	60	48	51	37
Unemployment†	4	5	7	8	7	7	12	14
Employment‡	55	39	46	27	55	44	45	32
N	26,424,898	14,075,254	615,242	330,098	28,341,113	15,107,695	839,742	458,043

*Proportion of population employed or looking for work 16 years old and over
†Proportion of the labor force that is not employed
‡Proportion of the labor force employed 16 years old and over

Source: Bureau of the Census, *1970 Census of Population*, vol. 1, *Characteristics of the Population*, chapter D, "Detailed Characteristics," part 34, New York; part 32, New Jersey; part 40, Pennsylvania (Washington, D.C., 1973); Bureau of the Census, *1980 Census of Population*, vol. 1, *Characteristics of the Population*, chapter C, "General Social and Economic Characteristics," part 34, New York; part 32, New Jersey; part 40, Pennsylvania (Washington, D.C., 1984).

1980 must be explained to a great extent by the greater labor-force participation of females. Table 4–3 shows as well that while the employment of male householders declined sharply while, even with the advent of the crisis, that of female householders remained relatively stable.

Given this context of relative growth in female employment, it is striking that, contrary to the trend shown for women in other groups, the participation of Puerto Rican women in the labor force declined from 1960 to 1970.[20] Tables 4–4 and 4–5 show that in 1980 the labor market activity of Puerto Rican women was still limited when compared to other groups of women in the region. Studies considering the period from 1960 to 1970 found that Puerto Rican women participated less in the labor force than white women even after controlling for education, fertility, and other individual characteristics, suggesting that these offer a limited explanation of this low labor-market activity.[21] Researchers have then begun to examine the labor market conditions in the Middle Atlantic states where women of the various groups were incorporated, displaced, and limited in employment as they came to constitute the labor supply of particular economic spheres. Here we will suggest some of the tendencies related to the slow expansion of Puerto Rican female employment over the last decades but also those related to the limits of that expansion.

We can initially consider that the changes in the occupational structure illustrated in Table 4–6 have resulted in an upgrading of the educational requirements in the Middle Atlantic region's labor market. Disproportionally confined to the lower strata of the working class, Puerto Rican and other migrant women have been limited in their participation in the expanding professional, clerical, and sales occupations because of their lower levels of education. White women were least likely to be in these lower strata. Their comparatively higher educations and the fact that they had held these occupations since the beginning of the century made them the most likely target of efforts to restrain wage levels when these occupations expanded.[22] It was their labor force participation that clearly increased in the region from 1960 to 1970.[23] Tables 4–7 and 4–8 indicate that greater numbers of white women had high school or college educations than did other groups of females, and consequently that they were the most strongly represented in professional, clerical, and sales positions among women in the region in 1980. Nevertheless, as economic expansion used up the most available labor reserves and improved workers' bargaining position during the 1960s, there was a

Table 4–6. *Women's Occupations in the Puerto Rican Population in the Middle Atlantic Region, 1970 and 1980 Percentage*

Occupation	1970		1980	
	Total	Puerto Rican	Total	Puerto Rican
Managerial and related	3	2	7	4
Professional and technical	16	7	18	10
Sales, clerical, and related	45	35	44	41
Service, excluding domestic	14	12	15	13
Domestic services	3	1	1	1
Craft and related	2	2	2	4
Operatives, laborers, and related	17	41	12	27
N	5,499,283	90,649	6,707,101	144,974

Note: Occupational categories are not strictly comparable from 1970 to 1980. They were collapsed to make them more comparable. Farming occupations were not shown since they accounted for less than half of 1 percent of employed women.

Source: Bureau of the Census, *1970 Census of Population*, vol. 1, *Characteristics of the Population*, chapter D, "Detailed Characteristics," part 34, New York; part 32, New Jersey; part 40, Pennsylvania (Washington, D.C., 1973); Bureau of the Census, *1980 Census of Population*, vol. 1, *Characteristics of the Population*, chapter C, "General Social and Economic Characteristics," part 34, New York; part 32, New Jersey; part 40, Pennsylvania (Washington, D.C., 1984).

heightening of their demands and struggles.[24] Educational upgrading and the resistance of employed and unemployed workers to intensifying competition resulted in a relatively rigid earnings structure. Even in jobs employing high proportions of white women and other groups suffering discrimination, there was no significant undermining of earnings.[25]

With this rigidity in wages, new contingents were called upon to re-constitute labor reserves and maintain lower pay levels, even when other groups were available. The rigid sex concentration and higher educa-tional requirements of jobs employing white females maintained them in a highly segregated sphere of the labor market. It was found, for ex-ample, that those jobs with the highest proportions of white females in 1960 remained highest in white female concentration in 1970. As wages rigidified, however, opening jobs to one group who had suffered dis-

Table 4-7. Occupations among Ethnic Groups in the Middle Atlantic Region, 1980 (Percentage)

Occupation	Puerto Rican Total	Puerto Rican Female	Mexican Total	Mexican Female	Cuban Total	Cuban Female	Other Latino Total	Other Latino Female	White Total	White Female	Black Total	Black Female
Managerial	5	4	7	5	9	5	6	4	11	7	6	5
Professional	6	8	10	11	9	10	7	7	14	16	10	12
Technical	2	2	2	2	2	2	2	2	3	3	3	3
Clerical and related	21	34	16	27	18	27	16	23	19	35	24	33
Sales	6	7	6	8	9	8	6	7	10	11	5	5
Service (excluding domestic)	17	13	20	19	14	11	16	14	11	14	21	23
Domestic services	*	1	1	3	*	*	2	4	*	1	2	4
Craft and related	11	4	10	2	10	4	12	4	12	2	8	2
Operatives	24	23	20	19	23	27	27	32	13	9	16	10
Laborers and related	7	4	6	3	6	4	6	4	4	2	5	2
Farming, fishing, forestry	1	*	3	1	*	*	*	*	2	1	*	*
N	372,158	144,974	25,458	10,422	84,906	37,720	309,957	136,198	13,125,043	5,485,275	1,511,293	779,161

*Less than half of 1 percent of employed persons.

Source: Bureau of the Census, 1980 Census of Population, vol. 1, Characteristics of the Population, chapter C, "General Social and Economic Characteristics," part 34, New York; part 32, New Jersey; part 40, Pennsylvania (Washington, D.C., 1984).

Table 4–8. Education among Ethnic Groups in the Middle Atlantic Region, 1980 (Persons 25 Years Old and Over) (Percentage)

Education	Puerto Rican		Mexican		Cuban		Other Latino		White		Black	
	Male	Female	Male	Female	Male	Female	Male	Female	Male	Female	Male	Female
Less than High School	39	44	32	32	38	41	32	38	15	18	24	19
High School												
1–3 years	24	21	18	19	11	10	16	15	15	15	22	24
4 years	23	24	24	29	23	26	26	28	33	41	31	36
College												
1–3 years	9	8	12	11	12	11	14	11	14	12	14	13
4 or more years	5	3	14	9	16	12	12	8	23	14	9	8
N	266,574	330,039	16,922	18,404	51,237	59,862	181,884	219,738	8,676,043	10,053,161	964,842	1,281,384

Source: Bureau of the Census, 1980 Census of Population, vol. 1, Characteristics of the Population, chapter C, "General Social and Economic Characteristics," part 34, New York; part 32, New Jersey; part 40, Pennsylvania (Washington, D.C., 1984).

crimination also served to open them to other workers who were also discriminated against.[26] Therefore, even if in more limited numbers than whites, women of all groups responded to the demand in the growing professional, clerical, and sales occupations. Table 4–7 shows that there were higher proportions of women than of total employed persons of each ethnic-racial group in these occupations. Capital has always tended in this way to break up any enclaves that have privileged a particular group as the labor supply for a particular job sphere.

If we were to look at the stratification among Puerto Rican women, those participants in the labor force, in fact, appeared to some extent as a select group entering the highly segregated occupational sphere of white females. The limited educational upgrading among Puerto Rican women from 1970 to 1980 was accompanied by an increase in their labor force participation that thus appears to have been the response of better educated Puerto Rican women to expanding white-collar employment (Tables 4–5 and 4–9). In Table 4–7 we can also observe that employed Puerto Rican women were more concentrated in clerical and sales jobs than non-Puerto Rican Latinos, even when the latter had higher numbers with higher levels of education. Their shift toward these occupations was also more noticeable since in 1980, for the first time, there were more clerical workers than operatives among employed Puerto Rican women (Table 4–6).

Previous research had already shown that, particularly in terms of clerical jobs, employed Puerto Rican women had what is considered a more favorable occupational distribution than other migrant women, when compared to white women and to men in their groups.[27] Consistent with this occupational distribution, it was found that in 1970 and 1977 Puerto Rican women active in the labor market nationally experienced underemployment (in the form of part-time work and inadequate earnings) to a lesser extent than did Puerto Rican men. They were also less underemployed than Mexican and black women, two groups with higher labor force participation, and they showed underemployment rates similar to those of white and Cuban women, groups that had more members at the highest levels of education.[28]

This occupational shift of Puerto Rican women, however, must be regarded with qualified optimism. To begin with, it must be considered in relation to the deskilling and declining economic status of growing numbers of white-collar occupations. Indeed, the line between the employment conditions in low-level white-collar occupations and manufacturing

Table 4–9. Education in the Puerto Rican Population in the Middle Atlantic Region, 1970 and 1980 (Persons 25 Years Old and Over) (Percentage)

Education	1970				1980			
	Total		Puerto Rican		Total		Puerto Rican	
	Male	Female	Male	Female	Male	Female	Male	Female
Less than High School	28	28	53	60	17	19	39	44
High School								
1–3 years	21	20	25	21	15	16	24	21
4 years	28	36	17	16	33	40	23	24
College								
1–3 years	9	8	3	2	14	12	9	8
4 or more years	14	8	2	1	21	13	5	3
N	9,830,839	11,334,260	201,943	233,867	10,323,564	12,141,939	266,574	330,039

Source: Bureau of the Census, 1980 Census of Population, vol. 1, Characteristics of the Population, chapter C, "General Social and Economic Characteristics," part 34, New York; part 32, New Jersey; part 40; Pennsylvania (Washington, D.C., 1984); Bureau of the Census, 1970 Census of Population, vol. 1, Characteristics of the Population, chapter D, "Detailed Characteristics," part 34, New York; part 32, New Jersey; part 40, Pennsylvania (Washington, D.C., 1973).

jobs is blurring. Therefore, the fact that Puerto Rican women may be closer to white women in their employment conditions only means that they share with them a low status based on gender discrimination. Nevertheless, this change in occupational distribution suggests that those Puerto Rican women who have faced relatively more favorable employment opportunities have been more likely to be active in the labor force, even when this also implied higher unemployment (Table 4–5). It also means that they have become a labor reserve for white-collar occupations that were once largely the domain of white women.

Even if we considered the status of employed Puerto Rican women to be relatively positive, however, their improved circumstances must be seen alongside the greater number of those remaining pauperized and as reserves out of the labor market. A first consideration would be why, with the increasing integration of the Puerto Rican and U.S. economies and after four decades of massive migrations, Puerto Rican women in the Middle Atlantic states continue to manifest such low levels of education. It is possible that migration flows to the Middle Atlantic region could be reflecting the still limited educational advancements of Puerto Ricans on the island. Previous research suggests that it is second-generation Puerto Rican women who have higher levels of education, higher rates of labor force participation, and higher representation in white-collar employment.[29] The level of education of Puerto Rican women in the Middle Atlantic region was also affected by the fact that migrants from Puerto Rico to this area continued to be less educated than those moving into other areas, while better educated Puerto Ricans moved out of New York City and probably out of the region.[30]

Still, migration flows are not the only explanation for why the proportions of higher-educated Puerto Rican women in the Middle Atlantic region remained even more limited than other Latinos in an economy requiring increasing credentials. The educational system must implement programs that are responsive not only to the cultural and language diversity presented by these women but to the constraints imposed on women, particularly on working-class women, by their household and economic responsibilities. These are responsibilities that, if anything, may be more difficult in urbanized settings where women are likely to face them in greater isolation.

Educational achievement, however, is not the only factor determining labor market activity but one mediating opportunities under conditions of limited employment and increasing credentialism. Research comparing the labor force participation of Latinas in different regions in 1976 found that Latinas had the lowest proportion of peripheral jobs in the areas where they were concentrated and that education was a more significant predictor of labor force participation among island-born Puerto Rican women than among other foreign born Latinas.[31] In this context, it is important to recall that the region's labor market has not been able to absorb even those with better job qualifications. Capitalism has imposed limits on employment that have tended to maintain a labor reserve even in growing job sectors. Under the conditions of wage rigidity described earlier, and as the economy slowed down, labor demand in jobs requiring higher education slackened, so that they did not increase at a rate capable of absorbing all the available better educated women.[32] There may be even further restraints on employment if, as has been suggested by some researchers, economic crisis and stagnation are confronted by increasing productivity and technological development that may increase profits but limit the growth of service occupations.[33] The labor force participation of Puerto Rican women must in this respect be referred to their movement into these white-collar jobs and the conditions of competition and succession among workers in this occupational sphere. The limited growth of jobs requiring higher education and the availability of white women to fill the increasing positions may account for the lower labor force participation of Puerto Rican women even with higher levels of education.[34]

Even more important in explaining the economic status of most Puerto Rican women is to understand that the loss of manufacturing jobs in the region has hit them harder than other racial and ethnic groups. As the expanding labor-intensive manufacturing in Puerto Rico showed itself incapable of offsetting the declining employment in the tobacco and home needle industries, women from the island intensified their migration to the New York region after World War II.[35] Here, they actively responded to demands in textile and other labor-intensive manufacturing industries that had already begun to see runaway shops moving out of the area. Concerning suggestions that Puerto Rican women have low labor market activity principally because of their traditional cultural values, one must remember that they showed a participation rate of 40 percent in 1950, the highest for all ethnic and racial groups of women in the United States except the Japanese.[36] It was as their job sphere continued shrinking that, contrary to other groups, Puerto Rican women declined dramatically in labor force participation, particularly from 1960 to 1970.

It must be emphasized that the differences in Puerto Rican female labor force participation among cities over this decade were mainly accounted for not by the characteristics of Puerto Rican women but by differences in labor demand, particularly in the operatives occupations where they were most highly concentrated.[37] Their declining labor force participation was explained predominantly by the declining opportunities for low-skilled women in the New York area, the hardest hit by employment losses in manufacturing.[38] Although operative jobs were still an important source of employment particularly for island-born Puerto Ricans, by 1980 the highest proportion of Puerto Rican women were no longer found in operatives occupations (Table 4–6).[39] Having been concentrated as the labor supply for these jobs in previous decades, Puerto Rican women were the most affected by runaway shops and the decline of low-skilled manufacturing.

As jobs requiring low levels of education disappeared, other sectors of the economy expanded during the 1960s. In the meantime, increasing labor and community militancy and continued migration of blacks and Puerto Ricans to the region magnified the problem of inadequate employment opportunities there. This led to rioting in ghetto communities, but it also resulted in increased used of public support programs, especially Aid to Families with Dependent Children (AFDC).[40] Although the AFDC program never increased sufficiently to cover all eligible families, Puerto Rican and black women represented a large segment of those requiring welfare benefits. Even when the program was threatened by government budget cuts, Puerto Rican female family heads, still confronting employment cuts, remained disproportionately out of the labor force and highly dependent on public assistance in 1980.[41]

In the context of the declining economic alternatives and higher acceptance rates of families on welfare, it was found that the labor force participation of both males and females was lower in the New York City areas with higher AFDC incidence.[42] Given the labor market conditions described above, this finding cannot be attributed to voluntary withdrawals from the labor market but must be seen as a response to job displacement. Research analyzing Latinas' labor force participation in 1976 suggests that while the prevalence of low-skilled jobs among regions did affect their economic activity, attractiveness of welfare benefits was not significantly related to participation after controlling for other variables.[43]

Nevertheless, the availability of welfare benefits and other alternatives in the informal economy appears to have allowed Puerto Rican and black women the possibility of subsisting, without further undermining earnings, while they moved in and out of peripheral jobs. It has been argued that the availability of Puerto Rican workers maintained wages at low levels in New York from 1950 to 1960.[44] However, my research showed that from 1960 to 1970 the presence of Puerto Ricans and other minority and migrant workers (not disaggregated by sex) did not lead to further competition for jobs and declining earnings.[45] That is, the labor market activity of Puerto Ricans and other workers suffering discrimination was limited to responding to labor demand in lower-paid jobs and therefore did not intensify competition to the point of worsening the jobs' level of remuneration.

As earnings rigidified even in the lowest-paid positions, labor reserves had to be replenished to meet demand in these jobs. The low labor-force participation of Puerto Rican women must also be related to the availability and succession of these additional contingents in the lower-paying job spheres. In the first place, a greater increase in service occupations of Puerto Rican women with lower educational levels would have intensified competition with black and Mexican women, already more concentrated in these jobs. The availability of black and Mexican workers for this job sphere may have made it less necessary to open these positions to additional contingents.

The remaining textile and clothing industries, on the other hand, became open to Cuban and other Latinas, who showed higher labor force participation than Puerto Rican women and were disproportionately employed in these occupations in 1980 (Tables 4–4, 4–6, 4–7). One could ask whether the availability of these other Latinas increased job displacement among Puerto Rican women, or whether the latter's declining labor force participation opened the way to their succession by these other groups. It appears more the case that, as the Puerto Rican female labor supply became insufficient to undermine earnings directly, other Latinas were called upon to fill operatives' jobs.[46] Even when Puerto Ricans remained concentrated in lower-paying manufacturing and faced declining employment, additional contingents were probably necessary as reserves to maintain low wages in this job sphere because of the competition the industry faced from foreign producers. Additionally, sectors in textile and clothing production have been reconstituted and deskilled in a revival of sweatshops and home production that has created working conditions worse than those faced by Puerto Rican women in the previous decade.[47] The garment industry has historically been a niche for immigrant women, and despite deteriorating conditions the industry has apparently maintained this sphere even more open to them, as the higher labor-force participation of Cuban and other Latinas suggests. On the other hand, Puerto Rican women, a larger group that had constituted the labor supply for certain sectors of the garment industry during previous decades, reflected more sharply its tendency toward declining employment and working conditions.

Still, Puerto Rican women remain a source of labor for low-paying manufacturing along with other Latinas, and it is probable that they have also been caught up in the reappearance of sweatshops and home production. This reconstitution of low-paying textile and clothing industries could have contributed to the relative decline in manufacturing wages in the region compared to other areas of the nation.[48] The presence of non-Puerto Rican Latinas could have increased competition even further if, with increasing cuts in social services and the intensifying economic crisis, Puerto Ricans had again been participating more actively as the labor supply for these positions.

Loss of Jobs and Puerto Rican Female Family Heads

It is within this context of limited jobs, employment cuts, and the incorporation of new groups of workers into the labor supply that the pauperization of Puerto Rican women and their role as labor reserves must be understood. This appears to be particularly true for Puerto Rican female heads of families. As Table 4–2 shows the incidence of poverty among both total and female-headed families is greater among groups with lower proportions of employed householders. The fact that female family heads suffer the limits to employment still imposed on working women relative to men is fundamental in explaining their higher poverty rates. Puerto Rican female-headed families, the most affected by employment cuts, were the most likely to be poor.

Workers pressured by the scarcity of jobs and economic need tend to offer their labor for the lowest-paid positions. The disproportionate economic responsibilities of female heads of families impels them in most groups to have higher levels of employment than women as a whole and makes them more bound to accept poverty wages (Tables 4–2, 4–4). Even when female family heads appeared less likely to be poor if they were employed, they were also disproportionally represented among the working poor. With the exception of Puerto Ricans, female family heads were a higher proportion of employed householders under poverty than their proportion in their group as a whole (Table 4–2). The response to labor demand in menial services and peripheral manufacturing means that poverty among non–Puerto Rican Latino, black, and even white female heads of families is explained not only by their exclusion from employment but by the level of earnings offered in the jobs they do enter.

Among Puerto Rican female family heads, however, exclusion from employment does appear to be the fundamental explanation of poverty. Such women had much lower employment rates than other Puerto Rican women in other family settings whose employment rates increased (Tables 4–2, 4–4, 4–5). Yet, Puerto Rican female family heads constituted only 37 percent of the working poor as compared to forty percent of all family heads in their group. This situation is more characteristic of island-born Puerto Rican female family heads and remains so even after accounting for reduced demand in low-skilled occupations, attractiveness of welfare benefits, or individual characteristics.[49] This finding is consistent with previous research indicating that, more than Puerto Rican wives, it was Puerto Rican female heads of family who were most active in the labor force in previous decades but also the ones declining in labor force participation in the 1960s and 1970s.[50]

Further research is required to clarify the negative relationship between family headship and labor force participation that has appeared as characteristic of Puerto Rican women in the United States. Personal attributes and circumstances have been shown to be related to labor-force participation rates among Puerto Rican mothers in 1980. Some of these characteristics, like English language skills, presence of small children, access to family networks, and home ownership may have a greater impact on the labor market activity of single mothers than of those who were married.[51] It would still have to be determined why and how these characteristics and circumstances were related to a higher participation among Puerto Rican female family heads in earlier decades and to lower participation after 1960. In order to analyze the decline in the labor market activities of Puerto Rican female family heads, one would have to consider to what extent and why these characteristics have changed over time and how they may have been related to participation in the different decades.

The analysis must still be related to labor market conditions in the areas in which they have been concentrated. It was apparently Puerto Rican female family heads, more than other Puerto Rican women, who constituted the labor supply for operative occupations during previous decades.[52] They were thus apparently also the most affected by the loss of low-skilled manufacturing jobs in the Middle Atlantic region.[53] The disparity between those Puerto Rican women concentrated in more adequate jobs, and those outside of the labor force, may therefore produce a polarization of Puerto Rican families of different types. On one hand are husband-wife families with employed householders, who are improving in economic status at least in part because of the growing proportion of employed women among them. On the other hand are the growing proportion of jobless and inadequately employed Puerto Rican men and women, particularly Puerto Rican female family heads, who are maintained disproportionately out of employment and in conditions of poverty and dependency.

The conditions lived by Puerto Rican female family heads underscore the need to relate what has been called the "feminization of poverty" to the global class structure and to the particular allocation of women in this class analysis. Economic instability itself must be considered as a factor related in complex ways to family structure, inasmuch as it is poor women who are more likely to become heads of families. For jobless women or those employed in menial services, poverty may come soon after a divorce, widowhood, or teenage pregnancy, if they are left as the sole supporters of their families.

On the other hand, women who, because of their family resources or their own allocation in the labor market, belong to the dominant classes or the higher strata of the working class may not be as likely to become family heads or to slip into poverty if they do. Although Puerto Rican married mothers in 1980 were more likely to own homes and to have better educations than Puerto Rican single mothers—characteristics posi-

tively related to higher status and to higher labor force participation—
Puerto Rican single mothers who had higher proportions of home ownership, and were thus presumably of higher strata, also had higher labor
force participation rates.[54] This more privileged class status has been
more prevalent among white than among black and Puerto Rican
women. Given their disproportionate allocation as labor reserves or in
the lowest-paid jobs, a larger proportion of black, Puerto Rican, and
other migrant women are more likely to be poor when they become
heads of families.

Furthermore, poverty among female family heads must not be considered in isolation from the economic conditions of the men and other
family members of their group. Higher poverty and unemployment
among family members also means that women will more likely be limited to their own resources if they become heads of families. In this way,
many white women are less bound to face poverty, not only because they
are less likely to be heads of households, but because of their higher class
position and the economic stability of their families or their partners.
Left redundant by loss of jobs, a large proportion of Puerto Rican female
family heads have the fewest resources, not only because of their own
class position but because of the precarious economic conditions suffered by their families and the men to whom they relate.

Conclusion

Class, national origin, gender, family status, and regional location
are factors explaining the conditions lived by Puerto Rican women in the
United States. Puerto Rican women in the Middle Atlantic region have
suffered the incorporation, displacement, and succession among workers in the job market that typically occur when capital plays different
groups against each other in its search for lower labor costs. Thus, capital's tendency to shuffle and reshuffle groups in a process of succession
appears to have allocated white, black, and migrant female workers
where their levels of education could be offered at the lowest pay. In a
process that has stratified Puerto Rican women, a select group has been
incorporated to expand the labor reserve of white women and thus maintain low wage levels in the expanding sex-segregated professional, clerical, and sales occupations. Limited as migrants even when they possess
higher levels of education, most Puerto Rican women are allocated at the

lowest levels of the economic structure. They remain predominantly impoverished as potential or stagnant labor reserves, increasingly displaced by employment cuts and sharing menial service jobs and the manufacturing jobs that remain with blacks and new groups of Latinos. The low labor force participation of Puerto Rican women facing limited employment may be interpreted as an adjustment and a resistance to intensifying competition in the jobs they enter—white and black female spheres—and those in which they are succeeded by other Latinas.

Critics who attribute poverty to family instability and welfare dependency obscure these inherent tendencies of joblessness and declining earnings that allocate groups as the labor reserves of particular job spheres and leave those with less social and bargaining power in the lowest-paid positions. They ignore the system's inability to provide employment—much less adequate employment—for all workers and the fact that, in its different forms, the labor reserve becomes a dead weight depressing earnings throughout the entire job structure. If Puerto Ricans were to increase their labor force participation, it would be either in response to tendencies in job growth or by displacing other workers. Attempting to impose labor force participation under conditions of job losses is to produce such a displacement and to contribute further to deteriorating employment conditions.

Critics of welfare have particularly obscured the discriminatory employment conditions suffered by working women relative to men in their class when they become main family supporters. They have threatened to force employment among women without considering that the jobs available to them are even more limited than they are for men and usually offer only poverty wages. Requiring work without ensuring the availability of jobs that provide adequate livelihoods for all groups of earners may be reinforcing a system that borders on servitude.

One must consider, as well, that for a significant sector of the population, the downward pressure on earnings has required the employment of more than one member in order for families to live above the poverty line. This constitutes an especially difficult and even discriminatory situation for single-parent households, and particularly for female family heads, who are a majority among them and tend to face lower earnings and employment rates. For women, the need for additional earnings may constitute a pressure to maintain relationships for reasons very far from the ideal of romantic love and family values.

Attacks on welfare recipients appear to advocate marriage as if the use of welfare were caused by separation from unemployed, irresponsible male partners. Thus, welfare critics ignore the social processes and conflicts that now impinge on family relations. But the high divorce and separation rates prevalent in our society suggest a questioning of the patterns of female subordination and other social conflicts affecting what has been considered the norm of husband-wife families. Challenging these conventions still leaves women as family heads in the presence of children and dependents, increasing their economic responsibilities and their likelihood of poverty as they face discrimination and limited employment options. One of the conditions for more harmonious and equitable family relations would actually be the economic autonomy of women and female heads of households that would allow for their financial well-being. The answer to conflicted relations is not to enforce a particular family structure.

It is just as important to remember that one must not equate work solely with paid employment. Attacks on welfare have failed to regard poor women's household and family work as a social and economic contribution that deserves to be recognized, facilitated, and financed. Welfare recipients, and particularly female heads of households, are involved in domestic work, family responsibilities, and all forms of exchanges of goods and services that allow their households and communities to survive with minimal monetary earnings. If anything, the lower cost of these services may in fact become a subsidy for employers at all levels, who may feel less pressure to pay higher earnings for the subsistence of their workers.

Offered as a legitimizing response of the system by the state to its citizens, welfare entitlements may provide some possibility of resistance to further deterioration in employment and economic conditions. The resistance, however, has been limited and has offered most recipients the means to survive only in conditions of poverty. Welfare benefits would have to be transformed in order to offer the means for their social, economic, and personal advancement. Particularly for women, they would have to provide the kinds of support services required for them to face their multiple responsibilities. Just as important, an unbiased analysis of welfare programs would also have to recognize the capitalist economy's failure to create jobs and acknowledge that it imposes inadequate earnings, along with competition and inequality, among ample sectors of our population. The arena seems fertile for rethinking such a system.

NOTES

Acknowledgments: In writing this chapter, I benefited greatly from previous research done with Dr. Rosemary Cooney of the Sociology Department at Fordham University, New York. This is the revised version of an essay published in *The Commuter Nation: Perspectives on Puerto Rican Migration,* ed. Carlos Torre, Hugo Rodríguez Vecchini, and William Burgos (Río Piedras: Editorial Universidad de Puerto Rico, 1994), 255–85.

1. For a definition and discussion of the feminization of poverty as a worldwide tendency, see Hilda Scott, *Working Your Way to the Bottom: The Feminization of Poverty* (London: Pandora Press, 1984).

2. My analysis and critique of the concept of the feminization of poverty benefited greatly from the ideas presented in Linda Burnham, "Has Poverty Been Feminized in Black America?" *Black Scholar* 16 (March–April 1985): 14–25; and Linda Burnham and Miriam Louie, "The Impossible Marriage: A Marxist Critique of Socialist Feminism," *Line of March* 17 (Spring 1985). See also Ruth Sidel, *Women and Children Last* (New York: Penguin Books, 1987); Carmen Gautier Mayoral, "The Puerto Rican Model: Welfare for the Multinationals; Is Poverty Being Feminized in Puerto Rico?" (paper presented at Feminist and the Scholar conference, Barnard College, New York City, 1987).

3. Rosemary Santana Cooney and Alice Colón, "Work and Family: The Recent Struggle of Puerto Rican Females," in *The Puerto Rican Struggle: Essays on Survival in the U.S.,* ed. Clara E. Rodríguez, Virginia Sánchez Korrol, and José O. Alers (New York: Puerto Rican Migration Research Consortium, 1980), 58–73.

4. For one of the latest analyses linking poverty and female-headed families among Puerto Ricans, see Linda Chávez, *Out of the Barrio: Toward a New Politics of Hispanic Assimilation* (New York: Basic Books, 1991).

5. Diana M. Pearce, "The Feminization of Ghetto Poverty," *Society* 21 (November–December 1983): 370–74.

6. This trend of increasing numbers of female heads of families was already evident in the previous decade, as shown in Cooney and Colón, "Work and Family," 66.

7. See, for example, Chávez, *Out of the Barrio,* chapter 7. For an excellent response to Chávez's and similar arguments, see Rina Benmayor, Rosa M. Torruellas, and Ana L. Juarbe, *Responses to Poverty among Puerto Rican Women: Identity, Community, and Cultural Citizenships* (report to the Joint Committee for Public Policy Research on Contemporary Hispanic Issues of the Inter-University Program for Latino Research and the Social Science Research Council, Centro de Estudios Puertorriqueños, Hunter College, 1992).

8. The following are theoretical arguments elaborated in Alice E. Colón-Warren, "Competition, Segregation, and Succession of Minorities and Women in the Middle Atlantic Region Central Cities Labor Market, 1960 to 1970" (Ph.D. diss., Fordham University, 1984). See also Marlene Dixon, Susanne Jonas, and Ed McCaughan, "Reindustrialization and the Transnational Labor Force in the United States Today," *Contemporary Marxism* 5 (Summer 1982): 101–15.

9. Burnham, "Has Poverty Been Feminized"; Gautier Mayoral, "Puerto Rican Model."

10. Kirkpatrick Sale, *Power Shift: The Rise of the Southern Rim and Its Challenge to the Eastern Establishment* (New York: Random House, Vintage Books, 1976); Wolfgang Quante, *The Exodus of Corporate Headquarters from New York City* (New York: Praeger, 1976).

11. Ira Rosenwaike, *Population History of New York City* (Syracuse, N.Y.: Syracuse University Press, 1972); Colin Greer, "Remembering Class: An Interpretation," in *Divided Society*, ed. Colin Greer (New York: Basic Books, 1974), 1–8.

12. Rowland Berthoff, "British Immigrants in Industrial America," in Greer, *Divided Society*, 160–77; Helen Icken Safa, "Runaway Shops and Female Employment: The Search for Cheap Labor," in *Women's Work, Development, and the Division of Labor by Gender*, ed. Eleanor Leacock and Helen I. Safa (South Hadley, Mass.: Bergin and Garney Publishers, 1986), 58–74; Seth M. Scheiner, "The Negro at Work: Blacks in Harlem, 1865–1920," in Greer, *Divided Society*, 196–214.

13. Harry Braverman, *Labor and Monopoly Capital* (New York: Monthly Review Press, 1974), 155–67, 271–89; Ernest Mandel, *Late Capitalism* (London: New Left Books, Verso, 1978), 140–43, 190–92, 248–73.

14. Ruth Fabricant Lowell, *The Labor Market in New York City: A Study of Jobs and Low Income Workers in 1970* (New York: New York City Department of Social Services, Office of Research and Program Evaluation, 1975).

15. Karin Stallard, Barbara Ehrenreich, and Holly Sklar, *Poverty in the American Dream: Women and Children First* (Boston: South End Press, 1983).

16. Saskia Sassen-Koob, "Recomposition and Peripheralization of the Core," *Contemporary Marxism* 5 (Summer 1982): 101–15; Safa, "Runaway Shops and Female Employment," 62.

17. Braverman, *Labor and Monopoly Capital*, 155–67, 271–89, 424–47.

18. Sassen-Koob, "Recomposition and Peripheralization," 101–15; Stallard, Ehrenreich, and Sklar, *Poverty in the American Dream*, 23–26.

19. Ibid.; Frank Bonilla and Ricardo Campos, "Evolving Patterns of Puerto Rican Migration," and "Exclusion from Work: Race, Ethnicity, and Sex in the Formation of U.S. Labor Reserves," in *Industry and Idleness* (New York: Centro de Estudios Puertorriqueños, Hunter College, CUNY, 1986).

20. Rosemary Santana Cooney and Alice E. Colón-Warren, "Declining Female Participation among Puerto Rican New Yorkers: A Comparison with Native White Nonspanish New Yorkers," *Ethnicity* 6, no. 3 (1979): 281–97; Palmira Ríos, "Puerto Rican Women in the United States Labor Market," *Line of March* 18 (Fall 1985): 43–56.

21. Cooney and Colón-Warren, "Declining Female Participation," 288–90.

22. Valerie K. Oppenheimer, *The Female Labor Force in the United States: Demographic and Economic Factors Governing Its Growth and Changing Composition* (Berkeley: University of California Press, 1970), 14–16, 25–62, 96–126.

23. Colón-Warren, "Competition, Segregation, and Succession," chapter 6.

24. James O'Connor, *The Fiscal Crisis of the State* (New York: St. Martin's Press, 1973); Mandel, *Late Capitalism*, 248–73.

25. Colón-Warren, "Competition, Segregation, and Succession," chapter 6.

26. Ibid., 279–82.

27. George L. Wilber, Daniel E. Jaco, Robert J. Hagan, and Alfonso C. del Pierro, Jr., *Spanish, Americans, and Indians in the Labor Market*, vol. 2 (Lexington: Social Welfare Research Institute, University of Kentucky, 1975); Evelyn S. Mann and Joseph J. Salvo, "Characteristics of New Hispanic Immigrants to New York City: A Comparison of Puerto Rican and Non-Puerto Rican Hispanics," *Research Bulletin* (Hispanic Research Center, Fordham

University) 8, nos. 1–2 (January-April 1985); Colón-Warren, "Competition, Segregation, and Succession," 265.

28. Rosemary Santana Cooney and Alice Colón, "Puerto Rican Labor Underutilization" (paper presented at the Southwestern Social Science Meeting, Dallas–Fort Worth, Texas, 1979).

29. Marta Tienda, "The Puerto Rican Worker: Current Labor Market Status and Future Prospects," in *Puerto Ricans in the Mid 80s: An American Challenge,* ed. Robin Johnson (Alexandria, Va.: National Puerto Rican Coalition, 1985), 81–83.

30. Cooney and Colón-Warren, "Declining Female Participation," 293–94; Government of Puerto Rico, Junta de Planificación de Puerto Rico, *Características de la población migrante de Puerto Rico* (San Juan, P.R., October 1984), 22; Evelyn S. Mann and Joseph J. Salvo, "Outmigration Rates and Extra-regional Migration Propensity of Race and Hispanic Origin Groups, New York City, 1975–1980" (paper presented to the Population Association of America, San Francisco, April 3, 1986).

31. Rosemary Santana Cooney and Vilma Ortiz, "Nativity, National Origin, and Hispanic Female Participation in the Labor Force," *Social Science Quarterly* 64, no. 3 (September 1983): 510–23.

32. Cooney and Colón-Warren, "Declining Female Participation," 290–92.

33. William B. Johnston et al., *Workforce 2000; Work and Workers for the Twenty-first Century* (Indianapolis, Indiana: Hudson Institute, 1987).

34. Cooney and Colón-Warren, "Declining Female Participation," 281.

35. Alice Colón, Marya Muñoz, Neftalí García, Idsa Alegría, "Trayectoria de la participación laboral de las mujeres en Puerto Rico en los años 1950 a 1985: Estudio sobre la calidad de vida y la crisis económica en Puerto Rico" (paper presented at the Congreso Latinoamericano de Sociología, Brazil, 1986).

36. Cooney and Colón-Warren, "Declining Female Participation," 281.

37. Rosemary Santana Cooney, "Intercity Variations in Puerto Rican Female Participation," *Journal of Human Resources* 10, no. 2 (1979): 222–35.

38. Cooney and Colón-Warren, "Declining Female Participation," 294–95.

39. Tienda, "The Puerto Rican Worker," 72–83.

40. Frances Fox Piven and Richard A. Cloward, *Poor People's Movements: Why They Succeed, How They Fail* (New York: Random House, Vintage Books, 1979).

41. George S. Sternlieb and Bernard P. Indik, *The Ecology of Welfare, Housing, and the Welfare Crisis in New York City* (New Brunswick, N.J.: Transaction Books, 1973); Clara Rodríguez, "Economic Factors Affecting Puerto Ricans in New York," in *Labor Migration under Capitalism: The Puerto Rican Experience,* ed. History Task Force, Centro de Estudios Puertorriqueños (New York: Monthly Review Press, 1979); Frances Fox Piven and Richard Cloward, *The New Class War: Reagan's Attack on the Welfare State and Its Consequences* (New York: Pantheon Books, 1985), 16–17; Stallard, Ehrenreich, and Sklar, *Poverty in the American Dream,* 46–47; Mann and Salvo, "New Hispanic Immigrants," 6.

42. Elizabeth Durbin, "The Vicious Cycle of Welfare: Problems of the Female Headed Household in New York City," in *Sex, Discrimination, and the Division of Labor,* ed. Cynthia B. Lloyd (New York: Columbia University Press, 1975).

43. Santana Cooney and Ortiz, "Nativity, National Origin, and Hispanic Female Participation," 519–20.

44. Rodríguez, "Economic Factors Affecting Puerto Ricans in New York," 198.

45. Colón-Warren, "Competition, Segregation, and Succession," chapter 6.

46. Ibid.

47. Saskia Sassen, *The Mobility of Labor and Capital: A Study in International Investment and Labor Flows* (Cambridge: Cambridge University Press, 1988).

48. Alice Colón, "Some Indicators of Industrial Development and Employment Growth in the New York SMSA" (paper presented for the Urban Area Analysis Course, Fordham University (Fall, 1977–78).

49. Santana Cooney and Ortiz, "Nativity, National Origin, and Hispanic Female Participation," 520.

50. Cooney and Colón,"Work and Family", 70–72.

51. Janis Barry Figueroa, "A Comparison of Labor Supply Behavior among Single and Married Puerto Rican Mothers." In *Hispanics in the Labor Force: Issues and Policies*, ed. Edgardo Meléndez, Clara Rodríguez, and Janis Barry Figueroa (New York: Plenum Press, 1991), 183–202.

52. Tienda, "The Puerto Rican Worker," 68.

53. Cooney and Colón, "Work and Family," 70–72.

54. Barry Figueroa, "Comparison of Labor Supply Behavior," 193–95.

FIVE

Our Two Full-Time Jobs: Women Garment Workers Balance Factory and Domestic Demands in Puerto Rico

CARMEN A. PÉREZ-HERRANZ

arly feminist theorists, especially Marxist theorists, argued that women's emancipation would follow their incorporation into the paid labor force. However, recent studies carried out in developing societies indicate that women have been incorporated into the labor force on the basis of gender and that society's gender hierarchy has thus been maintained and reproduced. Moreover, contemporary working women must now contend with two types of work: salaried and nonsalaried labor. This chapter evaluates the impact of these processes on Puerto Rican women by examining the lives of a group of women working in the garment industry in western Puerto Rico during what many are calling the last stages of Operation Boostrap, an industrial development program that has defined the island's economy since 1947. In particular, this essay explores the question of whether incorporation into the island's labor force under Operation Bootstrap has promoted women's emancipation or continued their subordination.

Because of its capacity to employ a significant number of workers, the garment industry has played an important role in the island's economic transformation. It is undoubtedly one of the most successful light manufacturing industries promoted by Operation Bootstrap. The establishment of this industry on the island, however, dates back to the first decades of the century when needlework was carried out by women in their homes, most of them in rural areas, and when production was organized on a piecework basis. When the industry expanded in the 1950s, many women began working in the factories that were established in the island's urban centers. The western part of Puerto Rico became one area where the industry flourished both as homework and shop work, and this was one reason that I chose this part of the island to carry out my research. Many of the women who worked in the factories where I conducted my fieldwork in fact began working in this industry from their homes.

Information for this study was gathered through interviews with a total of 157 women who worked in three plants located in the towns of Mayagüez, Rincón, and Añasco. These interviews were conducted over a twelve-month period, and further ethnographic data was gathered through an in-depth study of the families of three women workers. During the time I lived with these families, I was able to gather data about the women's daily routines. I found all the women I interviewed very generous and open about sharing their personal lives with me, although younger single women, with rare exceptions, tended to be more shy and hesitant in answering questions. Married heads of households or widowed women were, almost without exception, the most outspoken, and they displayed keen awareness of diverse issues and problems related to their employment and workplace dynamics. Their attitudes and answers to my questions were in most cases very precise and honest. The use of in-depth interviews and the participant-observation technique (which included, living with these workers) provided me with a comprehensive and detailed view of the strategies used by women to deal with the double burden of work in their factories as well as in their homes.

During the period when the research for this study was conducted, many companies that were engaged in light industrial work began to relocate to other parts of the Caribbean, where lower wages and other business conditions were more appealing. Puerto Rico no longer offered a significant advantage in terms of tax waivers and other incentives to U.S. enterprises, especially to the garment industry, when compared to the benefits offered by other countries in the area. For example, Puerto Rico in the early stages of Operation Bootstrap had made low wages a cornerstone of its economic development program; however, during the 1960s and 1970s wages rose considerably on the island.[1] Although wage increases were once seen as a positive outcome of the development experience, now in comparison to the lower wages prevailing in other developing countries they were a liability. Thus, U.S. companies began to relocate or open new plants in other Caribbean islands. This was the case with one of the factories where I carried out my research. This relocation process demonstrates the impact of world economic trends—and therefore the new international division of labor—on the lives of women in Puerto Rico. As other nations in the Caribbean offer lower wages and other incentives to international firms, Puerto Rican workers have experienced unemployment, underemployment, and deteriorating work conditions. Many of the garment workers I knew began to look for new jobs as their factories began to close. The effects of these worldwide capitalist transformations on Puerto Rican women thus presented elements that favored this inquiry.

A review of the literature on women and development reveals that the impact of women's incorporation into the formal labor force has been of great interest to many scholars.[2] This topic has been analyzed from different perspectives by leading feminists, including traditional Marxists who insist that salaried work will bring about women's emancipation in society.[3] Puerto Rican feminists have also addressed these issues, but they have focused principally on the sphere of salaried work.[4] Thus, they have diligently studied women's attitudes toward wage work, their participation in labor organizations, the impact of women's wages on household income, and labor force participation rates of women workers at different historical periods. Although many recognize the significance of the problem of the so-called "double shift," there has been very little research analyzing how salaried women articulate work inside and outside the household. The supposition that emancipation will follow women's incorporation into the labor force should be part of studies not only in the area of salaried work but also, and most important, of investigations in the household sphere.

This study of women's wage and household work in Puerto Rico in the early 1980s specifically addresses the Marxist feminist idea that women's traditional household tasks in capitalist societies will eventually be assumed by the public and private sectors and sold as commodities (as has been the case with public education, nursing, and care of the elderly), and that this process will continue as women abandon the domestic responsibilities assigned to their gender to participate in the labor force. This transformation in women's domestic role can be observed clearly within certain sectors of developed societies, but the situation in developing countries seems quite different. Here, although women have joined the labor force in increasing numbers, there appears to be an almost unbreakable bond between wage labor and domestic responsibilities. Conservative theoreticians, particularly developmentalists, attribute this resistance to change to the inability of Third World women to part with their traditional roles.[5] Indeed, among feminists in general there are diverse opinions about the benefits of economic development on women, as Susan Tiano succinctly illustrates in her article on women and industrial development in Latin America.[6] In this brief essay Tiano presents three theories that have guided the research on women and development. The "integration thesis," for example, proposes that development will eventually integrate women not only into the labor force but into all spheres of society. Women's participation in the labor force, according to this thesis, will give them economic independence and therefore emancipation. In contrast, the "marginalization thesis" proposes that the development experience will result in women's isolation from all spheres, and hence the ultimate impact of development on women will be their further subordination. Finally, the "exploitation thesis" maintains that the integration of women into the workforce is fundamental to the process of development in most economically emerging countries, but that this experience will impose upon women a greater share of gender responsibilities, thus curtailing the possibility of full emancipation. This study of women who have been incorporated into the labor force of a rapidly developing nation, as a result of an economic development program that has become a model of progress and modernization in Latin America and the Caribbean, expects to shed light on these debates.

Background to Garment Workers' Experiences

The implementation of Operation Bootstrap and the establishment of manufacturing industries during the 1950s and 1960s offered island women the opportunity of performing wage work outside the home. Working-class women, therefore, were the first group of Puerto Rican women workers to feel the full impact of the development experience. Because women already had a great deal of experience in the needle industry, as many previous scholars have indicated, and because the first stages of Puerto Rico's development program attracted firms that required a largely female labor force, women became a great asset to the government and to the industries that became established on the island.

More important, dire economic conditions in Puerto Rico, and the lack of other employment opportunities for women at the time, forced many home needleworkers on the island to seek employment in the new garment factories. Thus, Puerto Rican women were incorporated into the island's development program and into the U.S. factory system. Throughout the 1970s and 1980s the manufacturing sector continued to be an important source of employment for women workers in Puerto Rico. In 1980, for example, of the 1.2 million women who constituted the island's female labor force, seventy-two thousand were in the manufacturing sector.[7] At that time this sector was outnumbered only by that of public administration, which employed about one hundred thousand workers.

Since the 1950s the demographic profile of women in the manufacturing sectors in Puerto Rico has varied. During the first stages of Operation Bootstrap, most of the women who participated in factory (mainly garment) work were single eighteen-to-nineteen-year-olds. After 1950 this age representation shifted radically as women's ages increased to the twenty-to-twenty-four (and older) age categories. The rising age distribution of female workers in the island's labor force in the last few decades has been the result of the longer retention of women in the Puerto Rican school system, an outcome of the Commonwealth government's emphasis on education.[8] Higher educational levels have also expanded job opportunities for women in the clerical, managerial, and professional sectors. More recently, other manufacturing sectors, such as electronics and pharmaceuticals, have become alternative sources of employment for Puerto Rican women. These industries, characteristic of the present stage of economic development on the island, were first brought to Puerto Rico in increasing numbers in the 1970s to alleviate the high levels of unemployment resulting from the flight of manufacturing plants to other countries. The establishment of more sophisticated industries has also been strongly promoted by the Puerto Rican government, which sees these enterprises as well suited to the island's better educated labor force that today is well prepared to perform highly specialized and complex tasks.[9]

This shift in policy has dramatically affected Puerto Rican women in the industrial sector in the last decade, especially garment workers, since more and more jobs were lost to the relocation of manufacturing to other low-wage sites. This occupational sector, which included operators and women in related positions, has shown a decrease since the 1970s. In 1970

25,449 women worked in manufacturing, while in 1980 there were only 20,726.[10] On the other hand female participation in electronics and related occupations has increased since 1970. While in 1970 1,588 women worked in these sectors, by 1980 there were 3,616.[11] This may be an indication that women industrial workers will eventually experience greater participation in this type of industry. This suggestion needs to be qualified by the fact that positions in the pharmaceutical and electronic plants require more advanced levels of training (such as college education and greater knowledge of English), which may ultimately provide jobs in this industry only to those with higher levels of education.

These changes in the direction of Puerto Rico's economic development program have not only affected women workers, they have also had an impact on male labor force participation. The shift caused by Operation Bootstrap, from an agriculturally based economy to one dependent on export manufactures—and more recently to one based on service processing—has failed to include large segments of the male population. Government attempts to increase the education and vocational training of men have resulted in the employment of only some sectors of the male workforce. Thus, many Puerto Rican men on the island are unemployed or work for only a few months at a time in federally funded seasonal jobs.[12] Others are often forced to migrate to the United States to help support their families. These conditions have affected the composition of workers' families in Puerto Rico, leading in some cases to the dissolution of nuclear households and to increases in women's responsibilities in the family. Now a wife and mother becomes the head of household, breadwinner, and in some cases the single parent. In sum, in an extremely short period of time Puerto Rican women have been forced to assume, in addition to their traditional female duties, tasks and roles for which they have not been historically socialized. This is true for single heads of households as well as for married women. The goal of this study, therefore, is to examine how working in the manufacturing sector in Puerto Rico in the 1980s has affected the lives of a select group of women garment workers.

Women's Work in the Garment Factories

My research involved observing the work dynamics of women in three different lingerie factories belonging to a U.S.-based manufacturing company with administrative headquarters in New Jersey. In the

1950s this company had begun moving its operations abroad and had closed some of its plants on the mainland. At the time I was conducting my research, the administrative offices of the company were located in an old factory building near Newark, and from there the company administered its operations and carried out the process of designing and developing new product models. These headquarters were also used as a training facility, and workers from various plants in Puerto Rico were routinely brought there to work on models of the company's products.

One of the three factories I studied was first opened in the 1950s by this firm in Mayagüez, the most important urban center in the island's southwest; the other two were established during the 1960s and 1970s in towns adjacent to Mayagüez. In the oldest plant, the one located in Mayagüez, management was in the process of reducing its production and relocating some of its workers to the other two plants. A significant number of these workers had been with the firm since it first began operations. They were among the oldest workers in the firm, and many were reaching retirement age. They were thus quite worried about the work reduction in the Mayagüez plant. The firm's explanation for the reduction was that sales in women's lingerie had decreased due to market changes; however, they knew the firm was at the same time opening a new plant in the Dominican Republic.

The three plants I studied had similar production routines. What varied among them was the number of workers in each, with the Mayagüez plant employing the smallest labor force. The atmosphere inside all three factories was extremely orderly—almost rigid. The women entered the work area by forming a line when the clock hit the hour. As they walked into the area, they were scrutinized by higher-ranking personnel who made sure they brought no personal belongings into the plant with them. (Employees were permitted to carry only their personal scissors to their work areas. Factory management claimed this procedure was necessary in order to prevent the theft of production materials hidden in purses or in other personal belongings.) The work area was divided into several stations where the different production tasks were performed. Each of these work stations had a supervisor or "floor lady," who was responsible for overseeing the work of the operators and stimulating their speed and quality of work. "Floor ladies" were also responsible for handling and informing their immediate supervisors of any problems that arose in their work area.

In the three factories the plant supervisors were all men. They reported directly to the plants' general managers, who were also men. The main function of these plant supervisors was to deal with problems related to all the work stations, but they also supervised the process of receiving, distributing, and shipping materials. They were also responsible for supervising the plant mechanics. Factory managers' offices were always located adjacent to both the production and administrative areas, which were distinctly separated by high walls. The entire administrative area in each factory was air-conditioned; the rest of the building was not. Along with the manager, other administrative personnel, such as accountants and secretaries, worked in these areas. All of these were women. This rigid hierarchy in the physical organization of the plants extended to the relations between workers and management. The general managers in all three factories were highly respected and in some instances feared. Although some of the managers tried to be somewhat relaxed with workers, all asserted their authority firmly. When dealing with female workers, either in the plant or administrative areas, the managers and floor supervisors displayed some very paternalistic attitudes. This paternalism was reflected in conversations in which managers appeared to express more concern over the well-being of the women workers than for matters relating to their work in the factory. On occasion a manager would mention that he had known a particular worker since she was a "child," and that he knew her relatives too. Although the paternalism of the managers was more obvious when they dealt with younger workers, it was evident when they spoke to older women as well. For example, while instructions to younger workers were always given in a very slow and authoritative manner resembling the way adults sometimes address children, interactions with older women workers, though carried out quite respectfully, appeared constantly to overemphasize the efforts of management to satisfy the needs of workers—that is, to take care of them.

There was obviously a very fixed hierarchy within the factories that corresponded to gender ranking. Males, with the exception of the dispatchers, always occupied the positions of highest authority. Managers spent the majority of the time in their offices, which were located in a separate area of the factory compound that was always closed. In two of the factories the managers' offices had windows facing the floors from which they could view the plant operations and signal instructions to floor supervisors. Once or twice a day, or as the need arose, the managers made floor rounds. On these occasions they chatted briefly with workers. Sometimes these verbal interactions included a reference to the manager's wife or mother, suggesting that labor and management were all related to a kind of factory "family," with mothers and wives serving as the connecting links. Indeed, each of the three managers had relatives who had worked for or were still working in the same manufacturing company. One manager was the son of one of the oldest women workers with the company. When his mother died, the other long-time workers at the plant usually, and not surprisingly, recalled her while interacting with him.

Work organization in the factory was closely related to social conventions that operated outside the workplace. Affinal and kinship relations were often the fundamental source for the relationships that developed among workers in the factory, but sometimes these social interactions became strained. This tension derived mainly from the pressure placed on workers by supervisors (the "floor ladies") over the quality and speed of production. Often workers felt threatened as supervisors openly manifested their power within the factory administrative hierarchy. Some workers believed that once an operator became a supervisor, she changed. The new supervisor was then seen by the workers as an accomplice of the factory administration.

In analyzing gender roles and positions in the factory, one might initially conclude that the women had assumed the submissive position historically associated with females in Puerto Rican society. Indeed, very few women wanted to carry out tasks that called for leadership. For example, managers in all three factories were having a hard time convincing women workers to become "floor ladies," even though this position entailed a salary increase. However, when asked, women workers often explained they were not willing to jeopardize their personal relations with other workers by becoming managers since this job required putting intense pressure on other workers. Similarly, although most women realized that the union representing them, the International Ladies Garment Workers' Union (ILGWU), was not doing its job adequately, none of them challenged the union leaders or put forth their own organized demands. They also did not resort to the union when they had problems relating to their work; instead they attempted to settle conflicts with their managers personally. For example, when workers found discrepancies regarding their work schedules, they generally addressed their concerns to management and used the union only as a last recourse. Workers argued that they had to engage in "personal strategies" in their workplaces because they perceived the union as being on management's side. What this also tells us is that women, both as workers and as union members, were desirous of preserving the close networks and kinship relationships they had established in their factories; they were fearful that more collective and overt forms of assertion would have affected these relationships negatively. Thus, in addition to formal union activities, workers adopted a variety of individual strategies that they believed helped them overcome the pressures they found in the factory system operating in Puerto Rico at this time.

Before discussing these strategies further, I would like to explain the kinship networks that defined the work atmosphere in these garment factories. As I have mentioned, most workers were related to other workers and, in some cases, to management. The personal histories of three managers in these factories constitute good examples of these relations. The three managers were native to the towns where the factories were located, and they knew most of the workers personally. In some cases, they were even connected to them through kinship relations, as was the case with the Rincón factory manager whose mother had worked for his company until her death. This gave this particular manager a family connection to the company spanning two generations. Meanwhile, there were numerous workers in this company whose co-workers included mothers, sisters, and cousins—all of whom worked in production or administration. Most of the secretaries and accountants in the factories were related to other workers. These kinship relations, of course, also included the males; some female workers had brothers or husbands working as dispatchers or mechanics in the factories. Furthermore, kinship ties transcended a single factory; that is, some workers were related to employees in the other factories as well.

It is clear that the factory system in Mayagüez operates by a complex hierarchy that incorporates elements that are external to the factory system, like family ties and other affinal relations. A significant aspect of this social structure is that there is no attempt to hide these ties; the relationships are public knowledge, and I was informed of them as soon as I began my fieldwork. This intricate hierarchical structure fulfills some important functions in these garment factories. For example, the system is sometimes used by managers to increase production and to maintain the distribution of power within a given factory. In the case of male managers the system takes on the nuances of paternalism as they personally bestow praises to women who perform their work well or scold those who do not. Although personnel evaluation systems exist in modern workplaces throughout the island, the personalistic system in effect in these factories, with its links to the social hierarchy and kin relations established by the workers, is reminiscent of the hacienda system operating in Puerto Rico until the first decades of the twentieth century.

In Puerto Rico, as in other Caribbean islands, the hacienda system was extremely patriarchal and made use of the kinship system to grant and exact favors from workers and to control production. Among these kinship relations was the system of *compadrazgo* (literally, coparenthood). *Compadrazgo* refers to the relationship that developed between parents and godparents after the ceremony of baptism. This relationship, sanctioned by the Catholic church, required the *compadres* (coparents) to assume responsibility for the child in case of the parents' death or some other misfortune. Godparents also assumed the role of advisers to the children and agreed to provide financial aid in case of need. In haciendas throughout the island, landowners were frequently involved in *compadrazgo* relations with their workers, a relationship that permitted the hacienda owner, as a godfather to the workers' children, further control over his labor force. In the modern garment factories where I conducted my research, *compadrazgo* relations were often established between workers and members of management. By christening a worker's child, the manager became the worker's *compadre* or coparent. This was beneficial not only to the manager but to the workers because it allowed for communication at a less formal, family-style level. Nevertheless, as in the old hacienda system, this type of communication tended to benefit management to a much greater degree than it benefited workers, especially with respect to female workers.

The closely knit relations prevalent among the workers were the result of several factors. First, because of the length of time this company had been operating in the area, workers had been able to attract relatives to work in the factory. Second, management apparently had an unofficial policy of hiring workers who were recommended by other employees, which enabled workers to bring family members into the factory when positions became available. Third, management apparently realized that family relationships gave them more control over their workers, either through the gratitude that workers felt for the opportunities they offered, or through the pressure they were able to exert on workers through the relatives who had recommended them. And fourth, workers, especially women, also felt quite comfortable with these kinship relations, which made the factory into an extension of their communities and families. Additionally, because workers' households are mainly located in rural areas, strong networks of support among families and neighbors have evolved. These rural community relations, which in most parts of the island are usually determined by kinship connections, are a very important source of support for women working in urban workplaces. Because significant sectors of these communities work in the same factories at the same time, women workers have access not only to information but also transportation to and from their jobs. It is important to note that in the factories women continue these interpersonal relationships by creating among themselves artificial kinship relations, such as *compadrazgos* (that is, baptizing each other's children).

The relations thus established or perpetuated in the workplace were often used by workers to cope with problems or gain advantages. Having relatives who looked after them, exerted influence in their favor, and controlled information allowed employees to feel more protected in the factory. This control was more evident among the older women, who were the most outspoken in the factory and employed kinship relations in more dynamic ways in order to put pressure on management. They spoke on behalf of family members by employing arguments that no Puerto Rican manager could ignore, such as: "When you were a kid, do you think your mother would have left you with someone else, if the night before you had had an asthma attack?" (This in fact was an argument used by one woman on behalf of a younger one who had been absent from work the day before). Younger women, with few exceptions, were generally more shy and often sought the mediation of an older worker when presenting claims or requests to management or labor union representatives. Younger workers, for example, allowed older women to accompany them to see managers about permission to be absent from work to take care of personal matters. The older women usually added weight to these and other pleas of younger workers, and did not fail to remind a manager of how his mother, wife, or sister would have felt in a similar situation. In some instances fictional kinship relationships were created, such as the designation of a union representative, who promoted a more relaxed atmosphere when the workers came to discuss their grievances, as "our factory mother."

As I have noted, from the women workers' perspective, the ILGWU represented management and thus was used only in those instances where it was strictly necessary. For example, they sought the union's help when it came to matters involving retirement pay and health insurance claims. As Helen I. Safa has noted, these benefits were very important ones for the workers; however, they were very unhappy with the quality of the health services and the amount of retirement pay the union provided.[13] Although workers saw these benefits as the ILGWU's most important accomplishments in the past, now they did not believe the union could accomplish much more. Thus, while most workers recognized the union's responsibility in managing their health and pension benefits, they used their own system of individual negotiations or their kinship relations, which they considered more efficient strategies, in addressing grievances or obtaining favors. In general, most women appeared to manifest an attitude of submission at work, considering confrontational tactics as "manly" and "too aggressive." Perhaps for this reason, they seldom asserted themselves in more direct and organized ways. Instead, they preferred to use more subtle strategies with which they were more comfortable and that gave them the results they desired. But this attitude of apparent submission contrasted sharply (as we shall see later) with their more assertive behavior in their households.

Finally, I would like to explore Puerto Rican women garment workers' perceptions of their wage-work experience. The women I interviewed had different attitudes toward wage work, often depending on their age. Younger women, particularly those who were still single, thought their work in the factory offered a good opportunity to establish friendships, and those who planned to marry saw their jobs as a means to earn the money they would need to establish their future homes. Among those who were young and already married, wage work was definitely a way to help in building their homes or at least to contribute a much-needed salary in the new household.[14] Most of the women in this group saw themselves working for the rest of their lives, but some thought their factory jobs were temporary because they expected to find better-paying jobs as clerical workers or as assemblers or quality inspectors in one of the area's newly established electronics factories. Some

middle-aged women expressed an eagerness to resolve financial problems soon so they could return to the home that many still considered "a
woman's place." However, those still raising children felt there was little
likelihood of leaving their jobs. The older women I interviewed told me
that although they had always wanted to remain at home, economic necessities forced them to work. One of these women had always yearned
to stay home but accepted the fact that "now I've been working for more
than twenty years, so I'll work until my retirement." In general, younger
women wanted to continue working in the future, yet most of them
longed for better-paying jobs, such as those in the clerical sector. Older
women, who had worked most of their lives, indicated dissatisfaction
with their jobs, but they too expected to work until retirement age in order to guarantee an income in later years. Similarly, they foresaw their
daughters working all their lives as well; however, they expected them to
be employed in better-paying jobs, preferably clerical ones. In the meantime, all were extremely concerned with the production decreases in the
garment factories.

Dynamics within the Household

During the course of my fieldwork, I interviewed many of the women
in their garment factory work stations. Because many of the women invited me into their homes, I also had the opportunity to observe their
household environments and the ways in which they interacted with
their families and friends. Additionally, as I noted earlier, I lived for a
brief period of time with the families of three of these workers. Two were
workers at one of the companies, and the third had worked in the factories for many years but at the moment was a union representative in
the area. While living with these women and their families, I was able to
observe not only the extreme difficulties women had in juggling the responsibilities of two very different forms of full-time work but also the
very different views they held of the formal wage-work sphere and of
their household and community responsibilities.

Throughout the course of my research I noticed that, except for the
kinship relations that were continued in the workplace, these women perceived their wage work and household and community work as somewhat
separate entities. They also indicated in many different ways that work at
the factory, and to a certain extent some of the relations they developed

in their workplaces, were different and less significant to them than work and relations within their households and their communities. For some, wage work was but a medium through which they supplemented their household income; for others having a paying job was a way of obtaining the "little extras" they or their families needed. Most of the women said that although they had friends at the factory, they seldom interacted with them outside of work, with the exception of those who were their relatives. One woman regretted this lack of communication:

It's sad, but I never see my factory friends elsewhere—that is, with the exception of those members of my family who live in my community and I see every day. The rest live in other *municipios* or barrios and with all the things you have to do at home, there's not much time to visit and socialize with people who live far away.

Thus, women workers in Mayagüez were forced to keep their family and community and workplace relationships separate.

Many garment workers in general liked their wage work, and some were quite sure that if they lost their jobs, they would look for another one. Thus it may seem contradictory that most of these women saw their main responsibility as their household work and the care of their families. But this apparent paradox may be explained by the fact that in their jobs women receive little gratification since their jobs pay low wages, provide no opportunities for advancement, and are often insecure. On the other hand, women workers probably feel very satisfied with the support and affection they receive in their immediate households and from their extended family networks. Still, the factory represents for these women a place where they can interact outside their closely knit communities and expand their relationships, albeit in a limited way. Obviously, these women always welcome and need their wages to help support their households, but while I was living with the three families, it became clear to me that household and community relations were their first priority. The centrality of household responsibilities in women's lives is best appreciated by observing the daily routines followed by the three women with whom I lived.

These women started their routines early in the morning—around five o'clock, at which time they had breakfast and began to prepare the main meal of the day. Then they attended to their husbands' and children's needs before departing for work. The youngest of these women was also responsible for transporting some of her co-workers to and from the factory. After a long day at work, some of the women picked up groceries in town and went home, where they resumed their domestic routines. The youngest of the women, however, had to pick up her small daughter at the babysitter's house before going home. The other two women, who were older, came home to take care of grandchildren until their mothers returned from work. Each weekday afternoon was assigned a different task: one day was devoted to the wash; one to ironing; another to yard work; and yet another to general housecleaning. Some preferred to attend to some of these tasks on Saturdays, although this day was usually set aside for shopping. All the women I met had developed an efficient management of time; they assigned almost every minute of the week to a particular chore. Nevertheless, when emergencies arose, they could be sufficiently flexible in their schedules to give a hand to a neighbor or relative who needed their help; yet by doing so they added another task to their busy schedules. Weekend nights were usually spent with the family, as women and children gathered to watch television or play games. Men would do the same with other males at one of the men's houses or at a bar, where they could drink and also watch television if one was available. The exception to this was the husband in the youngest couple's household; he spent the entire weekend with his family.

For these women celebrations of special events or holidays were extremely important. At Christmas their entire family gathered at their homes. These family gatherings also occurred on Mother's and Father's Days, and on the feast of the town's patron saint, which attracted the whole family to entertaining presentations and other social activities held at the town square. These activities were the highlight of these families' lives. In addition, each family often gathered at home to celebrate special occasions that were always organized by the women. For these festivities, women cleaned and fixed up their houses and decided what foods to prepare, dividing all this housework among themselves. Sometimes they would even make clothes for the entire family and tell the men what to wear to the event, or buy outfits for them. During these parties the women were in charge of the kitchen—serving the foods, making sure that everybody was well fed, and afterwards sharing in the cleanup. Men took part in the activity simply by enjoying the food, but at times the owner of the house would be in charge of buying and preparing the alcoholic beverages. Likewise, when a whole pig was roasted in the yard, the men would be responsible for this and only this. Very special occasions, like weddings, baptisms, and birthdays, were organized in the same fashion.

Women in the different kinship-related neighborhoods also shared responsibilities when problems arose. They helped care for children and the elderly in times of illness, death, or any type of family crisis by performing different kinds of chores, such as buying groceries and cooking. As noted above, women also provided transportation to and from work and did various errands for their neighbors, thus helping to support the closely knit networks they had established in their barrios.

Caring for their children, being housewives, carrying out the responsibilities involved in the running of their households, and maintaining their community kinship groups were for these women their first priorities. Motherhood, especially, continued to be seen as a fundamental activity for women in these communities and was considered by some to be the most important element in defining the female gender in Puerto Rican society. It also seems that by emphasizing the responsibilities traditionally assigned to their gender on the island, these women workers wanted to continue to draw a line between what they defined as female and male spheres of interaction. For them, mother-child and female-bonding interactions were still extremely important. Yet for most women workers in Puerto Rico today, the unchanging nature of women's family and household responsibilities continues to be one of the sources of the double burden of work. Not surprisingly, these confining definitions of the female gender favor men as they simultaneously oppress women. These women's continued celebration of motherhood and family life, therefore, may be a way of subconsciously refusing to see their own subordination. However, maintaining this traditional ideology in modern Puerto Rico has provided these women workers with much-needed space in which to experience greater gratification and more control over their lives than they have had in modern industrial workplaces in Puerto Rico.

One of the areas in their private world that has given these women a great deal of personal satisfaction is the control of information and decision making in their households. Among the garment workers I interviewed, those who had strong family networks benefited the most from the exchanges of information and support systems operating in their families. Support and information were usually given most freely by women who were heads of households and who were the oldest members of the family. Women in general had very strict control of information related to budget matters, childrearing and marital problems, and other personal issues faced by other women. They often used this power to their advantage. As problems arose within the households and decisions had to be made, older women assumed leadership positions and offered possible solutions to the problems. I observed in the decision-making process that the problems and alternatives offered as solutions were usually debated among a very small group of women in the household, if they were not decided entirely by the eldest woman. Thereafter, the male members of the family would be informed of the problem and given the one alternative the women had chosen to resolve the issue. The dynamics of this control of information were known and accepted by all members of the household, yet both men and women appeared to participate equally in the process of decision making. Thus, women controlled one of the most important aspects of domestic life, although husbands or other male members of the family were sometimes made to think that they were in control of information and decision-making processes.

There were exceptions to this rule among some of the families. For example, there was one couple in which the male actively participated in all types of tasks and decisions within the household. It should be pointed out, however, that this couple had no extended family network in the area. They were originally from another part of the island, and in addition they were return migrants, having spent many years living in New York City. Their migrant life experience and the absence of a family network nearby may help explain the male's strong role in this household's decision making. Most adult males living in the households I researched, however, generally assumed secondary roles in family activities. Although they interacted with the family and exerted some influence in their homes, in most cases they interacted principally with other male members of the family or with males outside the house. Most of them spent their free time in the neighborhood bars and public plazas, or on hobbies, such as raising fighting cocks or fixing cars—activities that still defined the male gender in Puerto Rico. The fact that men spent so much time outside their homes certainly limited their access to information, and thus women were able to control it and on occasion use it in their favor.

Conclusion

It is evident that proletarianization has taken place in Puerto Rico and that this process has affected women. Economic development is apparent not only in the physical transformation of the country but also in the definitive incorporation of women into the island's labor force. Although development and Puerto Rico's integration into the world capitalist system have brought widespread consumerism and other accompaniments of modernization, they have also perpetuated the uncertainty of employment in Puerto Rico's dependent economy. Regarding the impact of salaried work, especially its potential to foster the emancipation of women, I found that some of the women in the garment factories of Mayagüez might complain about their work and long to stay home; however, they know that they are unable to survive without their salaries. Furthermore, most realize that their daughters will also work for wages, and they see wage work as a normal part of life—even though they long for them to stay home and take care of their children too.

Nevertheless, these women have not remained totally unaffected by their wage-work experiences in Puerto Rico. Their incorporation into the labor force within the particular circumstances of the factory has spurred the development of an array of strategies, all derived from methods originally employed within their households. One of the most significant of these is the use of kinship relations to aid in facing and solving the problems of the workplace. Bringing kinship relationships into the factory provides workers with added security for dealing with the complex interactions that take place in the somewhat alien and male-dominated factory environment. In this world, women rarely attempt to assume or usurp men's traditional gender roles. This situation has led women to create new strategies for interacting within this context. Thus, women deal, individually or with the help of relatives, with their supervisors or managers in order to solve problems in the workplace rather than using union representatives or other resources. In so doing, women have developed a less-confrontational style of assertiveness in the factory. Assuming a "strong" attitude in the workplace would be very risky for women; only a few of them act "strongly," and when they do, they make sure that other aspects of their behavior conform to their definition of womanliness. One woman, for example, continually mentioned her family and husband and faith in God as evidence of her traditional female role.

She was an active leader in the factory and church and used both her family role and her religiosity to prove she was a "good woman." Perhaps this worker felt that she needed to maintain a balance between the image she thought she projected in her job as an "aggressive" worker and the prevalent female gender ideology in Puerto Rico at the time, which continued to define "woman" as a quiet, family-oriented, religious person. She probably believed that a rupture in this delicate balance of images would have threatened her networks of support, particularly those provided by other women, which she felt she needed in order to succeed in the factory and at home.

In this study the arena of household and community emerges as the highest priority for Puerto Rican garment workers. This sphere gave these women the support systems they thought they needed to maintain their carefully organized lives as wage workers. They believe they have created a balance between factory and household work by juggling the tasks that are inherent in a woman's "double shift" with the aid of a closely knit network of relatives and friends. They cannot envision a rupture in this balance because they believe their very survival depends on it. Family and friends are the ones who give a hand in any time of crisis. Women are not, therefore, "passive recipients of change and victims of forces they cannot generate or control."[15] They have constructed, using elements that are familiar to them, a vast array of strategies through which they have assumed important roles in two separate spheres of action. In this fashion they manage to survive in an economy and society that have imposed on them a double burden of work. Thus, this sector of Puerto Rican women, as members of the new international division of labor, manage to adapt to impositions resulting from the global expansion of the capitalist system in the 1980s.

Emancipation, as it is defined by many feminists, is not clearly apparent in the lives of these Puerto Rican female workers, but they do reveal a new kind of woman worker on the island. These women are now active members of the labor force with full awareness of their rights and responsibilities as workers. As we have seen, there has not been a drastic rupture with traditional female responsibilities in the Puerto Rican society, and, therefore, women continue to function as housewives and mothers at the same time they shoulder the additional burden of wage work. Nevertheless, women appear to have gained some control over the tasks that define their traditional roles. They have also developed strategies that have helped them create a comfortable niche in their new area of interaction, the factory. The latter has what some women call "uncomfortable" aspects, which they believe need to be worked out or overcome in the future. However, many are proud they have managed to work in these factories under these circumstances and have thus been able to support their families with their labor for many years. The younger generation is still learning to cope with the new factory environment. However, because factory work poses so many limitations to women's advancement as workers, many young women look forward to leaving the factory and doing other kinds of jobs, such as clerical work. Younger women see themselves as future wage earners on the island, and many have attained high levels of formal education, but their futures looks grim nevertheless. These young women expect to marry, share future households with a spouse, and build a house with the monies earned through their hard work. Yet they face limited job opportunities and will probably be among the next generation of migrants to the United States.

NOTES

Acknowledgments: This work is based on "The Impact of a Development Program on Working Women in the Garment Industry: A Study of Women and Production in Puerto Rico" (Ph.D. diss., Rutgers University, 1990). The research for this study was carried out under the direction of Helen I. Safa and was partially funded by the National Institute for Mental Health. Other aspects of this research are discussed in "De la casa al trabajo, del trabajo a la casa: Etnografía del proceso de trabajo en las fábricas de la industria de la aguja en Puerto Rico," in *Clases, mujeres y espacios: Tres construcciones etnográficas sobre procesos de mercantilización en Puerto Rico,* ed. Carlos Buitrago Ortiz et al. (forthcoming).

1. James L. Dietz, *Economic History of Puerto Rico: Institutional Change and Capitalist Development* (Princeton, N.J.: Princeton University Press, 1986), 249.

2. See Ester Boserup, *Women's Role in Economic Development* (New York: St. Martin's Press, 1970); Susan Tiano, "Women and Industrial Development in Latin America," *Latin America Research Review* 21, no. 3 (1986): 157–70; Helen I. Safa, "Gender and Social Science Concepts in Latin America" (paper presented at the Sixteenth Congress of the Latin American Studies Association, New Orleans, 1988); June Nash, "A Decade of Research on Women in Latin America," *Women and Change in Latin America,* ed. June Nash, Helen I. Safa, and others (South Hadley, Mass.: Bergin and Garvey, 1986); Lourdes Benería and Martha Roldán, *The Crossroads to Class and Gender: Industrial Homework, Subcontracting, and Household Dynamics in Mexico City* (Chicago: University of Chicago Press, 1987).

3. María del Carmen Baerga, "La articulación del trabajo asalariado: Hacia una reevaluación de la contribución femenina a la sociedad puertorriqueña (el caso de la industria de la aguja)," in *La mujer en Puerto Rico: Ensayos de Investigación,* ed. Yamila Azize (Río Piedras: Ediciones Huracán, 1987), 89–111; Lydia Milagros González, *Una puntada en el tiempo: La industria de la aguja en Puerto Rico (1900–1929)* (Santo Domingo, D.R.: Editora Taller, 1990); Isabel Picó, "Estudio sobre el empleo de la mujer en Puerto Rico," *Revista de Ciencias Sociales* 19, no. 2 (1975): 141–64; Marcia Rivera, "The Development of Capitalism in Puerto Rico and the Incorporation of Women into the Labor Force," in *The Puerto Rican Woman: Perspectives on Culture, History, and Society,* ed. Edna Acosta-Belén (New York: Praeger, 1986), 30–45.

4. See also, for example, Yamila Azize, *La mujer en la lucha* (Río Piedras: Editorial Cultural, 1985); Blanca Silvestrini, "La mujer puertorriqueña en el movimiento obrero en la década de 1930," *Cuadernos de la Facultad de Humanidades* (Universidad de Puerto Rico) 3 (1979): 83–104; Isabel Picó, "Estudio sobre el empleo," 141–64; Luz del Alba Acevedo, "Política de la industrialización y cambios en el empleo femenino en Puerto Rico: 1947–1982," *Hómines* 10, no. 2, (1987): 40–69.

5. Robert L. Heilbroner, *The Great Ascent: The Struggle for Economic Development in Our Time* (New York: Harper and Row, 1963).

6. Tiano, "Women and Industrial Development in Latin America," 157–70.

7. Estado Libre Asociado, Departamento del Trabajo y Recursos Humanos, Negociado de Estadísticas del Trabajo, *La participación de la mujer en la fuerza laboral* (San Juan, P.R.: Estado Libre Asociado, 1982), table 14.

8. Picó, "Estudio sobre el empleo," 150.

9. Pérez-Herranz, "The Impact of a Development Program on Working Women," 86–87.

10. Acevedo, "Política de la industrialización y cambios en el empleo," 68.

11. Ibid., 68.

12. Ibid., 90.

13. Helen I. Safa, *The Myth of the Male Breadwinner: Women and Industrialization in the Caribbean* (Boulder, Colo.: Westview Press, 1995), 74.

14. For further information on women's contributions to the household economy, see Helen I. Safa, "Female Employment and the Social Reproduction of the Puerto Rican Working Class," in *The Puerto Rican Woman: Perspectives on Culture, History, and Society* (New York: Praeger, 1986), 88–109.

15. Peggy Sanday, "Female Status in the Public Domain," in *Women, Culture, and Society,* ed. Michelle Z. Rosaldo and Louise Lamphere (Stanford, Calif.: Stanford University Press, 1974), 189–206.

SIX

Gender and Politics: Grassroots Leadership among Puerto Rican Women in a Health Struggle

MARYA MUÑOZ-VÁZQUEZ

T his chapter explores the ways in which a group of women workers organized and struggled to confront harmful incidents of gas emissions in their workplace in Puerto Rico in the 1980s. By incorporating the category of gender into its analysis, this study not only illuminates Puerto Rican working-class women's perspectives on politics and leadership but also challenges traditional academic thought on political action, which until recently has ignored women's political behavior and visions of politics.[1] Feminist critics have argued that the premise for this exclusion rests on the idea that political action is congruent with the "male" and not with the "female."[2] Another bias of mainstream political thought is its conceptualization of political activity as participation in formal power, or power from above, such as in party politics—as opposed to women's involvements in social movements or power from the community. Because working-class women have lacked the access to formal political power enjoyed by men and women with professional backgrounds, their contributions have rarely been the object of political analyses. This study recognizes working-class women's grassroots actions and leadership as definitely political, and demonstrates that a political perspective that includes woman-oriented political participation and leadership styles, derived from the interests and experiences of women, provides a more complex view of politics and its relationship to gender.

Since "gender" has a variety of meanings, I would like to explore here what the term has meant in connection with politics and the environment in recent feminist investigations. Within this context, one popular definition of gender has emphasized the historical subordination of women in every dimension of social experience. In this sense, gender symbolizes female-male interactions that are constituted through power, such as economic, political, sexual, and linguistic relationships—all of which have been male sources of power and which, according to some scholars, account for the continued marginalization of women.[3] However, some feminists speculate that this marginalization may lead to ways of thinking that are different from patriarchal views and practices, thus placing women in a position to challenge social schemes that are oppressive and allowing them to create oppositional categories that are nonoppressive.[4] Feminist research has extensively documented the existence of the sexual division of labor in many societies. Although no one pattern or formula for the division of labor exists, women generally are the ones who take care of families. Feminists argue that this social responsibility, and the ongoing contact with the concrete realities of everyday existence it entails, have led women to value caring, compassion, and sentiment and to acknowledge these as important in the sustenance of life.[5]

Feminist researchers have also documented the fact that in many Third World countries women historically have been engaged in subsistence agricultural-silvicultural activities, as part of their family responsibilities. Their knowledge of and respect for nature's immense diversity have become guiding principles not only in their own economic activities but in other spheres of their lives as well. Thus, women are struggling against the destruction of nature by many modern polluting industries, and in their struggle they have challenged prevailing economic, political, and scientific paradigms of development. For Vandana Shiva and other scholars involved in this struggle, modern Western postcolonial development has come to mean the commercialization of a nation's economy in order to generate surplus and provide for the accumulation of wealth.[6] Specifically, the destruction of natural resources, dispossession of lands, and displacement of women and indigenous people from productive and sustainable agricultural activities have often resulted from the expansion of the industrial sector.[7] In sum, industrial development has destroyed the productive capacity of women by taking away their control of the land, water, and forests, and by destroying the capacity of nature to renew itself. In the process of utilizing a nation's resources, therefore, modern Western development has linked economic production to the destruction of nature.[8] In recent years, however, this idea of "production as destruction" is being countered by women who have struggled to promote the concept that production should be for the sustenance of life.

In their feminist struggles women are also adopting concepts, such as harmony in diversity and power without violence, that challenge patriarchal political "truths." Women's practices and voices thus constitute categories of thinking that are contributing to political, scientific, and economic transformations. But this definition of gender, signifying a distinct way of being and thinking for women, is under scrutiny. Initially, criticism focused on the interpretation that women personify an essential nature, as if all women were automatically the repositories of certain virtues or visions; some feared that this might suggest that women were somehow morally superior to males. More recent critics claim that from this perspective the cultural and social differences (such as class, age, education, race, and ethnicity) among women appear not to have a great deal of relevance and that this, ultimately, could lead to a polarized view of women and men or to stereotypical views of "woman" as a universal being. Nevertheless, I believe the concept of "woman" as the originator of new thoughts and processes and actions has a great deal of validity in political theory since it can allow for new theoretical and practical dimensions of concepts that we have previously ignored but that now have the potential of contributing to social transformations.

One political concept that is being redefined by women in contemporary societies is the idea of leadership in political struggles. Kathleen B. Jones has proposed that the understanding of political leadership in modern times has been based on rules, prescribed skills, and the effective use of power and techniques that often are devoid of principles other than utility. Expressions of compassion, love, and pain are interpreted from the dominant experience as exaggerations, weaknesses, and irrational behavior, and thus are not considered consistent with leadership qualities.[9] Jones asserts that this traditional way of understanding leadership has undermined female power, and she points to the structural implications that connect leadership to the concept of "authority" as a possible explanation for this.[10] In traditional political spheres leadership is achieved by behaving authoritatively, so that, for her, the very definition of the term "authority" is what lies at the root of the separation of women from the process of "authorizing" or leading in political struggles. Jones argues that the rationality of authority poses a definite separation of the realm of cognition from the realm of belief and feeling and creates an arbitrary restriction to formal rules that establish a dichotomy between compassion and authority. Some sort of surrender of private judgment— that is, submission to the judgment of another—is entailed in the concept of authority. Submission is achieved by acquiescing to the rationality of the discourse, a set of formal rules, a commanding tone, dispassionate expressions, and the "masculine" mode of communication (including assurance, assertiveness, and unqualified declarations). "Female" hesitancy and other patterns of expression that are interpreted as marks of uncertainty or confusion are not considered authoritative. But Jones believes that the female political experience will lead to a redefinition of authority into a contextual, relational process of communication and connection. Examining women's leadership experiences in the workplace, Karen Sacks defines "woman-centered leadership" as the mobilization of already existing social networks, mediation of internal conflicts, consensus building, and coordinating, compromising, and politicizing the notions of responsibility and respect.[11]

From a mainstream political perspective, therefore, leadership has meant the ability to organize and mobilize a group in order to promote specific ends. The dynamic set up by such a mobilization is directed to partially transforming the conditions of social development, and the ability to mobilize assumes the possession of certain skills and knowledge.[12] The leader must have an understanding of the context of power and the possibilities of change, the ability to offer incentives or impose sanctions that will sustain the required participation from the "followers," the skills to act as a spokesperson, and the ability to communicate clearly, confront, and authorize.[13] Ultimately, leadership is the act of decision, presupposing the ability to direct mass action, in which "friends" or allies are mobilized against "enemies." But from a gendered perspective, leadership becomes a collective and dynamic process, a complex set of relationships and negotiations, rather than a mobilization of parallel and individual actors.[14] Instead of emphasizing the notion of individual acts or rights, an egalitarian vision of social organization, implied by women's collective efforts, seeks a participatory and collective style of decision making.[15] Within this framework, leadership means the ability to bring forth the personal by politicizing the experiences of everyday life, encouraging the expression of sentiments such as care and compassion, and developing the values of equality and respect through organization and mobilization. In one of her early works Sheila Rowbotham pointed out that women, in order to create alternatives to oppressive conditions, had to question the accepted way of seeing political movements and look at themselves historically through their own cultural expressions, actions, organizations, and ideas. To achieve this, women had to come together, learn to trust one another, and explore the traditional ways in which they had been socialized, including the inhibitions against self-assertion they had internalized.[16] This chapter explores how women workers at the Guanajibo-Castillo Industrial Park in Mayagüez, Puerto Rico, examined their own gendered views of political action in a collective decision-making process that generated new definitions of leadership, and thus challenged the political and industrial structures and ideologies that were endangering their lives.

Women's Participation in Puerto Rico's Health Struggles

In the past four decades Puerto Rico has become a production site for high and medium technologies. This development is part of a strategy for a new international division of labor based on the industrialization of peripheral areas, including Puerto Rico, where from 1947 to 1965 the predominant capital investment was in low technology-industries with labor-intensive processes, notably textiles, shoes, clothing, and construction. After 1965, however, investment was channeled into high-technology industries (for example, oil refineries, petrochemicals, pharmaceuticals, and chemicals). Some intermediate-technology industries, like electronics and machinery, were also established.[17] As so many scholars have noted, this transformation in Puerto Rico's economy has brought a series of problems, the most obvious being unemployment.[18] But because the majority of high- and intermediate-technology industries discharge hazardous wastes into the water, air, and soil, serious environmental and occupational health problems exist on the island as well.[19]

Some of the more notorious contaminating industries are located in the areas of Cataño, Bayamón, and Toa Baja (Gulf Oil and thermonuclear power plants), Peñuelas and Guayanilla (Arochem Oil Refinery and thermonuclear plants), Yabucoa (Sun Oil Refinery) in the Industrial Park of Mayagüez (where potentially toxic substances such as polychlorinated and aromatic solvents are used). Other areas that have been severely affected by the generation of hazardous industrial wastes include: Ciudad Cristiana, where large deposits of mercury, lead, arsenic, and PCBs, among other substances, have polluted the entire vicinity; Juana Díaz, where mercury and polychlorinated solvents have been found in the water supply; and the Barceloneta-Arecibo region, whose water system has also been compromised by discharges of acetonitrile, carbon tetrachloride, and mercury. There are currently some two hundred areas in Puerto Rico being studied as possible illegal dump sites for industrial hazardous waste. These examples represent only some of the more serious problems.[20] In spite of the fact that several environmental groups on the island have pressed the Puerto Rican government to take a stronger stand against the growing problem of industrial pollution, the government has been unable to challenge the companies involved. Neftalí García Martínez, a well-known organizer in Puerto Rico's environmental struggles, sees the island government's inability to protect its environment and its people—especially its industrial workers—from the dangers of environmental contamination as a manifestation of the limitations of the island's colonial status and of the failure of federal regulatory agencies such as the Environmental Protection Agency (EPA) and the Occupational Safety and Health Administration (OSHA) to operate effectively in Puerto Rico.[21]

In response to the crisis of environmental pollution, the affected communities and workers, and their scientist allies, have been organizing themselves and disseminating information to deter construction of additional hazardous industries, improve the mechanisms for environmental protection, and arouse a pro-environmental consciousness throughout the island. Since the 1960s it is estimated that more than ninety communities have been engaged in environmental health struggles.[22] The most successful of these include blocking the construction of nuclear power plants on the island between 1969 and 1976, halting the installation of a "superport" for large oil tankers and refineries during the 1970s, and delaying the dumping of hazardous waste in certain landfills. Communities have also been able to obtain compensation for workers (the majority of them women) contaminated by mercury in a Beckton-Dickinson thermometer factory in Juncos and to former employees (six women and one man) of the Parke-Davis pharmaceutical factory who suffered work-related illnesses, including cancerous cysts (requiring mastectomies), depression, headaches, and gastrointestinal disorders.[23]

In nearly all of the environmental and occupational health struggles in Puerto Rico, women have been visible as spokespersons, coordinators, and members of committees. The reasons for women's involvement in these struggles vary. First, the tendency toward occupational segregation by sex in the last four decades has resulted in many women working in the garment, electronics, and electrical parts industries, all of which pose high health risks.[24] According to Annette Fuentes and Barbara Ehrenreich, the National Institute of Occupational Safety and Health (NIOSH) lists electronics as one of the industries with the highest health risks due to a production process that uses toxic chemicals, including solvents, acids, and paints.[25] Workers in the garment industry, 77 percent of whom are women, have also been exposed to health hazards. Men, too, have been affected, particularly those working in oil refineries, petrochemicals, and the cement industry.[26]

A second reason for women's extensive participation in environmental and occupational health struggles is that poor urban women are quite probably the social sector most affected when pollution strikes their community. They usually spend more time in the community because of their socially assigned household chores and thus experience heavier exposure to any existing toxic substances. It has also been proposed that low body weight, which has been related to lower resistance to toxins, increases vulnerability to the effects of pollution. Pregnant women are especially at risk, since they carry their developing fetuses with them into polluted environments.[27] Additionally, from the moment that contamination puts the lives and health of families at risk, women are usually the ones who take care of sick children and spouses. This implies long hours of waiting in health centers and often receiving—especially in cases of environmental or occupational illness—inadequate treatment. Finally, women have been at the forefront of initiatives to combat the economic and social problems that have affected their communities, and these efforts have sharpened their organizational and leadership skills.

The Incidents in Guanajibo-Castillo Industrial Park

The gas emissions at the Guanajibo-Castillo Industrial Park in the city of Mayagüez in the 1980s represent one of the most significant examples of the environmental health problem in Puerto Rico. These episodes also illustrate dramatically how the gendered segregation of work determines and structures women's experiences with regard to health hazards in the workplace. I became familiar with the situation in Mayagüez through a feminist organization that had been assisting the workers in their struggle. The women workers were looking for a variety of avenues of support and asked to consult a psychologist. It was in this capacity that I worked with this group from 1986 to 1988 and became one of the scientists who assisted the Comité Pro-Rescate de Nuestra Salud (CPRNS) (Committee to Rescue Our Health) in gathering and analyzing information related to gas emissions and their impact on workers in the factories. Along with other committee members, I attended demonstrations, participated in the committee's monthly meetings, and helped organize conferences and discussions at various universities about the workers' situations. A colleague at the University of Puerto Rico arranged a practicum for graduate students in community psychology, and they, along with professors and a group of advisors, assisted the workers during this two-year period.

The method I utilized to gather my data is called "observation through participant activism," and it is based on the following principles: that knowledge about a group is derived from an interchange between the researcher and the members of the group involved; that research should respond to the needs of marginal communities or social sectors and strengthen their capabilities of achieving their political goals; and that the relationship between the observer and the observed should be part of a dialogue of collective analysis in which all should engage in order to achieve the group's goals.[28] As researchers, we were fully aware of the limitations inherent in the "observation through participant activism" methodology, such as the fact that community members may have felt undue pressure to adopt strategies suggested by the researcher-participant. Another serious limitation is that the scientists were able to leave the committee at any time, whereas committee members could not disengage themselves from the struggle and its consequences as easily. Nevertheless, becoming part of these workers' struggles gave us a more personal perspective on their problems and a greater sense of responsibility and concern for the group and its mission.

The Guanajibo-Castillo Industrial Park was built in the 1950s under Puerto Rico's post–World War II economic development program. The project included a waste-water treatment plant and sewer system for the newly located industries. At present, there are twenty-nine factories located in this industrial complex, including two pharmaceutical companies, six electronics plants, and nine clothing factories. As early as 1983, workers in the complex began to notice gas emissions that traveled like a cloud throughout the industrial park. From 1983 to 1987 more than sixty incidents of gas emissions were observed.[29] Based on evidence compiled from various sources, a scientific consultant for the workers concluded in 1985 that the gas emissions originated principally from the pharmaceutical, electronics, and electrical-products industries, and that they contained toxic substances that had not received proper treatment. These substances, in the form of volatile liquids and gases, found their way into a sewer system designed for carrying sanitary wastes and pluvial water; the sewer system then leaked into the Industrial Park and its surroundings. It was also determined that some of the emissions originated from the waste water treatment plant and from direct emissions into the atmosphere.[30] On January 25, 1985, there was a significant leak that resulted in the evacuation of almost all of the two thousand workers in the industrial park and required the hospitalization of more than four hundred individuals. Symptoms reported by the persons affected at the time of the emissions were: nausea; vomiting; dizziness; fainting; difficulty in breathing; irritation of the eyes, nose, and throat; and numbness in the face and arms.

Those most affected by the gas emissions were the employees of the clothing factories, who were mainly women, and the neighbors directly north of the park. Male workers in these factories were also affected. Apparently, the use of air conditioners in the electronics plants prevented the gas emissions from entering these buildings and thus protected those workers; but no such equipment existed in the garment factories.[31] When the first emissions occurred, workers tried unsuccessfully to demonstrate that their health problems were directly related to exposure to the chemical substances in the emissions. Together with the committee's scientific advisors, workers and neighbors generated various studies and pressured the Puerto Rican government to conduct further investigations. One of these studies was based on sixty-four medical records of workers who had been exposed to contaminants. It contained diagnoses by a team composed of general practitioners, internists, neurologists, psychiatrists, and pulmonary specialists, and indicated that 9 percent suffered from neuropathies (peripheral nerve disorder that produces weakness and numbness); 50 percent had upper respiratory tract (nasal and pharynx) problems; 20 percent presented persistent complaints of arthralgia (pain in the joints), myalgia (general muscular pain), and generalized weakness; 14 percent were afflicted by bronchial asthma; 9 percent had hair and skin problems; 20 percent had difficulties with eye movement; 11 percent suffered from depression; and 6 percent experienced impaired concentration and loss of memory. A team of clinical psychologists evaluated thirty-two of the workers and neighbors and confirmed a pattern of emotional and cognitive disturbances that, according to the scientific literature, was consistent with those found in other workers exposed to organic solvents, leading the team to conclude that the impaired concentration, memory, and emotional functioning of the Mayagüez workers was related to their exposure to toxic substances.[32]

Meanwhile, investigations conducted in 1987 by the Environmental Quality Board for the Puerto Rican government in order to identify toxic substances present in the industrial complex found the following solvents: dichloromethane, 1,1,1-trichloroethane, perchloroethane, toluene, ethylmethylbenzene, xylene, and 1,2-dichloroethylene.[33] A study published in 1988 by the University of Puerto Rico at Mayagüez verified the presence of these solvents and also confirmed the existence of inorganic substances such as chlorine, ammonia, and carbon monoxide.[34] A review of the literature of the health effects of organic solvents, such as those identified in the Guanajibo-Castillo Industrial Park in Mayagüez, indicates a correlation between exposure to these toxic substances and specific health problems, including impairment of the central nervous system (loss of memory, depression, fatigue); problems of the peripheral nervous system (neuropathy); and skin and respiratory problems, among others.[35] Thus, the Guanajibo-Castillo Industrial Park experience clearly illustrates that the toxic substances utilized in industries can have negative effects on workers as well as on residents living near the plants where there are improper waste disposal systems and inadequate pollution control mechanisms.

In order to evaluate the devastating impact of these substances on individual workers, I would like to focus on two CPRNS members. Born in 1951, M is married with one small child and she has a high school education. Because of her verbal abilities, she was chosen to speak at rallies, marches, and university conferences, and to serve as a spokesperson in CPRNS meetings with Puerto Rican government officials. M's observations of the Guanajibo-Castillo case and her suggestions for committee work were always very sound. She noted that following the toxic emissions, she began to feel numbness in various parts of her body and pain in both her arms and legs; she also experienced moments of disorientation that were followed by anxiety and insecurity. M was one of the people diagnosed with neuropathy. A, another worker affected by the gas emissions, was born in 1943, completed the fifth grade, is married, and has four children. During one of the gas emission incidents, she lost consciousness; later, when she returned to work, she suffered from fainting spells. Eventually, A had to leave her job because she found it difficult to remember the things she had to do and constantly suffered from headaches, anxiety, depression, and hallucinations. She also required help when she left the house because, as in M's case, she became disoriented. All these health problems created tense relations within her family. Although A had been a productive garment worker for ten years and, according to her husband, had always taken excellent care of her home, the quality of her personal life was now seriously compromised by the toxic emissions. Nevertheless, A attended the committee meetings regularly, demonstrated great interest in what was being said, and participated in all of the group's activities, including marches, pickets, and public hearings.

In evaluating their experiences, both M and A indicated that they had never before suffered from this combination of symptoms or from disorientaion. I should add here that many other women workers reported similar disorientations. While in a very familiar place—the town square, for example—they would suddenly experience momentary lapses of memory and not know where they were. Or they might prepare breakfast for their spouses and, instead of placing the food on the table, throw it in the garbage can. While the workers' committee and their scientific advisors concluded that their physical health had been seriously impaired by exposure to toxic substances, their employers and the Puerto Rican government insisted that the levels of contamination that had occurred were not enough to explain their health problems. Instead they attributed these to a mass psychogenic effect resulting from a combination of hyperventilation, hysteria, and stress—in other words, they argued that the breathing difficulties, nausea, fainting spells, dizziness, and other symptoms the workers suffered were generated by the stress of work conditions, odors in the environment, and fear provoked by the previous gas emissions.[36] Thus employers conveniently ignored workers' complaints, and the Puerto Rican government refused to impose tighter environmental regulations or fine the companies involved. Neither provided the workers with the assistance they needed for their disabilities.[37]

Gendered Grassroots Leadership in Mayagüez

Guanajibo-Castillo's CPRNS was organized during the fall of 1983 and was expanded and strengthened in mid-1985 in response to one of the worst incidents of gas emissions. Cielo Martín and Santos Feliciano, both of whom were employed in garment factories in the complex at the time of the gas emissions, were the original organizers of the committee. Both of these women had had previous organizing experiences, unlike most of the other workers: one had been a labor organizer as well as a political activist; the other had been active in church gatherings. Another worker who had been badly affected by the gas emissions, Monserrate Cruz, was also very active in the steering committee of the CPRNS, and in 1986 she became its president. Typically between thirty and seventy people, the majority of them women, attended CPRNS meetings. Three or four men whose health had been negatively affected and three or four husbands usually attended as well. The total membership of the CPRNS was approximately seventy workers and twenty community residents, while its steering committee consisted of a president, vice president, secretary, treasurer, and some members at large. To aid it in its struggle, the CPRNS procured the assistance of Misión Industrial, a community-based organization well known for its defense of Puerto Rico's environment; the Unión de Trabajadores de la Industria Eléctrica y Riego (UTIER), the electrical and water supply workers' trade union; and Organización Puertorriqueña de Mujeres Trabajadoras (OPMT), a feminist organization. The committee also enlisted, through the assistance of the environmental organization and other grassroots agencies, the services of various scientists, doctors, psychologists, and lawyers, some of whom donated their time. The monthly meetings held to plan strategies and address other matters were attended on a regular basis by the steering committee, some committee members, several representatives from the above-mentioned organizations, and a few graduate students and scientific advisors. Other scientific advisors attended meetings whenever their expertise was deemed necessary.

In order to appreciate fully the enormous importance of garment workers' activism in the CPRNS, we should, even if only briefly, explore the rigid class and gender divisions that defined garment factories in the late 1980s in Puerto Rico. In the Guanajibo-Castillo industrial complex the production departments of the garment factories were housed in long, one-story structures with poor lighting and ventilation, yet the women's jobs involved intricate assembly operations that required manual dexterity and good eyesight. Most of the women worked with fairly simple but noisy machinery to complete repetitive tasks. The work was also arranged so that each worker depended on the production of the other workers in her group to complete her quota. The male employees, on the other hand, worked at individual tasks, such as cutting fabric, carrying heavy loads, or doing janitorial work. Managerial control was derived not only from the way in which the work was organized but also through the imposition of rules and restrictions; supervision was highly authoritarian. After the controversy over gas emissions began, new rules, for example prohibiting workers from listening to the radio, were arbitrarily enforced. As in other industrial workplaces throughout the island, upper management was disproportionately male and worked separately in air-conditioned offices. An environment divided along gender and class lines was clearly in place in Guanajibo-Castillo Park. Women's struggle for a healthier workplace, therefore, was not only a challenge to industrial companies' use of dangerous production methods but also to the patriarchal organizational structures present in the factories.

Women's Collective Decision Making

At the monthly meetings of the CPRNS I noticed that collective decision making was a major concern among the women members, especially among its most active leaders. The preoccupation with collective decision making among women political activists has several theoretical justifications. First are those that have to do with sensitivity to other people's points of view, particularly those whose interests are at stake. Second, by participating in decisions that affect them people can give direction to their lives instead of passively depending on others. Third is the realization that most political experiences are too complex to be represented adequately by one or even a few points of view, and that the collective process of decision making admits the experiences, points of view, values, and knowledge of everyone who is involved. Collective decision making, in this context, contains three distinct conceptual elements: solidarity formation, goal setting (giving direction to the struggle collectively), a collective planning of political strategies.

The difficulties of establishing a collective decision-making proc among the women of the Guanajibo-Castillo Industrial Park were ill trated on several occasions during my involvement in their struggle. O difficulty throughout the struggle had to do with internal differences o tactics and strategies. A conventional approach to grassroots political tion would employ pickets and demonstrations to pressure the gove ment to confirm the presence of toxic substances in the park, advise t offending industries to implement pollution controls, and assure tl workers got appropriate medical care. However, most of the women wo ers initially preferred a different approach to pressing their case. As cc mittee leader Cielo Martín noted, the organization of work in the g ment factories did not lend itself to open communications in the eve some sort of political action was needed. Specifically, workers were quired to produce their daily quotas without talking, which would fo them to communicate surreptitiously with their co-workers and risk e missal or other reprisals. Accustomed to proceeding cautiously in their tempts to influence those in power, most of the women at first preferi to try quietly negotiating with the government rather than to use me aggressive tactics such as pickets and demonstrations. They expected t for the most part government officials would sympathize with their cau

The tension between these two orientations became apparent d ing monthly committee gatherings. In a January 1986 meeting to disc the results of a workers' health assessment survey, one male organi proposed a demonstration in front of the capitol building in San Juar a way to make the public aware of the emissions in the park. He cc mented that he had made this suggestion previously but that the wom on the committee had responded that their ill health did not permit t kind of activity and so no action was taken. Some women now argu that they could not participate in public demonstrations because of th precarious economic situation. They also worried that if their nan were publicized, they would be subject to reprisals. Although Mar acknowledged the importance of pressure tactics, she supported women in this instance.[38] Later, however, most of the women in CPRNS came to recognize the importance of picketing and other pi sure tactics in advancing the group's goals. In fact, they were very s prised at how effective these tactics were in persuading Puerto Rican g ernment administrators (mostly male) to initiate the actions the workers demanded.

Martín's concern with collective decision making in the CPRNS was apparent in the ways she encouraged the other women to become more active in the meetings. Sometimes she specifically raised the issue of how women could better participate in the committee's deliberations, making their active involvement—and learning about political organizing and environmental issues in general—part of the committee's strategies.[39] Her approach contrasted markedly with conventional approaches to political activism, where learning is not viewed as a strategy of group action. Yet, as the CPRNS came to realize, this supposition limited the input of workers in the committee's proceedings. Thus, CPRNS leaders encouraged the learning process not only during committee deliberations but also in workshops it created for its members. During the two years that I worked with the CPRNS, five workshops were organized, four of them by women.

In one workshop, women workers, committee advisers, and graduate students met to analyze workers' experiences with physicians from the State Insurance Fund (SIF), which was considering their claims. At this meeting women shared personal horror stories about their visits to these doctors. Even before asking the women about their symptoms, the SIF doctors advanced their diagnoses and in the process revealed their gender and class biases: women were experiencing difficulty in the factories because they were menopausal or were having problems with their husbands. And they prescribed without hesitation what they judged to be the "necessary medication" for women with "psychiatric problems." After their medical consultations, many women said they felt humiliated, angry, and depressed. Some felt unable to challenge the doctors' diagnoses, while others attempted to pressure doctors to take their complaints more seriously (such as by ordering laboratory tests). The women also became more aware of the reasons, including the possibility of a conspiracy between SIF and the industrialists, for the doctors' diagnoses and treatment, which often involved the prescription of antipsychotic medications. During this workshop one of the committee's advisors, a woman psychiatrist, recommended that when visiting doctors in the future, women should take certain precautions: questioning their medical diagnoses; formulating strategies to challenge discrepancies in diagnoses; and asking about the possible side effects that could result from the medications that were prescribed. This new strategy enabled the women to better articulate their concerns. At another workshop, organized by Monserrate Cruz, a respiratory therapist informed the workers that a diagnosis of respiratory disease in medical practice was usually based on a sociomedical history of the patient coupled with a test of pulmonary function, and that physical evidence of lesions was not required for this type of diagnosis.[40] This was contrary to what doctors had been telling women. Knowing how to confront doctors is an important aspect of occupational health struggles. It empowers workers to press their conviction that their illnesses are caused by exposure to toxic materials, in spite of the doctors' denials. Thus it strengthens their capabilities to advance their rights and pursue remedies through negotiation and pressure tactics.

In this section we have seen how listening to women's voices provides us with a different perspective of grassroots leadership and political thought. For the workers in the Guanajibo-Castillo Industrial Park, collective decision making was an element of significant value, equal to the importance of planning political actions in mainstream political thought. The basic processes of collective decision making—that is, solidarity formation, collective goal setting, and collective strategizing—permitted these women workers a broad understanding of and an immediate response to the political and social elements of their struggle. They also prepared the way for some women in the collective to advance into positions of leadership. By opening these new possibilities for action and leadership, collective decision making became a useful political strategy in the struggle for a cleaner and safer work environment in the Mayagüez garment factories in the 1980s.

The Integration of Body, Mind, and Environment

As the foregoing discussion has shown, the controversy in the Guanajibo-Castillo case focused on the health effects of the toxic gas emissions on workers and on nearby residents. While workers spoke throughout the struggle of the impact of the gas emissions on their mental health, the CPRNS strategy was to demonstrate that they were physically rather than emotionally sick. The committee's objective was to challenge the contention of the industries involved, and of the Puerto Rican government, that workers were manifesting "mass psychogenic effects" or "hysteria." The CPRNS chose this strategy to avoid suggesting the stereotype of the "hysterical personality." Nevertheless, by delimiting the issue in this manner, the committee accepted one of the most basic premises of the scientific reductionist paradigm—that is, the notion of "physical reductionism," whereby everything reverts to the organism. This was in direct contrast to the industrialists' psychological reductionism, which implied that the psyche was the source of the workers' ailments. By focusing exclusively on the physical effects of the gas emissions, however, the committee excluded the issue of emotions from the dialogue. Yet women had spent countless hours during their monthly meetings expressing their pain, sadness, depression, and anger over the effects of the contamination of their persons and their workplaces. In their discussions women recognized that their entire person, both physical and psychological, was affected by the emissions and that an understanding of the totality of this experience was important in the process of healing and indemnification for their injuries. From a gendered perspective, this expression of sentiment—that is, CPRNS women's repeated statements concerning how they felt about their health at committee meetings—is part of women's grassroots political behavior, even if many men in the CPRNS viewed this behavior as interfering with the task of strategizing.

The subjective expressions of the women factory workers of Mayagüez regarding their experiences with gas emissions in their work sites represent one kind of critique of dominant scientific thought about the way in which a situation as complex as the one in the Guanajibo-Castillo Industrial Park is understood. Stanley Aronowitz has noted that most reductionist scientific research "cannot conceptualize the notion of the body-subject, that is, a body that interacts with the world and that has conscious and unconscious aspects that constitute its mental and physical functions."[41] By failing to take the position that women's emotional health as well as their physical health was damaged, the committee may have missed an opportunity to counter the unsound and false arguments presented by the island government and mainland industries regarding this important health controversy. Instead of posing the question in terms of physical or emotional illness, the committee could have better articulated the argument if it had asked how persons are affected (both physically and emotionally) by exposure to toxic substances, known to affect the cognitive and emotional enters of the central nervous system, in circumstances that present other kinds of stresses as well. In the case of the women we knew, these included authoritarian management and the requirement that they perform repetitive tasks in hot and noisy work settings. These women were also exposed to a variety of toxins, in repeated incidents, over prolonged periods of time. Could the committee have presented the evidence of organic damage at the same time it linked it with the multiple emotional and social health aspects? The committee did address some of the limitations of the reductionist model, but it did not do so on the important issue of the women's and men's health diagnoses. Thus, it failed to adopt an alternative body-mind approach.

Regarding the diagnosis of hysteria, the detrimental effects of this kind of label for women are well known. When considered from a limited point of view, hysterical responses appear to be the opposite of rationality; and, as so many feminist scholars have noted, rationality is typically associated with the masculine. From a broader perspective, hysterical responses have been viewed as a consequence of violent structures faced by women and as having meanings related to oppressive conditions in their lives.[42] Women attribute a very different significance than men do to the expression of emotions. For women, emotional expressions are part of our identity as human beings; they link us to others—especially when we share sadness and pain. They are legitimate forms of human expression that enable others to know us and support us. For men in positions of authority, such expressions are perceived as weakness, irrationality, or loss of self-control. Indeed, this is how various government administrators in Puerto Rico reacted when the workers expressed their feelings about their illness and the socioeconomic consequences of their ill health.

Notwithstanding the CPRNS decision to concentrate on the workers' physical health, the actions of the committee clearly demonstrated the importance of the feelings of women. We believe this form of interaction should be an integral part of women's political struggle, for feelings inform the interests that give direction to our struggles, help us to understand the false dichotomy between rationality and emotion, and can indicate alternative courses of action. The open expression of feelings also presupposes that harmful dynamics among members of grassroots committees will be more readily confronted.

Conclusion

This analysis of women's grassroots activities in the Guanajibo-Castillo health struggle between 1983 and 1989 would be incomplete if the gains won by CPRNS members under such difficult conditions were not noted. Not insignificantly, the committee was able to obtain extensive media coverage, and it successfully disseminated information on their case to the public. Through their work, the CPRNS members were able to gain credibility among the residents of the Mayagüez area and with some of the doctors at the State Insurance Fund. They also increased the awareness of many communities on the island with regard to the potential health risks of polluting industries in Puerto Rico. The struggle of these women workers is very historic because they dared to confront an establishment of powerful male industrialists, heads of government agencies, and a medical profession that was not always willing to listen to them. Ultimately, they induced the Puerto Rican government to investigate the problems of gas emissions in the area and to gather scientific data pertaining to pollution of organic solvents and their health effects in general. More important, the CPRNS succeeded in getting the industries at the Guanajibo-Castillo Industrial Park to discontinue the use of some of the dangerous chemicals in their production processes in favor of less harmful ones.

The Guanajibo-Castillo environmental struggle helped the women workers develop grassroots leadership skills and political knowledge, and as a result they came to understand the social forces that shape the course of an environmental struggle. The women became spokespersons, confronted an entrenched political establishment, and affirmed their beliefs, positions, and values. They also observed and analyzed the forces and manifestations of women's subordination to men in our society as State Insurance Fund doctors, heads of government agencies, and former supervisors at the factories responded to their claims with class arrogance and sexism. The committee had some setbacks, too. For example, one of the most important legal cases, demanding compensation for damages by the women and men whose health had been impaired by the emissions of toxic chemicals, was settled in favor of the industrialists in 1989. The failure of the CPRNS to win this aspect of the struggle was partially due to the fact that the workers lacked the economic resources needed to win the case. In contrast the industrialists had more than twenty lawyers and various experts to support their position.

Mainstream political thought and practice presuppose a patriarchal view of power and social transformation, and they determine which behaviors are political and which traits define leadership. In some political struggles, mainstream political thought joins together with the dominant scientific thought to establish a false dichotomy between the cognitive realm and the realm of beliefs and feelings, between the personal and the political (or scientific), a dichotomy that is in many ways contrary to women's political interests. By recording women's political behaviors and listening to their voices from a gendered perspective, a different view of what contitutes the political emerges. This view is derived from women's experiences of oppression and, therefore, proposes nonoppressive categories of political struggle such as solidarity, participation, and dialogue.

Analyzing the environmental health struggle of workers and residents of Mayagüez allows us to develop alternative conceptions of what the political encompasses and to strengthen grassroots movements through the creation of alternative strategies. Cielo Martín believes that, "in general, men involved in politics have a preconceived notion of how to go about a struggle, but it's not congruent with reality; movements have to be and are much more creative than this." The women and men of the Guanajibo-Castillo Industrial Park who experienced the toxic contamination of their workplace had few options with regard to the health and economic issues they confronted. Nevertheless, these workers decided to meet the challenge and struggle for a healthier and safer environment for themselves and for their community. Through their struggle they have opened up options for other people affected by environmental pollution on the island and, thus, have taught the Puerto Rican people some powerful political lessons.

NOTES

Acknowledgments: I wish to thank the women from the Comité Pro-Rescate de Nuestra Salud (Committee to Rescue Our Health), and my colleagues, for their most valuable suggestions concerning the text: Cielo Martín, Santos Feliciano, Monserrate Cruz, Doris Vázquez, Idsa Alegría, Alice Colón, Awilda Palau, and Ruth Silva Bonilla.

1. Mainstream political thought refers to the traditions, ranging from liberalism to the Marxism of the Second International, that define Western political writings. Mainstream political scholars generally have ignored women's perspectives in their political discourses.

2. Kathleen B. Jones and Anna G. Jónasdóttir, "Introduction: Gender as an Analytical Category," in *The Political Interest of Gender: Developing Theory and Research with a Feminist Face,* ed. Kathleen B. Jones and Anna G. Jónasdóttir (London: Sage Publications, 1990), 1–10.

3. Ibid., 6–8.

4. Vandana Shiva, *Abrazar la vida: Mujer, ecología y supervivencia* (Montevideo, Uruguay: Instituto del Tercer Mundo, 1988), 23–36.

5. Jones and Jónasdóttir, "Introduction," 11, 32.

6. Shiva, *Abrazar la vida*, 23; Andre Gorz, *Ecología y libertad: Técnica, técnicos y lucha de clase* (Barcelona: Gustavo Gilly, 1979), 11–47; Carolyn Merchant, *The Death of Nature: Women, Ecology, and the Scientific Revolution* (San Francisco: Harper Publications, 1983).

7. Shiva, *Abrazar la vida*, 23–36, 62–78; Merchant, *Death of Nature*, 1–41; Ynestra King, "The Ecology of Feminism and Feminism of Ecology," in *Healing the Wounds: The Promise of Ecofeminism*, ed. Judith Plant (Philadelphia: New Society Publishers, 1989), 19–27.

8. Shiva, *Abrazar la vida*, 23.

9. Kathleen B. Jones, "Toward the Revision of Politics," in *The Political Interest of Gender: Developing Theory and Research with a Feminist Face*, ed. Kathleen B. Jones and A. Jónasdóttir (London: Sage Publications, 1990), 14.

10. Kathleen B. Jones, "On Authority: Or, Why Women Are Not Entitled to Speak," in *Feminisms and Foucault: Reflections on Resistance*, ed. Irene Diamond and Lee Quinby (Boston: Northeastern University Press, 1988), 119–34.

11. Karen B. Sacks, "Gender and Grassroots Leadership," in *Women and the Politics of Empowerment*, ed. Ann Bookman and Sandra Morgen (Philadephia: Temple University Press, 1988), 77–94.

12. Daniel Camacho, "Introduction," in *Los movimientos populares en América Latina* (Mexico City: Siglo Ventiuno, 1989), 15.

13. Sacks, "Gender and Grassroots Leadership," 77–96; Frances Fox Piven and Richard A. Cloward, *Poor People's Movements: Why They Succeed, How They Fail* (New York: Vintage, 1978), 1–39; Frances T. Farenthold, "Introduction," in *Women Activists: Challenging the Abuse of Power*, ed. Anne Witte Garland (New York: The City University of New York, 1988); Jones, "On Authority: Or, Why Women Are Not Entitled to Speak," 122.

14. Sacks, "Gender and Grassroots Leadership," 77–96.

15. Ibid., 77–96.

16. Sheila Rowbotham, *Women's Consciousness, Man's World* (Baltimore: Penguin Books, 1973), 36.

17. James L. Dietz, *Economic History of Puerto Rico: Institutional Change and Capitalist Development* (Princeton, N.J.: Princeton University Press, 1986), 182–311.

18. Ibid., passim.

19. Neftalí García Martínez, "Economía política de los problemas ambientales" (unpublished manuscript, Servicios de Científicos y Técnicos, San Juan, P.R., 1984); Neftalí García Martínez, "Lucha ambiental y defensa de los recursos naturales," *Pensamiento crítico* 11, no. 57 (1988): 12–19.

20. Neftalí García Martínez, "Las luchas populares en Puerto Rico: Hacia una nueva estrategía de desarrollo" (unpublished manuscript, Servicios de Científicos y Técnicos, San Juan, P.R., 1991); Neftalí García Martínez, "El problema de los desperdicios peligrosos y domésticos en Puerto Rico: Alternativas para su solución" (unpublished manuscript, Servicios de Científicos y Técnicos, San Juan P.R., 1987), 1–10.

21. Neftalí García Martínez, "El colonialismo, los recursos naturales y el ambiente," *Pensamiento crítico* 11, no. 51 (September–December 1986): 16–20.

22. Interview with Neftalí García Martínez, San Juan, P.R., March 1987.

23. García Martínez, "Las luchas populares," 1–10.

24. For a discussion of women's occupational distribution under Operation Bootstrap, see Luz del Alba Acevedo, "Industrialization and Employment: Changes in the Patterns of Women's Work in Puerto Rico," *World Development* 18, no. 2 (1990): 231–55.

25. Annette Fuentes and Barbara Ehrenreich, *Women in the Global Factory* (Boston: South End Press, 1984), 19.

26. See, for example, Ida Susser, "Union Carbide and the Community Surrounding It: The Case of a Community in Puerto Rico," *International Journal of Health Services* 15, no. 4 (1985): 561–83.

27. Lila Pastoriza, ed., *Impacto del ambiente en las mujeres* (Buenos Aires: Centro de Apoyo al Desarrollo Local, 1992).

28. Paulo Freire, *Pedagogy of the Oppressed* (New York: Herder and Herder, 1970); Orlando Fals Borda, *Conocimiento y poder popular: Lecciones con campesinos de Nicaragua, México y Colombia* (Mexico City: Siglo Ventiuno, 1985); Awilda Palau, "Las investigaciones con la técnica de observación: 'Para quién y desde dónde?'" in *Contribuciones puertorriqueñas a la psicología social comunitaria*, ed. Irma Serrano García and Wayne Rosario Collazo (Río Piedras: Editorial de la Universidad de Puerto Rico, 1992), 305–18; Ruth Silva Bonilla, "Debate de teoría y método en los trabajos de investigación en las ciencias sociales" (Centro de Estudios, Recursos, y Servicios a la Mujer, Centro de Investigaciones Sociales, Universidad de Puerto Rico, Río Piedras, 1986, unpublished manuscript); Sandra Morgen, "It's the Whole Power of the City against Us! The Development of Political Consciousness in a Women's Health Care Coalition," in *Women and the Politics of Empowerment*, ed. Ann Bookman and Sandra Morgen (Philadelphia: Temple University Press, 1988), 99.

29. Marya Muñoz-Vázquez, "Psicología social comunitaria y la contaminación ambiental: El caso de Mayagüez" (Department of Psychology, Universidad de Puerto Rico, Río Piedras, 1986, unpublished manuscript).

30. Neftalí García Martínez, "Algunas hipótesis y conclusiones sobre los escapes de gases en el Complejo Industrial Guanajibo de Mayagüez" (Servicios de Científicos y Técnicos, San Juan, P.R., 1985, unpublished manuscript).

31. Neftalí García Martínez, "Las emanaciones de sustancias químicas en el Complejo Industrial Guanajibo, Mayagüez" (paper presented at the Twenty-first Interamerican Congress of Psychology, Havana, Cuba, 1987). Our initial observations indicated that such substances did affect some of the workers in the electronics industries.

32. Margarita Alonso, "Preliminary Review of Medical Records: Guanajibo Industrial Park, Mayagüez, Puerto Rico" (Servicios de Científicos y Técnicos, San Juan, 1988, unpublished manuscript); Reinaldo Ortiz Colón et al., "Relación entre la exposición a sustancias tóxicas y el funcionamiento intelectual y afectivo de obreras textiles puertorriqueñas" (Department of Psychology, Universidad de Puerto Rico, Río Piedras, 1993, unpublished manuscript).

33. Government of Puerto Rico, Junta de Calidad Ambiental, "Investigation of Incidents at the Barrio Guanajibo Industrial Park, Mayagüez, Final Report," No. PE 769 (San Juan: Environmental Resource Technology Company, 1987).

34. "Estudio sobre las emanaciones tóxicas de la zona industrial Guanajibo-Castillo de Mayagüez, Puerto Rico" (Colegio de Ingeniería, Centro de Investigaciones, Universidad de Puerto Rico, Mayagüez, 1988, unpublished manuscript).

35. Heidi Figueroa, "Solventes orgánicos y neurotoxicidad: El caso de los hidrocarburos policlorados" (Department of Psychology, Universidad de Puerto Rico, Río Piedras, 1986, unpublished manuscript).

36. Government of Puerto Rico, Junta de Calidad Ambiental, "Investigation of Incidents at the Barrio Guanajibo Industrial Park, Mayagüez, Phase II," No. PG 4332 A (San Juan, P.R.: Environmental Research and Technology Company, 1988).

37. Marya Muñoz-Vázquez, "An Analysis of the Role of Urban Working-Class Women in Puerto Rico in Environmental Issues and Sustainable Development" (paper presented at the Symposium on Women and Development sponsored by the Center for the Study of Women and Society, City University of New York, New York City, September 1991).

38. Interview with Cielo Martín, Mayagüez, December 1992.

39. Ibid.

40. Comité Pro-Rescate de Nuestra Salud, *Proceedings of the Committee: Informe de Práctica,* June–December 1986, 18–20.

41. Stanley Aronowitz, *Science as Power: Discourse and Ideology in Modern Society* (Minneapolis: University of Minnesota Press, 1988), 336.

42. Ruth Silva Bonilla, "La salud y la enfermedad mental: Apuntes sociológicos a la discusión del tema," *Revista de ciencias sociales* 25, nos. 1–2 (1986): 21–36; see also Ruth Silva Bonilla, "La fijación de estereotipos sexuales en el discurso médico-psiquiátrico relativos a las histerias en las mujeres" (Centro de Estudios, Recursos, y Servicios a la Mujer, Centro de Investigaciones, Universidad de Puerto Rico, Río Piedras, 1995, unpublished manuscript).

SEVEN

Negotiating Gender, Work, and Welfare: *Familia* as Productive Labor among Puerto Rican Women in New York City

ROSA M. TORRUELLAS
RINA BENMAYOR
ANA JUARBE

his chapter concerns a group of Puerto Rican migrant women who have been absent from the formal labor market for more than a decade. For a variety of reasons they have not been part of the labor force during this time and hence are not even counted in the unemployment rolls. Although the principal means of support for almost all of them is Aid to Families with Dependent Children (AFDC), all of these women feel deeply connected to work. Not only do they have extensive employment histories, they also espouse a strong work ethnic and, as homemakers, view themselves as performing invaluable work. Indeed, raising children, keeping a family together, and being in charge of the domestic sphere have become their primary social and gender responsibility—in effect, their principal work experience.

In addition to nurturing and sustaining their immediate families, these Puerto Rican migrant women also feel an enormous sense of responsibility for maintaining the extended group of relatives and close friends who constitute their *familia*. The work that these *puertorriqueñas* perform in caring for their families is therefore more extensive than what women perform in an average mainland family but is very typical of the family work that other women do in the States. Incorporating the perspectives of women who are not currently involved in wage labor, but nevertheless consider themselves to be workers, in a collection on Puerto Rican women and work challenges us to broaden the very definition of productive labor to include domestic labor—an idea advanced for years by many feminist and Marxist scholars.[1]

Because some of these women and their families are supported by public funds, this chapter also enables us to reconsider the current sociopolitical debate that poses a dichotomy between welfare and wage labor in relation to Puerto Rican women. Since 1988 the federal Welfare Reform Act, as well as many other initiatives introduced by individual states, have required that welfare recipients perform wage work in exchange for public monies.[2] An underlying assumption in "work-fare" programs is the idea that welfare recipients lack a work ethic and that they would be content to remain chronically dependent on the state if they were not forced to become self-reliant. A related claim that concerns Puerto Ricans specifically is that they migrate to the United States in order to exploit higher welfare entitlements than those available on the island. Overall, the most virulent charge is that dysfunctional family structures and practices lead to and are reproduced by welfare participation. These moral indictments expand beyond individual women into the arena of the family, which is depicted in terms of pathology and social disintegration. All these assertions portray Puerto Rican, as well as other women of color, as an economic burden on the state and a moral liability to society. In New York City, Puerto Rican and African American women are the principal targets of these stereotypes because they compose the bulk of the city's welfare recipients.[3]

Countering these cultural deficiency arguments are structural analyses showing that economic transformations in the twentieth century have defined and limited economic opportunities for Puerto Rican women, both on the island and in the United States.[4] However, in this chapter we argue that theories of cultural deficiency or behavioral deviance need to be challenged by exploring women's life-goals and experiences. We believe that in order to get beyond externally derived stereotypes, research and public policy have to take a closer look at the interplay among the structural, cultural, and ideological factors that affect women's life cycles at different historical moments. We further argue that the Puerto Rican women on welfare whom we interviewed have a very different understanding of the relationship among *familia*, work, and welfare than those who espouse deviancy or deficiency explanations. These women see themselves as chief architects of a very active process through which they negotiate these interconnected arenas in their lives. Thus, they do not view being on welfare as a negation of wage work but rather as a resource that has allowed them to take care of their homes, raise their children, and fulfill what they consider is a fundamental cultural, social, and productive role.

Given the instability they experienced in the labor market, the marked decline in household income, and the deterioration of their immediate social environments, they view their decision to use welfare at the child-rearing stage of their life cycle as strategic to their survival in this country. We base our analyses of women, work, and welfare on an extensive study carried out with sixteen Puerto Rican women in East Harlem between 1986 and 1991. We met these women in 1986, when they enrolled in a literacy program developed by the Centro de Estudios Puertorriqueños (Center for Puerto Rican Studies) of Hunter College of the City University of New York. (This educational initiative has since matured into the El Barrio Popular Education Program, an independent, community-based organization in East Harlem.) All of the women were first-generation migrants, born and raised in Puerto Rico, whose ages generally ranged between the late thirties and the sixties, although there was one very dynamic eighty-year-old in the group. With few exceptions, they were single mothers (that is, women who had never formally married or were separated or divorced) and heads of households whose yearly incomes were well below the poverty line. Most had participated in the formal labor market earlier in their lives and now received public assistance. These women therefore represent a sector of New York's Puerto Rican migrant community that has experienced intensified social marginalization and persistent poverty, especially in the past two decades. According to some scholars, this condition has been caused by the flight of manufacturing from the city, which has left Puerto Rican migrant women without their traditional source of employment. Scholars have also noted that with little or no formal schooling, and limited functional command of English, Puerto Rican migrant women have had little chance to qualify for the service jobs that now dominate New York City's working-class economy. Looking at the current fiscal crisis in the city, coupled with cuts in federal funding, we forecast even harder times for them.

As part of our research in the El Barrio Popular Education Program, we gathered extensive life histories from this group of women.[5] We used their personal narratives in order to get a deeper sense of the experiences that influenced the individual and collective transformations we observed as the women participated in the educational process of the program. By reproducing their own words throughout the chapter, we also recognize the need to represent and analyze critically Puerto Rican women's own perspectives on the important social and personal issues in their lives.[6] Finally, in order to better understand these women's struggles for dignity, a better future for their children, respect for what they contribute to society, and the right to define culturally relevant and appropriate pathways for achieving their goals, we have used the concept of cultural citizenship. Cultural citizenship identifies ways in which cultural communities define their sense of rights, responsibilities, and contributions to a culturally diverse society. In this essay we argue that the women of the El Barrio program understood their individual struggles for improved life chances for themselves and their children as reflective of a collective struggle of the working-class Puerto Rican community to which they belong. In this process, they were and are engaged in the affirmation of collective cultural rights as women, as members of the working class, and as Puerto Rican colonial migrants. As their narratives unfolded, we became acutely aware of the saliency of the issues of work and welfare in their lives, as daily sources of social and cultural discrimination around which they had defined gender, labor, and cultural rights.

The Experience and Expectation of Work

If we examine the relationship of wage work and welfare historically—even within the limited scope of our sample—we see that, contrary to popular belief, Puerto Rican women on public assistance have been part of the formal workforce and have the potential to return to it. Thus, their histories and goals have been very much shaped by an experience and expectation of wage work, however fragmentary and structurally limiting their participation in the labor force may have been in the past. For many of the women, migration to the United States in fact was motivated by the need for jobs and desire for economic advancement. Remembering her days in Puerto Rico, Minerva Torres Ríos recalled: "I was growing up and life was getting more expensive. So I said, 'Well, I'm going to go to New York and at least I'll be able to help my family financially.' So I did. My cousin sent me a ticket and I came." Once in the States, these women manifested an understanding of the issue of work that was more complex than simply their participation in wage labor. Since childhood these women had been socialized into what generally has been called "women's work," which traditionally has included domestic labor, child care, sewing, and other forms of manual labor. At particular points in their lives, they might have engaged in these forms of work in the home, in a formal workplace, or in both settings. But, for these poor and working-class women, defining as work only as those activities for which they were paid was an artificial division between wage labor and housework, particularly since the jobs they performed for wages were often an extension of the work done at home. Regardless of the context of their work, at home these migrant women saw themselves as fulfilling a very productive obligation for society—performing the type of work that they as women were entrusted to carry out as part of their female roles in Puerto Rico. They did not consider becoming welfare recipients as a strategy for cheating the state but as one that enabled them to continue to exercise what they considered their reproductive and social responsibilities.

For most of the women in our study, the personal story of work began in their childhood years in Puerto Rico. Inscribed in their memories was a girlhood shaped by a concern for economic survival, for many had been born into families who—as a consequence of the tremendous upheavals in the island economy during the first half of the century—had become part of the rural proletariat, living on below-subsistence wages. Educational opportunities for these women had also been extremely limited. Because schools often were located at great distances from their homes, and because attendance was often not enforced, their formal education was sporadic. Whether in the countryside or in towns, as young girls they had been forced to contribute to the economic survival of their families. Since this was a gendered arrangement, typically they were called upon to assist with immediate needs in the home. This meant becoming responsible for household chores, child care, sewing or embroidering for the home needlework industry, or being hired out as child domestics.[7]

In most cases they were pulled out of school, if they were enrolled at all, although they noticed that boys were allowed to continue their basic education in preparation for future employment. Ultimately, this process served to socialize them into their adult family and mothering roles and prepare them for "women's work"—work they performed either in their own homes or for wages. For example, Erlinda Romero was never sent to school; instead, she worked as a *niñera* (nanny), taking care of other people's children:

People would pay me to look after their kids. Well-to-do people. Poor people don't pay. I was always getting jobs here and there. My mother was very fussy and she would pull me out of my jobs and take me home. But after a while, when the money ran out, she would send me out to look for another job. She was the one who decided whether I could work or not. Because I was young. She was always keeping an eye on us.

On the whole, responding to the pressure of the family's economic survival, these women had little or no room for exploring personal talents or dreams. The encouragement normally associated with high achievement was a luxury in their world.

Parents too were subjected to these pressures, which often prevented them from attending to the developmental needs of their children. Leticia Quiroz sadly remembered her mother's reaction to her difficulties in school: "Yes, my mother pulled me out of school when I was in the fifth grade. Because she said that even a donkey was smarter than me. 'You're not going to learn anything, so you are going to stay home and clean house.' Clean and cook. So I didn't go to school." But in her testimony, Erlinda Romero linked children's lack of education to the difficult choices parents faced: "We were born in the countryside. My mother had ten children and my father died when I was just months old. My mother was left to raise all of us by herself, and so she struggled. Three of us girls were not able to go to school." One long-lasting repercussion of this experience is that it initiated a process whereby these women became tracked into the lowest level of employment options, since as children they did not receive the educational foundation to prepare them for the occupational structures they would face as adults in another societal context. Nevertheless, as we noted above, the desire to *buscar ambiente* (to find a better life) was always a major factor in considering migration to the United States. In Luisa Jovellanos's words:

Sometimes you have to test new waters. You have to seek fortune somewhere else. Right? Well, we didn't need to come here because we owned our house . . . and my father worked. But my mother wanted to find better opportunities for me, you know, so that I could go to school and build a future. So she brought me here.

With one exception, the women we interviewed arrived in New York after World War II, and most of them recalled being able to find abundant factory jobs regardless of their educational level. But many of these were bottom echelon jobs in the garment industry.[8] It is important to note here that although the late 1950s is often cited as the beginning of the decline in employment opportunities for Puerto Ricans in the United States, many women did not begin to feel the full effects of the decline until the mid-1970s.[9] As Marta Velázquez put it:

> At that time, around 1963, wherever you went you did not need a lot of training. You didn't have to have any education. There weren't so many requirements as there are now. And today, there aren't as many jobs as before, when you could find a job anywhere. Many of the factories have closed down.

During these years these women worked under highly exploitative conditions, yet women perceived factory jobs in the metropolis to be a step up—an avenue to progress. Even though the availability of jobs at this particular moment presented some women with what they believed was the best strategy to *superarse*, or get ahead, in some cases, the appeal of a paycheck prevented some of them, especially the young women, from thinking in more long-range terms and taking advantage of educational opportunities. Flor Tirado was encouraged to go to school but soon abandoned the idea in favor of a weekly salary:

> My mother enrolled me in night school. She wanted me to go to school and learn. But the classes were in English and I didn't catch on, because since I didn't know [how to read and write] Spanish, I couldn't learn English. I was there for a while but then I got a job and I dropped school. I went to work. I didn't earn a lot then. But I loved it. I loved the money and I forgot about school.

The vision of opportunity that most of these women had when they first came to New York has since faded. From the mid-1970s to the late 1980s, the erosion of stable manufacturing jobs, the flight of companies to offshore production sites, and the reorganization of light manufacturing, not to mention the growing world of "high-tech" and financial markets, have pushed these women further to the margins of employment.[10] Even if they contemplated working in the few remaining jobs in the manufacturing sector, some women feared the high volatility of this labor market. It is this fear of job loss that explains Leticia Quiroz's use of public assistance: "Sometimes I think if I go back to work and don't like the job or if I get fired, what will I find? Jobs are very hard to find today." In the meantime the growth of public service-sector jobs during this period did not greatly benefit this group of first-generation migrant women. Most of these jobs required levels of English-language proficiency and educational skills that Puerto Rican migrant women, especially the older ones, lacked. Relocation to places where economic prospects might be brighter was also out of the question, since these women lacked the finances required for such a move. Declining job opportunities in the mid-Atlantic region, and the inability to profit from employment in expanding sectors of the economy therefore led these women to view welfare as a means of surviving the negative impact of the economic transformations of the times.

However, mainstream analyses have often blamed unemployment and welfare reliance on individual shortcomings, turning a structural problem into a personal one. Even those who attribute the rise of so-called underclass behaviors to a chronically "weak attachment" to the labor market fail to question the validity of the cultural arguments that classify these behaviors as "deviant."[11] In our view, the unavailability of decent jobs and real labor incentives has great bearing on the attitudes and strategies that people develop to deal with exclusion. The factors Andrés Torres and Frank Bonilla identify as inhibiting today's potential entrants into the labor market were just as significant twenty years ago for young women with families to support:

> The rise in working-class poverty, the polarization of earnings within the labor force, and the decline in opportunities for long-term stable employment generate a perception among potential entrants to the labor market that participation is not worth the sacrifice involved in taking low-paying, dead-end jobs.[12]

In the case of the women we interviewed, there was a reluctance to subordinate what they perceived as the needs of their children and families by taking the unstable minimum-wage jobs that were available in the 1980s. At play here was a dual sense of social responsibility. At one level they performed the mothering role of picking up children from school, supervising them in the home, and making sure they did not get into trouble on the streets. This was not an insignificant task, given the embattled neighborhood conditions in which they lived. However, in their concept of *familia* women also demonstrated a sense of responsibility that went beyond motherhood—that is, they embraced women's pivotal role in forming and maintaining the family unit, however it was constituted in contemporary Puerto Rican society. It is this strong cultural connection between woman and the family that led these migrant women to consider taking care of their own families as their primary "job." They were poor women, restricted in their access to employment and in their ability to command a reasonable salary with which to support their children, but they still defended their right to fulfill the full range of their familial responsibilities, which in some cases extended beyond childbearing into the grandparenting years. Therefore, their use of public assistance must be viewed from the perspective of women who continually negotiated changes that might threaten their families' unity and well-being and that frequently involved sacrificing their own personal desires, needs, and labor-force participation in the process.

The Move to Welfare

All but three of the women we interviewed had been on public assistance at some time in their adult lives. In contrast to the perception that Puerto Rican women exchange their economic dependence on men for dependence on the state, our case studies revealed a more complex dynamic at play. The women became welfare recipients for a wide variety of reasons, after exhausting other possibilities, and through different chains of events. This microcosmic view shows us that Puerto Rican women on welfare are not a homogeneous group and that a complex set of circumstances have governed the choices available to them. In all cases, however, we saw a combination of cultural expectations and structural conditions coming into play, sometimes allowing women a degree of latitude and other times severely restricting their alternatives. A condition that affected almost all of these women, as we noted earlier, was their displacement from the workforce due to factory closures. The loss of a job often initiated a spiraling-down process. Becoming unemployed was for some of them a transitory stage but, given the contraction of the manufacturing sector, usually not to another job. Therefore, losing their jobs typically meant a declining standard of living, the loss of medical benefits, and an overall weakening of their families' safety nets. Because many of these women lacked the educational skills to compete in our technologically advanced labor force, they were unable to command decent employment in a changing economy. For example, Flor Tirado once operated machines in a yogurt-cup factory. When the plant closed, she did not apply for a filing job in a nearby plant for fear that her inability to read and write would be too much of a liability: "I was afraid that I would confuse the letters. If not, I'd be earning good money there today. And I wouldn't be claiming welfare."

The move from wage work to welfare was governed by other factors as well. We have learned that limited economic options, together with cultural and gender priorities, played a prominent part in these women's separation from the formal labor force. Moreover, their commitment to motherhood and family was also fundamental in shaping the decisions they made with regard to wage work. Later in life, economic circumstances forced them to work outside the home, but they grew up expecting to marry and to become mothers. As children, they were socialized into placing the economic needs of the family unit ahead of their own desires and potentialities. It is clear from their stories that when they formed their own families as adults, they again subordinated their personal needs to those of their kin. Within this social framework, it is not surprising that child-rearing and family would emerge as their primary work and responsibility as women, and for many poor Puerto Rican mothers this came to mean soliciting welfare to support their families. In some instances women were able to quit their jobs, having married men who commanded a steady income and could support a family. True to the American middle-class ideal, they became housewives in nuclear family households with a male breadwinner, even if only temporarily.[13] Marriage and a male income allowed them to exercise an option—to stay home and raise their children instead of going out to work. Erlinda Romero, for example, was employed in a factory that made artificial flowers when she met her husband:

> I was already eighteen. I met this man. He was a good man. He fell in love with me. I accepted him because I was all alone here. I didn't have anyone. So he married me. He worked as a hotel manager. He supported me, we had two children, and so we lived, and struggled, and struggled. My husband worked for twenty years, and we were together for twenty-five.

For some women, the "choice" to be housewives and stay-at-home mothers was also conditioned by a gender socialization based on a patriarchal ideology that ascribed decision making and authority in the marriage to the man. Raquel Cossío recalled that, "El nunca quiso que yo los diera a cuidar a nadie ni nada." (He [her husband] never wanted me to let anyone else take care of them [their children]). So, instead of pursuing a job outside the home or going to school, she stayed home and worked at raising her children. Gender socialization notwithstanding, dependence on a husband's income did not prove to be a source of long-term stability for some of the women since Puerto Rican men have also suffered considerably from declining economic conditions.[14] The case of Luisa Jovellanos clearly illustrates this. She and her husband first went on welfare in the ninth month of her second pregnancy. She was working at the time but was forced to quit her job because her boss insisted that it was placing too much physical stress on her. She recalled, "So he [my boss] gave me a letter and I went to welfare and they opened my case right away . . . and since then I have been drawing welfare. I included my husband in the application because at that time he was out of work. So the two girls, my husband and me all received welfare." Given Mr. Jovellanos's precarious employment options, the family did not have any other choice but to rely on welfare as a means of support.

Among the women we interviewed, becoming the head of the household and with no prospects of obtaining a decent job was cited as a major reason for eventually turning to welfare. A single mother with several small children, no extended family upon which to rely, and with little formal education and few marketable job skills had few possibilities open to her. The decision to migrate, especially in the post-sixties period, was governed more by the fact that women could not find jobs in Puerto Rico, where they did have a network of family and friends, than by some preconceived plan to "milk" the government by migrating to the mainland where welfare entitlements were greater. However, as we have explained, the shrinking labor market in the Northeast did not offer more stable employment in the new setting.[15] One single parent, Paquita Ramírez, was already a mother of five when she arrived in New York in 1979. Coming from a background of extreme rural poverty and illiteracy, she had virtually no chance of accessing employment either in Puerto Rico or in New York. Even if she could find a job, she would have to contend with the unavailability of adequate child care. For her, becoming a welfare recipient represented stability for her family. Knowing that as an American citizen she was entitled to AFDC support, she fought to get it, standing her ground when the caseworker tried to coerce her into returning to Puerto Rico:

> It seems like the caseworker I got didn't like me. She wanted to give me tickets to go back . . . I said no, that I had come from Puerto Rico to find a better life for myself and my children, and I created a scene. Then, another social worker said to her, "Well, if Mrs. Ramírez doesn't want to go back, open her file because we aren't going to put her out on the street with five minor-age children." So they opened my case.

Separation or divorce was another condition that led to welfare. In becoming the main providers in their families, the women either had to find a job or another source of income. Some tried to explore their options in the labor force, only to be faced head-on with the hard realities of a constricting labor market. For example, when her youngest child reached the age of sixteen, Cecilia González separated from her husband and immediately looked for work. She found a job in a garment sweatshop, which turned out to be a "fly-by-night" operation that left her suddenly unemployed. She then went on to a series of short-term factory jobs, the last of which she lost because of factory relocation. She was then employed through an agency as a homecare attendant for senior citizens. Since this work paid very little, she was forced to work at night cleaning offices. She commented:

> Any which way, things were tough. While I was working those two jobs, and since I've always suffered from asthma and allergies, I got very sick. I had to give up my jobs. I fought to get "disability," but I didn't get it. [Meanwhile] I would have to drag myself to work because I was very, very sick. They [her employers] were the ones who gave me a letter to apply for welfare.

Not to be overlooked among the various circumstances leading to welfare is the impact of job stress on women's emotional well-being. Marta Velázquez had worked for twenty-three years in a factory and was the sole supporter of her two children. Her story illustrates the high levels of stress experienced by many single mothers:

Well, sometimes it was the pressure, the pressure of the orders they would give me to fill, but it wasn't that I couldn't fill the orders. It was that the work wasn't finished. So, sometimes I needed twenty-five packages to send to this place or that, and often I wouldn't get the materials to send. So the boss would make me tense. It wasn't my fault but he made me feel that it was.

Her poor state of mental health, due to excessive stress on the job, eventually forced Velázquez to become unemployed shortly before retirement age, causing her to lose the right to a pension and thus to go on welfare.

A View of Welfare from Within: Indignity versus Cultural Right

Arguments about underclass behavior have long claimed that persons on public assistance are content with "sponging off" of the state. However, the Puerto Rican women in our program were active agents in their own struggles for advancement. The very systemic constraints that limited them also drove them to use welfare strategically. At the same time, this arrangement exacted a heavy price of indignity, for rather than receiving recognition and validation for prioritizing family, the education of their children, and, indeed of themselves, these women were socially stigmatized as "unworthy." A particularly humiliating aspect of the welfare experience for Puerto Rican women was the workfare program. According to the 1988 Family Support Act, parents whose youngest child was three years of age or older were obliged either to work in "informal" jobs or to study as a precondition for continued state support, but the act stipulated they were not to draw full-time wages.[16] Instead, they were offered supplements to their monthly welfare check, on the order of twenty to thirty dollars a week, to pay for carfare and lunch expenditures while on the job. Aside from the fact that this subsidy did not cover the actual cost of subway travel and budget lunches, it was perceived by the women as another form of degradation they were forced to endure. Moreover, when the hours they worked were calculated against the sum of their monthly check, they were actually working for far below the minimum wage.

For many of the women we interviewed workfare was a powerfully negative wage work experience. Julia Avilés's story dramatically portrayed the hardships the women generally experienced:

I was sent to clean up empty lots. We went to one on 170th Street, near Walton Avenue [in the Bronx]. I thought I was going to vomit from the stench of urine. The drug addicts that would come out of hiding with their needles hanging from their arms would say, "Don't throw my stuff away!" In the rain, in the snow, there was no toilet; we had to knock on doors and ask people's permission to go to the bathroom!

Her testimony, along with that of many others, illustrates the manner in which social policy locks women out of any real productive structure, simultaneously stripping them of their dignity. Julia Avilés recognized that she was being required to perform the most menial of tasks—cleaning public waste. For middle-aged women who had successfully raised children and who played by society's rules, being required to work at such demeaning jobs was perceived as a lack of social respect and a violation of their human dignity. Avilés refused to comply with the workfare program and declared her sense of indignation by saying: "Todo el mundo decía, 'Esto es una poca vergüenza lo que tiene el gobierno. Esto es una humillación.'" (Everyone used to say, "This is shameful, what the government offers us. This is humiliating"). Another woman's story illuminates how the structure of the welfare system has prevented women from using workfare as a stepping stone to regular employment. After being placed in the workfare program, Marta Velázquez was sent to do filing at a welfare office. She noticed:

Welfare gave me $128 dollars bimonthly. I think they gave me $28 dollars a week to work thirty-six hours. So I said to them, "I know how to handle the files. Why don't you hire me to do the job and take me off of welfare?" "Oh, no. Because you need the high school diploma." The high school diploma to take this file and put it in the cabinet!

Her comment underscored the absurdity of welfare employment guidelines. She went on to tell how she lost the assignment in the welfare office because of a brief illness. By the time she was ready to return, they had reassigned her clerical job to someone else.

At issue here are not only the structural constraints that the welfare system may place on women's struggles to get ahead but the degree to which these limitations violate their values, ethics, and sense of entitlement. Terms such as *humillación, poca vergüenza,* and *indignidad,* which the women invoked to describe the situations in which welfare placed them, signify transgressions at both the personal and cultural levels. Reacting to the disrespectful treatment she received at the welfare office, Eloísa Hernández declared in an indignant tone of voice: "Somos pobres pero tenemos dignidad," (We are poor, but we have dignity). She invoked this saying, often expressed in Latino cultures, because for her it contained a world of truth. It acknowledged that she lives in a social structure in which people are unequally and differentially treated. It also recognized, through the plural subject "We," that poverty is a shared condition rather than individual misfortune. The saying also validated her oppositional stance. Despite the difficulties she faced, she did not see herself as passive or a victim of social circumstance. Rather, she openly affirmed more basic human values. *Dignidad,* then, emerges as a cultural resource in the face of disempowering structural forces.

Throughout these life histories, we noted repeated instances in which the women articulated "vernacular" claims and understandings of civic rights and human dignity, based on their concepts of welfare entitlement and administration. One of Luisa Jovellanos's stories exemplified the ways women actively resist the welfare system's treatment of the recipient. On the surface, Jovellanos fitted the stereotype of the long-term welfare dependent: once on welfare, she did not pursue reentry into the labor force, even though she had some elementary education and a substantial employment history. After separating from her husband, she decided to raise her six children alone, not wanting to give them "another father" or entrust them to someone else's care. She tells how, upon failing to receive her monthly check, and concerned for her children, she immediately went to see her local caseworker. She arrived at the welfare office at nine in the morning with all six of her children and was kept waiting until noon. Finally, as her spontaneous, bilingual reenactment of outrage attests, she rebelled against this inconsiderate treatment:

> Entonces yo voy y le digo a la investigadora [So I go up to the investigator and say], "Hey, listen. I stay here *desde* [since] nine o'clock in the morning. Look at my kids. I no eat breakfast, I no eat lunch, I no eat nothing. What happen? *What happen?"*
> Ella me dice [she replies], "Never mind. No is my family."

Yo digo [I say], "What!" Porque ella dijo que los hijos míos
no eran familia suya [because she was telling me that my children were no concern of hers]!

After a heated argument, Jovellanos said that a supervisor intervened
and told the caseworker: "You are supposed to attend to her because
those are little children. Her children are babies, they aren't teenagers,
and babies don't know the meaning of 'We don't have any food' when
they are hungry."

Luisa Jovellanos's determination that her children's well-being
should not be threatened by bureaucratic negligence was never motivated by a desire to "live off the state." Through her account we come to
understand that she was affirming her prerogative to have children and
to insure their survival. In a larger sense, the story illustrates many migrant Puerto Rican women's perceived right to fulfill the gender responsibilities that were socially entrusted to them since childhood. More significantly, in seeking justice for herself Luisa Jovellanos was voicing, albeit
indirectly, a demand on behalf of a cultural community that has com-
monly suffered ill treatment from the welfare bureaucracy. These links
between the individual and collective dimensions of social demands are
highlighted in Blanca Silvestrini's incisive analysis on cultural rights and
the law. Before the law, she states: "Claimants are viewed as individuals.
Once separated from their group, they lose the strength that the community provided, because they had originally defined their claim as mediated by their participation in a cultural community."[17] Even when Luisa
Jovellanos's story was framed in terms of personal indignation, it expressed the larger social referent of class and gender oppression. Her
sense of entitlement and rights, based on a traditionally constructed cultural identity as Puerto Rican woman and mother, poor and single head
of household, exemplifies her notion of cultural citizenship. Hence, her
understanding of citizenship—of belonging, participation, equal rights,
and contribution to the social good—rests upon the culturally and mate-
rially derived concepts of social responsibilities and justice.

Ironically, however, asserting traditional cultural roles, and the right
to nurture and provide for their families, has placed many single women
household heads in a subordinate position in society. By refusing to recognize work in the home as productive labor, social policy and attitudes
have cast these women as unworthy citizens, unwilling to contribute to

the social product. Conservative political and social thinkers see these women as failures because they have not reproduced the patriarchal nuclear family structure, with a male breadwinner at the helm. This gender ideology always defined our concept of the model family and determined community supports for poor women. Mimi Abramovitz points out that even in colonial times communities differentiated between "deserving" poor women (those who became household heads through widowhood or a husband's disability) and "undeserving" ones (those who became head of a household through divorce, having children out of wedlock, or by remaining single).[18] Nancy Hewitt has also noted that middle-class white women reformers of the nineteenth and early twentieth century preserved this concept of the "domesticated den" as the centerpiece of their reform programs:

> Aid was offered to individual families who most closely resembled the privatized ideal. Thus, alms were distributed to "respectable" families in impoverished neighborhoods. Birth control was dispensed to married women in stable relationships. . . . Poor women in urban and rural areas were forced to hide, limit, or relinquish their communal modes of child care and healing to gain access to public health programs, nursing services, and well-baby clinics. Americanization courses taught immigrant daughters to emulate bourgeois lifestyles and to evacuate the crowded stoops and communal kitchens for the privatized home.[19]

It is this traditional ideology of ideal motherhood and family life that has guided our welfare reform programs and underlies the punitive measures of the state against women on welfare.

As in the past, the ways in which racial, class, and gender biases intersect in the social definition of deviant behavior become evident the further one is from the married, white, middle-class, wage-earning, nuclear family model.[20] Poor women of color have had to fight for the right to hold and maintain values of motherhood, especially when these might be realized within nontraditional family formations. Patricia Hill Collins reminds us that women-centered networks of community-based child care have historically characterized the reproduction of African American communities.[21] Similar extended family and "othermothering" relationships are highly valued by Puerto Rican women, for whom the practice of sharing responsibilities, human resources, and limited material means of sustenance has deep cultural roots. Not to be ignored is the tremendous importance of such forms of mutual support that have enabled women to carry out work both within and outside the home. By claiming welfare as an entitlement or a public service to be rendered with dignity, women like Luisa Jovellanos assert their belief that they are deserving workers and productive contributors to society. They are, as we have shown above, women who are upholding the social contract they learned as young girls in Puerto Rico. At a deeper level what is at stake here is a redefinition of different women's contributions to the polity and an expanded, culturally based concept of women's citizenship rights.

The Legacy of Welfare Mothers: The Second Generation

A common argument in the public discourse about welfare and the underclass is that children who grow up on welfare are likely to reproduce that dependence in their own adult lives. The socioeconomic position of their children was not one of the criteria we used to select our narrators. Yet, interestingly enough, we found that the vast majority of their grown children held jobs and that some were college graduates and worked as semiprofessionals. We found only one instance of "hard-core" drug involvement and criminal history in the group. Another mother talked about the detrimental psychological effect her alcoholism had on her children. Yet the vast majority of the next generation was employed in the formal labor market. It was not clear whether their position in the workforce offered any possibility for upward mobility since our inquiry did not include gathering systematic profiles of the children. However, references in their mothers' life histories indicated that most of them worked in low-paid service sector jobs, which would still place them in a highly insecure economic position. Nevertheless, these findings raise questions about the cultural reproduction of poverty and antisocial strategies of survival.[22] The women in our study were first-generation migrants and thus not in a youth cohort. By these indicators, therefore, they did not belong to the so-called underclass. However, the cultural explanations for the growth of the underclass still point the finger backward; that is, along with economic position, the social behaviors and cultural practices of parents are often alleged to be root causes that pave the way for the fall from poverty into the underclass.

Our data suggest that, through a variety of strategies, this group of poor Puerto Rican women advanced their children to what they consider a higher level. Raquel Cossío proudly declares:

I have four children, and all have their high school diploma. [When they were little] I would take them to school every day. I never let them go to school unaccompanied and I would bring them home for lunch every day. I took charge of them until they finished high school. I devoted myself to them and to running the house.

In most cases, these women's children went through elementary and high school in the 1960s and 1970s, a period in which the drop-out rate was lower than in the 1980s.[23] Even those who did not go to college became situated in the workforce. The real question, then, is whether the nation's economic structures are able to deliver any degree of stability to this and future generations of workers. All the recent economic indicators show that unemployment, underemployment, and working for poverty wages will continue to rise and that more and more people will need to rely on public assistance entitlements.[24] Moreover, there is growing evidence around the world of a condition of chronic unemployment, what some might call a permanent social space of nonwork.[25] The evidence points directly to economic crises rather than to dependency behaviors as responsible for the reproduction of poverty.

Despite their structural exclusion from employment, the women in our study have continued to espouse the American dream, holding on to the notion that social advancement is achievable through work and education. However, they did not measure advancement only through economic mobility in the labor market. The women in our study who had been part of the labor force in the past saw their own wage work, as well as their work in the home, as critical factors in their children's ability to progress. A few of them were even able to combine their child-rearing activities with wage work at home. During the time her own children were growing up, for example, Flor Tirado operated a small daycare center in her house and prepared lunches to sell to workers in a nearby factory. Once her children were older, she took a night job in an office supply factory, leaving her husband in charge of child care. For her, as for most of the women, the goal was to fulfill those dreams of progress, if not for themselves at least for the next generation.

I wanted to get ahead. I wanted to do something. At least, I wanted to have a little house, open a small business, to achieve something and provide for my children and everything. I saved [money], and I don't regret that I spent it on my children, so that they could go to school. I don't regret spending my money on them. Because, even if I have nothing today, I have them and they were educated. They are my legacy, proof that I achieved something.

Thus, these migrant women creatively combined multiple forms of labor in the effort to sustain a home environment conducive to the education and development of their children.

Conclusion

The overall assessment we make regarding these women's relationship to work and the state is that they negotiated their social circumstances with contradictory effects. On the one hand, asserting their culturally constructed roles as mothers brought them rewards and was a source of strength and creativity. Regardless of the real prospects of economic mobility for their children, the women felt a great sense of accomplishment "de haber echado pa'lante a la familia" (for helping the family get ahead). Esther Martínez, in an essay entitled "My Sacrifices Paid Off," speaks for many of the women: "My children are now on their own and I feel good about the sacrifices I made for them, because they have shown their appreciation and have fulfilled my hopes that they would finish school and command better jobs than those their father and I had." On the other hand, in some cases, the affirmation of culturally defined gender roles and rights brought a decline in economic power and in all cases a decline in social esteem. Moving from labor force participation to public assistance did not strengthen their own material life chances. "Being on welfare" meant having to accommodate to very low living standards and to few opportunities for social mobility. Moreover, the women found themselves circumscribed by an ever-shrinking arena in which to affirm and secure class or gender rights. They became isolated from certain group contexts such as the workplace, which provided a regular social network and a potential collective force for challenging social inequities.

A number of factors coalesced to place these Puerto Rican women in a position of increased marginalization. Structural changes in the New York City economy from the 1960s to the 1990s altered their ability to command an above-subsistance wage through unskilled and semiskilled jobs. The women spoke forcefully about the systemic obstacles to advancement they encountered over the years. These included the disappearance of manufacturing jobs and the scarcity of effective training programs to address changing skill requirements in employment. These structural transformations coincided with parenting stages in their life cycle. Nurturing and reproducing the family influenced the women's decisions regarding participation in the formal labor market. They stayed home and raised their children themselves because they were responding in part to a culturally informed view of the role of women in the household. But, as we have argued, this commitment to the primacy of family did not represent for them a negation of wage work, for their concept of work was fundamentally defined by their domestic responsibilities. Hence, they viewed themselves as being engaged in a productive function that merited, even if it did not command, a wage. Symbolically, welfare took on the attribute of wage work, constituting a stable, even if meager, source of income.

Another major factor contributing to the complex situation in which these women found themselves was a change in family structure. As a consequence of transformations in the labor market, Puerto Rican males also became massively unemployed and unable to command sufficient income to support their families. In addition, domestic conflict often resulted in the estrangement of adult male breadwinners from the family unit. Thus, the burden of providing for their families economically was added to the female responsibility of child rearing. Left without traditionally prescribed sources of support with which to fulfill their role, women were forced to reassess their situation and options. The disappearance of stable jobs, the paucity of acceptable child-care arrangements, and the precarious economic position of other adults in the household left welfare as the most viable means of meeting both child-rearing and financial obligations. As we have noted, in most cases the women went on public assistance after having struggled with poorly paid part-time or unsteady jobs and having exhausted or lost other income-producing possibilities, and they did so hoping to halt the downward-spiraling process that threatened their families' existence.

At a later stage in their lives, some women may have sought reentry into New York City's labor market; however, their intent was complicated by the transformed nature of existing jobs. Training for employment in the service sector, which today defines the city's economy, was not widely accessible. Moreover, the dramatic rise in unemployment among the working class made it especially difficult for older women to compete with younger workers for the few decent jobs available. Nilda Rolón's story offers a good example:

> I hustled and looked for many jobs. I looked for work as an at-tendant; as a nurse's aide; in school lunchrooms; senior citizen lunchrooms; well, I hustled. And to date I haven't found anything, because times are really tough. There's no work, and employers these days want young people. I would dress well, wear perfume; I would be well groomed. I had all my documents with me, you know. I ended up feeling very dejected and troubled.

Public policies with regard to welfare and job training have been heavily dependent on a cultural model of deficit, which more recent academic and policy debates term as "underclass" behavior.[26] The model is further supported by popular media images that accentuate crime and images of social deviance and family disintegration.[27] Consequently, the solutions that such analyses propose are punitive in character and disempowering in their results. The accounts that we gathered portray, instead, women who have a keen understanding of complex class and gender factors, but who see as well the concrete structural binds that have restricted poor Puerto Rican women in their daily lives and in their future aspirations. Rather than the stereotypical images of dependency and passivity, the narratives bring into focus the range of ways in which Puerto Rican women have negotiated adverse circumstances and developed their own responses to poverty conditions. Their stories reveal many strengths and contributions, which have been rendered socially invisible. More important, they suggest the need to recast social policy in ways that harness the human and cultural resources available in poor communities, encouraging community-initiated solutions to persistent poverty and exclusion.

If we have learned anything from this investigation, it is the importance of placing people's own perspectives, voices, and histories at the center of analysis. Doing so has allowed us to reconceptualize work and welfare as complementary rather than antagonistic spheres and to understand that challenges to economic and social inequity from disenfranchised communities may sometimes be expressed in cultural terms. Thus, the conflicts in which the women in our study became engaged over the course of their reproductive lives were not only struggles over denial of specific entitlements but affirmations of different conceptions of rights. Seen in this way, their social responsibilities toward children and family became not only a primary productive activity—that is, work—but also a cultural right to be valued and supported by the society. At the same time, these responsibilities also embody the right of access to meaningful wage work. By claiming the right to be responsible mothers, these Puerto Rican migrant women have opened a new space for appreciating the positive dimensions of cultural communities and for recognizing that equity and difference are not mutually exclusive definitions of social life. By affirming broader views of the concepts of citizenship and work, they have pushed further the boundaries of political and economic inclusion.

NOTES

Acknowledgments: This chapter was one of the last pieces of scholarship produced by Dr. Rosa Torruellas before her untimely death from cancer in 1993. In the last two years of her life, Rosa had become actively engaged in research on Puerto Rican women and welfare. Her research was a result of her close involvement with women in her community through the El Barrio Popular Education Program, which she created and directed for six years. Rosa was also working with a team of island and U.S.-based Puerto Rican women researchers on an extensive project on Puerto Rican women and the welfare state. Her work would have constituted one of the most significant Puerto Rican contributions to scholarship and policy research in the field of women, work, and welfare.

This chapter is an elaboration of chapter 3 in our larger study, *Responses to Poverty among Puerto Rican Women: Identity, Community, and Cultural Citizenship,* Report to the Joint Committee for Public Policy Research on Countemporary Hispanic Issues of the Inter-University Program for Latino Research and the Social Science Research Council (New York: Centro de Estudios Puertorriqueños, Hunter College, 1992).

1. An extensive literature exists on this subject. See, for example, Rosemarie Tong, *Feminist Thought: A Comprehensive Introduction* (Boulder, Colo.: Westview Press, 1989); Michele Barrett, *Women's Oppression Today: Problems in Marxist Feminist Analysis* (London: Verso,

1980); Zillah R. Eisenstein, ed., *Capitalist Patriarchy and the Case for Socialist Feminism* (New York: Monthly Review Press, 1979).

2. Nancy Fraser, *Unruly Practices: Power, Discourse and Gender in Contemporary Social Theory* (Minneapolis: University of Minnesota Press, 1989), 144–85.

3. Office of Program Planning, Analysis, and Development, New York State Department of Social Services, *Hispanic AFDC Recipients in New York City: Barriers to Employment and Self-suffiency* (Albany: New York State Department of Social Services, 1991), table 1, 25.

4. Salient studies include Centro de Estudios Puertorriqueños, History Task Force, *Labor Migration under Capitalism: The Puerto Rican Experience* (New York: Monthly Review Press, 1979); Palmira Ríos, "Puerto Rican Women in the United States Labor Market," *Line of March* 18 (Fall 1985); Andrés Torres and Frank Bonilla, "Decline within Decline: The New York Perspective," in *Latinos in a Changing Economy: Comparative Perspectives on Growing Inequality*, ed. Frank Bonilla and Rebecca Morales (Newbury Park, Calif.: Sage Publications, 1993), 85–108.

5. For a description of our methodology and the kinds of interviews we conducted, see Rosa M. Torruellas et al., "Testimonio, Identity, and Empowerment," *Centro de Estudio Puertorriqueños Bulletin* 2, no. 6 (Summer 1989): 76–86; Rina Benmayor, "Testimony, Action Research, and Empowerment: Puerto Rican Women and Popular Education," in *Women's Words: The Feminist Practice of Oral History*, ed. Sherna Berger Gluck and Daphne Patai (New York: Routledge, 1991), 159–74.

6. For further information on the literacy program see Félix Cortes, "Las letras hacia la conquista de la vida," *Centro de Estudios Puertorriqueños Bulletin* 2, no. 6 (Summer 1989): 71–73; Rosa M. Torruellas, "Alfabetización de adultos en 'El Barrio': ¿Destrezas básicas o educación popular?" *Centro de Estudios Puertorriqueños Bulletin* 2, no. 6 (Summer 1989): 66–70.

7. Important studies on the needlework industry in Puerto Rico include Blanca Silvestrini, "The Experience of Puerto Rican Women in the 1930s," in *The Puerto Rican Woman: Perspectives on Culture, History, and Society*, ed. Edna Acosta-Belén (New York: Praeger, 1986), 59–74; Lydia Milagros González, *Una puntada en el tiempo: La industria de la aguja en Puerto Rico (1900–1930)* (Santo Domingo, D.R.: Editora Taller, 1990); María del Carmen Baerga, *Género y trabajo: La industria de la aguja en Puerto Rico y el Caribe* (Río Piedras: University of Puerto Rico, 1993).

8. The low status of Puerto Rican women in the garment industry during the 1950s and 1960s has been well documented. See Altagracia Ortiz, "The Labor Struggles of Puerto Rican Women in the Garment Industry in New York City, 1920–1960," *Cimarrón* 1, no. 3 (Spring 1988): 39–59. For the impact of the work in the garment industry on Puerto Rican women and their families see Rina Benmayor et al., "Stories To Live By: Continuity and Change in Three Generations of Puerto Rican Women," *Oral History Review* 16, no. 2 (Fall 1988): 1–46.

9. For a general discussion of the decline of the New York metropolitan region, see Torres and Bonilla, "Decline within Decline," 85–107.

10. Ibid., 86–90.

11. "Spatial concentration of poverty, welfare receipt and crime, and intergenerational transmission of culture or structural position all contribute to the social context in which poverty may occur. When this context reinforces weak labor force attachment, an under-

class can be said to exist." Martha Van Haitsman, "A Contextual Definition of the Under-class," *Focus* 12, no. 1 (Spring–Summer 1989): 27–28.

12. Torres and Bonilla, "Decline within Decline," 102.

13. As a middle-class ideal, the notion of the nuclear family (consisting specifically of a mother, father, and two children) was also promoted in Puerto Rico as part of systematic efforts to control the population, especially during the 1950s.

14. Walter Stafford, "Racial, Ethnic, and Gender Employment Segmentation in New York City Agencies," in *Hispanics in the Labor Force: Issues and Policies*, ed. Edwin Meléndez, Clara Rodríguez, and Janis Barry Figueroa (New York: Plenum Press, 1991), 159–80; Frank Bonilla and Ricardo Campos, *Industry and Idleness* (New York: Centro de Estudios Puer-torriqueños, Hunter College of CUNY, 1986), 25–59; Sonia M. Pérez, "Puerto Rican Young Men and Economic Instability: Implications for Puerto Rican Family Poverty," National Council of La Raza report, Washington, D.C., 1992.

15. Bonilla and Campos, *Industry and Idleness*, 40.

16. Office of Program Planning, Analysis, and Development, *Hispanic AFDC Recipients in New York City*, 6.

17. Blanca Silvestrini, "The World We Enter When Claiming Rights: Latinos and the Quest for Culture" (History Department, University of Puerto Rico, Río Piedras, 1990), 8.

18. Mimi Abramovitz, *Regulating the Lives of Women: Social Welfare Policy from Colonial Times to the Present* (Boston: South End Press, 1988), 75–100.

19. Nancy Hewitt, "Beyond the Search for Sisterhood: American Women's History in the 1980s," in *Unequal Sisters: A Multicultural Reader in U.S. Women's History*, ed. Ellen Carol DuBois and Vicki L. Ruíz (New York: Routledge, 1990), 10.

20. Maxine Baca Zinn, "Family, Feminism, and Race in America," *Gender and Society* 4, no. 1 (March 1990): 68, 79.

21. Patricia Hill Collins, *Black Feminist Thought: Knowledge, Consciousness, and the Politics of Empowerment* (Boston: Unwin Hyman, 1990), 119–23.

22. Nicholas Lemann, "The Other Underclass," *Atlantic Monthly*, December 1991, 96–110.

23. In the 1980s Aspira, a Puerto Rican educational organization, found that the school drop-out rate among Puerto Rican youth in New York City had climbed into the 75 to 80 percent range. See Aspira, "Racial and Ethnic High School Dropout Rates in New York City" (New York: Aspira, 1983). Currently, these rates have declined to around 50 percent, but this is still a formidable figure and an urgent community problem.

24. Jason DeParle, "Fed by More than Slump, Welfare Caseload Soars," *New York Times*, January 10, 1992, A1; Todd S. Purdum, "Spiraling Welfare Roll Dominates Dinkins's Report Card," *New York Times*, September 18, 1991, B1.

25. Paul Grell, *Etude du chômage et de ses conséquences: Les catégories sociales touchées par le non-travail: Histoires de vie et modes de débrouillardise* (Montreal: Groupe d'Analyse des Politiques Sociales, University of Montreal, 1985).

26. Linda Chávez, *Out of the Barrio: Toward a New Politics of Hispanic Assimilation* (New York: Basic Books, 1991), 139–59; William Julius Wilson, *The Truly Disadvantaged: The Inner City, the Underclass, and Public Policy* (Chicago: University of Chicago Press, 1987).

27. Lemann, "The Other Underclass," 96–110.

EIGHT

New Tappings on the Keys: Changes in Work and Gender Roles for Women Clerical Workers in Puerto Rico

GERALDINE J. CASEY

This chapter explores the changing gender and class relations among contemporary women clerical workers in Puerto Rico.[1] More than 30 percent of all employed women were clerical workers in 1990, exceeding their rate of participation in any other single occupation.[2] Women were previously concentrated in the manufacturing sector as machine operators in the textile, food processing, garment, and electronics industries—a legacy from the late 1940s and 1950s campaign for rapid industrialization known as "Operation Bootstrap."[3] Today, clerical work outstrips women's participation in other sectors of the service economy, and it is often accompanied by high levels of gender stratification, just as the education and health care fields are. It is also an integral part of the "high-tech" electronics, communications, and financial industries that dominate Puerto Rico's "postindustrial" service economy. This rapid expansion of clerical work took place in the 1960s and 1970s, in the wake of Operation Bootstrap's demise, the expansion of the public sector, and the shift from manufacturing to service industries.[4] During these years automated clerical work was identified as one of the next links in the chain of twentieth-century modernization projects in Puerto Rico, promising prosperity for workers and an end to the long-standing problem of chronic unemployment on the island. This chapter will examine these assumptions in light of the structural employment patterns and experiences of women clerical workers in Puerto Rico in the early 1990s and the tensions over gender equity and class mobility that today define the world of clerical work. The essay will also discuss the strategies women office workers have developed to mediate, resist, and collude with gender stereotypes, mobility myths, and changing class identities in the context of Puerto Rico's colonial political economy.

Images of Clerical Work and Upward Mobility

Images of the importance of clerical work permeate the popular culture of Puerto Rico today. In metropolitan San Juan, secretarial training schools and business institutes line the avenues, promising jobs and affluence to those who enroll. In rural areas, cars with loudspeakers attached to their roofs circle town plazas and side streets blaring the schedule of upcoming classes. Popular magazines codify and expound upon the appropriate styles for office fashion and furnishings, while ads touting the new office technology fill store windows, newspapers, and the airwaves. More important, computerized clerical work figures prominently in contemporary narratives of upward mobility. Entrepreneurs anxious to tap into this ideology have established computer training institutes throughout the island. One person commented that these enterprises spring up like *cuchifrito* (fried pork) stands along the side of the road. The proliferation of these institutes is due, in part, to the profits available to managers for administering federally guaranteed student loan programs. Although job placement rates for graduates are low, professional training schools continue to attract students because of the high interest in clerical work and related careers.

An example of this interest in clerical work is seen among service organizations and advocacy groups that work with poor, unemployed women that may have different goals but identify computerized clerical work as a vehicle for women's personal empowerment. One these groups, the Proyecto Caribeño de Justicia y Paz (Caribbean Project for Justice and Peace), a national ecumenical organization involved in social advocacy work, proposed to establish small-scale, cooperative enterprises in which women would operate word-processing workshops.[5] Poor unemployed women themselves have internalized the notion that computerized clerical work constitutes a viable strategy for their economic success. This assumption is clearly visible in sociologist Linda Colón's 1988 film, *Desigualdad social y pobreza* (Social Inequality and Poverty), which included interviews with members of "Atrévete," a grassroots group of women residents in the Luis Llorens Torres public housing project in

San Juan.[6] As these women discussed the role of computer training programs in their self-help agenda, the camera captured a row of new computers lining the rear wall of the community room where the interviews
took place.

For women employed in blue-collar manufacturing jobs, the promise
of white-collar clerical work constitutes a powerful narrative of social mobility. This plot finds poignant expression in the research by Puerto Rican anthropologist Carmen A. Pérez-Herranz on women garment workers in western Puerto Rico during the 1980s.[7] When asked about their
aspirations for the future, the majority of women in her sample responded that they wanted to be secretaries. If they thought they were too
old to change occupations, they hoped their daughters would be able to
become secretaries or clerical workers.[8]

These views from outside the world of office work provide the cultural backdrop and social context in which clerical workers are situated.
The clerical workers I interviewed expressed a range of views concerning their work expectations and job satisfactions; however, they shared
an overriding concern about the low salaries, job insecurity, and limited
opportunities for advancement associated with their employment, as
well as the negative perceptions people had of them as clerical workers.
The latter issue is well illustrated by Margarita Pérez's experiences as director of the Caribbean Project for Justice and Peace. Before her commitment to liberation theology led her to change careers and eventually
to assume leadership of the Caribbean Project, Pérez had worked as an
executive secretary and had succeeded in working her way up to a managerial position as director of personnel for an American paper company. One of her functions as director of the Caribbean Project was to
receive visiting scholars, but often when she mentioned her previous
work experience,

> they seem so embarrassed and surprised in response. They say
> things like, "Oh, I thought for sure you were trained in sociol-
> ogy or history." And that is meant to be a compliment. As though
> that was the only way to become an organizer, a leader. And they
> talk as if I should be *proud* they thought that of me.

Pérez, on the other hand, valued her secretarial background because
she believed her leadership skills, including her analytical abilities, had

developed while she was a secretary. To her it seemed elitist for anyone to think a secretary could not be a political leader.

Organizing for Change in the Office

Women office workers at the University of Puerto Rico (UPR) and in their trade union, La Hermandad de Empleados Exentos No Docente (HEEND) (Brotherhood of Exempt, Non-Teaching Employees), constituted the majority of the women I interviewed for this project. Of the three thousand clerical and technical workers employed at the eleven campuses of the UPR, 70 percent are women and 90 percent are members of HEEND, which has been in existence since 1972. The presence of HEEND at UPR represents part of the history of labor militancy and political radicalism at this university, which has far exceeded the political practice of clerical workers in other institutions on the island.[9] Through HEEND, clerical workers have successfully challenged dominant ideologies and expectations about women in order to form new structures and organizations, including an on-campus day-care center for workers' children; occupational safety and health committees; counseling services; cultural workshops in poetry and silk screen; and their own musical group, Las Pleneras de la Hermandad (Union Singers). Women clerical workers and their union at UPR have also participated in campaigns against domestic violence and sexual harassment on the job.[10] The respect university workers and their trade union have earned in the larger Puerto Rican society is suggested by the fact that a full-length photo portrait of HEEND past president Ana Milagros Santiago, shown addressing workers and students at a UPR strike in 1984, was included in a photographic essay on the history of Puerto Rican women from 1899 to 1985 in a special women's issue of the social science journal, *Hómines*.[11]

One member of HEEND is Luci Arroyo, who has worked as a secretary at the Río Piedras campus of UPR for twenty-three years. She joined HEEND after twenty years on the job. Although she does not attend HEEND meetings, Arroyo decided to become a member anyway: "It was only right to join because of all the work the union does for us." She has lived in San Juan for more than half her life, but she was born and raised in a rural town and continues to affirm her connection with the language and popular culture of rural working people. For example, in response to a simple demographic question about the year of her birth, Arroyo noted, "I was born in 1947, behind some sugar sacks at the refinery" (*detrás de unos sacos de la central*). She clarified her reply by explaining that she was not born in a hospital but at home with the help of a midwife, and she went on to describe growing up under very difficult economic conditions. Later she revealed that her personal work history reflected substantial changes in her employment and social position: in addition to getting her secretarial training, she earned an associate's degree in secretarial sciences and has completed thirty credits toward her B.A., including all the basic courses plus classes in education and the humanities. At the time of our interview, her three-year-old child had just been accepted into the on-campus day-care center that HEEND initiated for UPR employees. In light of her work history and life experiences, it is interesting to note that Luci Arroyo did not believe her job as a secretary constituted upward mobility:

> Gerrie, it's a job. It's just a job. I worked in the shoe factories in Barceloneta when they had work. Full-time, until the companies left. Then I was unemployed. I went to secretarial training school in Manatí. . . . But I couldn't find work. There were no jobs. So I came to San Juan. I got a job as a secretary and I went to stay with my aunt in Río Piedras. I lived with her for eight years. Because that's where I could get a job.

Comparing her job to those of her sisters and sisters-in-law who worked in private-sector pharmaceutical plants, Arroyo observed: "There is much less pressure on you here [at UPR] than in the pharmaceutical companies. Of course, they get more money. But there is no security. My benefits here are better, very good. But they give us *sueldos de hambre* [starvation wages] and there's no place to go." For women like Luci Arroyo, then, clerical work is not a vocation; it is just another way of making a living.

On the other hand, Elizabeth Correa, a UPR secretary in her early twenties, was a member of Professional Secretaries International (PSI), an organization that stresses technical skills and professional clothing styles as vehicles to career advancement. PSI workshops in technological skills are combined with fashion shows that promote the "appropriate image" for professional secretaries. All PSI events are thus imbued with the ideology of upward mobility as the organization strives to counter the portrayal in popular culture of secretaries as fluffy-headed, sexy coquettes. But sometimes PSI's perspective of clerical workers as "professionals" conflicts with that of the HEEND, which organizes political mobilizations and mass actions to achieve its goals at UPR. For example, when a loud group of protesting university workers with HEEND picket signs passed her office in March 1990, I asked Elizabeth Correa what she thought. She was not impressed: "Look at them. They are so vulgar, with their chants and picket signs. Marching through the campus like that, in sneakers and T-shirts! That is not right. That is not the way to do things." Contrastingly, activists within HEEND doubt the capacity of voluntary professional organizations like PSI to advance the position of clerical workers. Ana María Pérez, a thirty-year-old secretary at the Río Piedras campus and a national officer in HEEND, commented:

> You can act like a professional, you can dress like a professional, but that doesn't mean the boss is going to treat you like a professional. Or pay you like a professional. All the technical training and style—that is no guarantee for respect. It doesn't mean very much without a written contract.

It is interesting to note that after Elizabeth Correa passed the PSI exam and received her certificate as a licensed professional secretary, she transferred to another office on campus in search of advancement. At the time of our next conversation, in the summer of 1992, Correa was working in the private sector but only on a temporary contract. She reiterated her belief in the need to professionalize secretarial work, but she also expressed frustration over her inability to secure full-time work and career advancement. Paying careful attention to the PSI guidelines for professional success did not resolve the fundamental social and economic problems she faced.

Some workers, such as Marisol Rivera, an administrative assistant with eighteen years of experience working at the Carolina campus of the University of Puerto Rico, supported the goals of both organizations. Rivera was an active member of HEEND and had also been active in the metropolitan San Juan chapter of PSI. She believed her commitments to both organizations were interrelated: "I'm a professional secretary. And I'm a professional with my trade union. That is the only way we're ever going to get anything."

The preceding sketches indicate the range of perspectives clerical workers have about their work. The overwhelming majority of workers I interviewed were proud of the work they did. At the same time, they expressed serious frustration over the bureaucracy and lack of resources they confront in their offices, along with their low salaries and the limited opportunities for advancement available to them. Nevertheless, most expected to continue working in this field. Thousands of other women today are training to become secretaries in Puerto Rico. However, rising unemployment and underemployment is forcing many of them to migrate to the United States in search of work.[12] Even with computer training, clerical workers do not believe their current jobs guarantee upward mobility or job security. In 1990 the unemployment rate for clerical workers was 28 percent. This was higher than the unemployment rate for women machine operators (23 percent) and women in other service occupations (14 percent).[13] Low salaries were a pervasive concern among all the women I interviewed.[14] Obviously, clerical work has not been a panacea for women workers on the island.

To improve their situation, increasing numbers of clerical workers at UPR are joining organizations such as HEEND or PSI or, as in the case of Marisol Rivera, both organizations. In the early 1990s there was a dramatic increase in HEEND membership. In January 1990 more than 90 percent of the clerical and technical bargaining unit at UPR agreed to pay the agency fee (comparable to a union dues checkoff) to HEEND for the first time. This option was a new clause in the bargaining agreement negotiated between UPR workers and management in the fall of 1989. Management was confident that the majority of workers would decline to enroll. After 90 percent of the workforce agreed to sign up, university management arbitrarily canceled this clause of the contract. In response, HEEND initiated a successful work stoppage, which shut down the university until management agreed to comply with the original agreement.

In my experience as a trade union organizer among university clerical workers at Boston University, and in my general research on the topic, the issue of union dues and checkoff is always considered a difficult if not impossible demand around which to organize workers. Asking workers to go on strike over their right to pay the union *more* money is never an easy move. A manager at the Río Piedras campus reported to me that university administrators had agreed to the clause assuming that workers would not sign up for the payroll deduction. The personnel office expressed confidence that university workers were "too professional," "too white-collar," and too concerned about their paychecks to agree to pay the agency fee. Yet UPR clerical and technical workers overwhelmingly agreed to the income deduction, and they were willing to go on strike to defend the integrity of their trade union in this matter.

Clerical Workers' Gender, Class, Race, and National Identities

In Puerto Rican offices identities based on gender, class, race, and nationality are mobilized and reconstructed through the dynamic of struggle and accommodation between clerical workers and managers.[15] Supervisors and office managers invoke popularly held assumptions and call upon traditional values as a means of labor discipline. They also use "scientific management" procedures and new technologies imported from the United States to control women's labor. However, Puerto Rican women clerical workers are not passive recipients of these approaches. They also call upon tradition and modern strategies to substantiate their claims for equity and respect in the workplace.

With regard to the social relations of work, women clericals at UPR mobilized their own interpretations of gender and class identity. Significant numbers of them accepted the traditional role of women as subordinate caretakers that was projected by management. Some women believed that acquiescence and cooperation were effective strategies to enhance their position. Other women privately disagreed with management decisions yet affirmed the right of supervisors to set policies and define cultural norms in the workplace. Still other women decided to challenge prevailing assumptions by building and participating in new organizational forms such as HEEND and PSI. Rather than schematize these responses as discrete patterns of behavior, it would be more useful to trace out the complex and contradictory nature of their interplay, for the same woman can manifest one or more of these responses, even during the same day. We may be able to better define how different interpretations of gender and class identity are mobilized in the clerical workplace in Puerto Rico.

Gender Issues among Clerical Workers. The structural position of secretaries in Puerto Rico is highly gendered because gender stratification is so pronounced in the island's labor market; as of 1980, thirty-nine out of every forty secretaries were women.[16] While men were employed in clerical occupations, only one man in my research had the job title of "secretary," and he worked in the military offices of the ROTC program at one of the UPR campuses. The gender stratification of clerical work increases preexisting tensions between men and women in Puerto Rico. Unemployment rates for men are consistently higher than those for women in the workforce, and this pattern appears to be increasing as the Puerto Rican economy continues to lose its manufacturing base through automation and plant departures. There is also a rising gender gap in education in Puerto Rico—that is, women attend and graduate from school at all levels in higher numbers than do men—that will definitely affect employment in white-collar service sector jobs, which place a premium on the increased literacy and the socialization skills associated with higher education.[17]

These gender issues tend to increase the tensions between men and women in general. But for one woman I interviewed, the gender issue became quite personal. She noted that "in Puerto Rico, women have all the drive" to advance themselves and their families economically, but they are expected to maintain the double duty of housework and child care at home. At the same time, this woman bitterly complained that working women feel obligated to let their husbands think *they* are the breadwinners, the powerful ones in the family. At this point in the interview, she was in tears. Mediating the contradictions of gender role expectations in the intimate zone of family relations can be a terrible burden for working women.

Established gender ideologies also have a profound impact in the clerical workplace, for they shape job expectations and the daily work process. At a day-long conference to commemorate National Secretaries' Week (NSW) in 1991, one group of secretaries generated a master job description itemizing 124 discrete tasks the women were called upon to perform. Eighteen of the twenty secretaries participating in this workshop were from private-sector firms; all of them worked for male managers or supervisors. Itemized tasks that were assumed to be standardized, routinized, and gender neutral (typing, taking dictation, opening the mail, answering the phone, scheduling appointments, and filing) were described by these secretaries in a caretaking language consistent with traditional female roles (finding things, reminding people, picking up after others, organizing the mess). Workshop participants listed a host of other duties that they considered "personal work"—tasks unrelated to their formal job description but that they were required to do anyway. These included ordering flowers, picking up the boss's dry cleaning, and purchasing and wrapping presents for his family and friends. In addition, one secretary was required to go to her supervisor's home, after work hours, to help his wife prepare for dinner parties. Another was expected to collect reference materials for her boss's children at community libraries and then to complete their homework. A third secretary reported that she was expected to transcribe into English all social interactions and written materials for her supervisor from the United States, who, after three years in Puerto Rico, had not learned a single word of Spanish. All of these tasks call upon stereotypical assumptions about women's traditional roles as nurturing household managers to extract additional labor from them as workers, but this gender stereotyping is in contention. At the conference, as secretaries volunteered various tasks they performed to help construct the master list, when one of these personal tasks was mentioned other women would interrupt and interject a range of comments: "That's not fair"; "Wait a minute, you don't have to do that"; or "That work shouldn't be part of your job description."

At the same time, many women clerical workers internalize prevailing assumptions about gender roles and accept the rigid gender division of labor. I asked women to evaluate clerical work as a possible future job for their children. Among those secretaries who considered it a positive option, several women were explicit that it would be an acceptable career for their daughters but not for their sons. One women raised the concern that her son's gender identity might be negatively affected by working in a woman's field; as she put it, "he might get his cables switched, from positive to negative."

Cultural assumptions about secretaries in Puerto Rico are also highly gendered. The image of a female secretary sitting on the male boss's knee is still pervasive in the popular culture of Puerto Rico.[18] Several different meanings are embedded in this particular cultural icon: it confirms (male) managers' desire to have a young, attractive, and attentive female secretary at their service; it suggests that the only way a woman can maintain her job is through her sexual powers; and it encourages women to view other women as competitors and sexual predators. In April 1990, on the outskirts of San Juan, the sexual attitude in this icon was dramatically expressed on an advertising banner (*cruzacalle*) strung across the highway in front of one of the motels that cater to the somewhat illicit afternoon trade: "We Guarantee the Lowest Rates for Secretaries' Week." This practice was challenged by a group of women attending a PSI seminar during National Secretaries' Week the following year. They decided to picket any motel that displayed this kind of sign, although they expressed great discomfort at the idea of even being in the vicinity of these establishments.

Traditional gender roles also shape the ritual cycle of office holidays among clerical workers in Puerto Rico. Celebrations are marked by the giving of highly gendered items such as candy, greeting cards, and flowers by male bosses to female workers. St. Valentine's Day, which emphasizes romance and sexuality, and Mother's Day, which celebrates women's traditional maternal role, have a prominent place in the clerical work calendar. These holidays have no intrinsic relationship to office work, yet they have become occasions for elaborate office parties and intense gift giving directed toward secretaries and other women clerical workers.

At the same time, occasions that celebrate the role of women as workers, such as National Secretaries' Week in April, have been romanticized and sexualized. During NSW in 1990 and 1991, print media were filled with ads for perfume, jewelry, and clothes, projecting the secretary as a sexy, alluring coquette—someone to buy for, someone to please. Male supervisors provide elaborate gifts of candy and floral bouquets, and they sponsor outings to fashion shows, concerts, dances, and romantic dinners for their secretarial staff. Women supervisors participate in these activities at a reduced level, but their parties usually take place in the office. In exchange for these gifts, it is expected that women workers will subordinate their independent judgments, needs, and desires to those of their gift-giving supervisors. Thus, the ritual cycle of office celebrations functions, in part, as a form of labor discipline.

However, the campaign to bring emotions, cultural celebrations, and personal life into the workplace is not simply a manipulation on the part of supervisors. Clerical workers have also struggled for the right to bring their private lives and celebrations into the workplace. For example, women fought for and won the right to display family photos, plants, and mementos on their desks. Furthermore, family responsibilities and cultural proscriptions against unsupervised socializing for women mean that clerical workers in Puerto Rico have neither the time nor the cultural permission to gather together after work, as men often do. Consequently, women must bring their celebrations into the workplace, in the form of office parties and luncheons. These office celebrations of holidays, birthdays, and wedding showers partially signify a workers' victory. Yet supervisors' ultimate control of these celebrations, because they control the office space and rhythm of work, reinforces managerial authority.

New contours in the world of clerical work in Puerto Rico, however, are challenging traditional assumptions about women office workers at UPR. The introduction of computers and other office technologies demands new skills, greater literacy, and more independent thinking from clerical workers. UPR job descriptions now include a requirement for computer literacy in such software packages as WordPerfect, Lotus, and Windows. PSI emphasizes these characteristics in their efforts to change the nature of holiday celebrations by encouraging secretaries to boycott office-sponsored lunches and fashion shows and to demand instead that bosses spend their money on professional training for their secretaries. UPR offices with female supervisors also are altering celebrations by reducing or removing their sexual nuances. Parties in these offices have become potluck lunches, and sometimes one box of candy will be purchased and left on the front desk "for the whole office to share." In part, this shift reflects the inability of women managers to associate themselves with the romantic and sexual allusions embedded in holiday celebrations. It may also reflect the weaker buying power of women supervisors or a more developed awareness about issues of gender equity among some female supervisors.

HEEND organizes alternative celebrations for UPR workers on National Secretaries Day and Mother's Day by producing posters and greeting cards that emphasize women's collective work and their history of participation in Puerto Rico's social struggles. HEEND reproduces original poems and art created by university workers as a way of affirming their belief that workers are capable of critical and creative thinking. Poems by famous Latin American writers, such as Pablo Neruda and Nicolás Guillén, are also reproduced on posters and greeting cards to mark these new "holidays" of women workers. The gender and class relations embedded in clerical workers' holiday celebrations are clearly in contention in contemporary Puerto Rico.

Class Issues among Women Clerical Workers.   The analysis of class position and working-class consciousness among women clerical workers in Puerto Rico presents particular problems. The office is a contested work space, a divided zone where surface-level commonalities regarding dress codes and job descriptions mask profound differences among workers. In this work zone the fluidity of class relations is particularly significant: Does clerical work constitute an advancement, providing upward mobility for working-class women? Or does it signify proletarianization and downward mobility, especially for women from middle-class families who earned college degrees in the liberal arts and developed professional job aspirations?[19] For women from blue-collar, working-class families, whose point of reference for female employment has been industrial production, secretarial jobs are an advance. But women from middle-class families who hold college degrees in the liberal arts and maintain professional expectations often describe the clerical occupation as a "dead-end" job. For example, one clerical worker, a single mother and the head of her household, worked next to another woman whose husband had a professional job in the private-sector banking industry. They shared the same office space, did the same job, and brought home the same salary, yet they experienced very different social realities. Clearly, class identity among contemporary women clerical workers is shaped by factors outside the workplace. The complexity of class composition, reflected in different family backgrounds, educational levels, current marital status, household composition, and the employment or unemployment of husbands and other adult family members, challenges us to rethink some basic assumptions about the nature of the white-collar working class in Puerto Rico.

The fabric of social life in the 1990s is dramatically different from the reality encountered by women clerical workers who entered the workforce in the 1950s. In the 1950s and 1960s women workers in general were mobilized in large numbers to participate in Puerto Rico's "Operation Bootstrap," as the program was known in the United States. The transition from the Operation Bootstrap model of public ownership of key resources and equal distribution of social services to the contemporary model of privatization and downscaled social services has had a profound impact on the quality of clerical workers' lives. Under Operation Bootstrap, women worked in manufacturing jobs as machine operators, packers, inspectors, and seamstresses.[20] Massive public funding supported extensive infrastructure development in utilities, transportation, and plant construction, as well as social programs in education, health, and housing—all designed to improve the productivity of labor.[21] Although

Operation Bootstrap's educational emphasis was on training for industrial production, clerical workers also received educational support during this period. Students who graduated from UPR with degrees in secretarial sciences, for example, were eligible for full tuition scholarships and stipends to pursue graduate courses in business management and secretarial science education at universities in the United States.

Contemporary educational and ideological campaigns that mobilize women to participate in the world of computerized clerical work are as intense as the earlier campaigns of Operation Bootstrap, but with some very important differences. Recruitment and training are no longer considered the social responsibilities of government or political parties. In past decades the social engineering projects of the Popular Democratic Party relied upon large-scale popular mobilization. Today, this approach to mobilizing labor has been replaced by sophisticated advertisements and media campaigns that promise individual advantage and promote individual choice. Instead of attending free government schools and training workshops, contemporary women clerical workers have to seek out and pay for their own job training.

Another factor that shapes women clerical workers' class identity in recent years is the recent sharp rise in unemployment. While the number of clerical workers nearly doubled between 1975 and 1990, from 54,000 to 103,000, the unemployment rate for clerical workers rose from 18 percent to 28 percent. The 1990 figure was higher than the unemployment rate for women service workers (14 percent) and for women machine operators (23 percent), even though these latter face the constant threat of plant closings. Ironically, the same office technology that raised the prestige of clerical work in Puerto Rico has also eliminated thousands of clerical jobs.[22]

In addition to working women who are unemployed, the number of women permanently out of the workforce is also growing. In 1990, 28 percent of women in Puerto Rico were employed, 3 percent were unemployed, and fully 68 percent were listed as being "out of the workforce." The term "out of the workforce" includes housewives, students, the retired, and the handicapped, but the category also masks a large proportion of hidden unemployment. Under the heading "housewife," I found many women who had trained for careers and once worked as clerical workers only to find themselves forced to stay home because they had lost their jobs. Likewise, many students reported that they would prefer full-time employment, but they could not get it. Attending college had become an economic strategy; women relied on scholarships and guaranteed federal loans as an alternative source of income.

Women clerical workers who find full-time employment report that their salaries are not sufficient. A large number of women clericals at UPR hold second jobs, working evenings and weekends. These second jobs, performed after regular working hours, are necessary to augment low salaries. Many UPR clerical workers negotiate private contracts for typing, word processing, and editing of materials for students and faculty members, work they do after regular working hours. In addition, during working hours, clerical workers pursue a wide range of sales activities, earning small commissions for mail-order businesses in jewelry, clothes, office equipment, home furnishings, and kitchen goods. Women also organize a large number of raffles and candy sales for their churches, their children's schools, social and political organizations, and for HEEND.

Puerto Rico's chronically high unemployment rate, and the numbers of people (women and men) who are permanently out of the workforce, have a tremendous impact on the lives of all working-class women, including full-time clerical workers. The nearly 70 percent of all women who are out of the workforce are the sisters, mothers, daughters, nieces, in-laws, and neighbors who form the kin and friendship networks of employed women. Technically considered unemployed or underemployed, these women are engaged in a range of economic activities in the informal sector. They provide crucial labor for the social reproduction of families and communities. At the same time, they place additional social and economic demands on employed clerical workers. Clerical workers at the UPR help women in their networks secure orders for the goods and services these informal workers provide. UPR workers also secure work contracts for unemployed male relatives in automotive and appliance repair and construction work. Elaborate arrangements of reciprocal child care and economic assistance also operate between employed women clerical workers and their mothers, adult siblings, and in-laws who are out of the workforce.

The connections between women who are employed as salaried clerical workers and women who are unemployed or working in the informal economy provide additional resources but also place tremendous economic, social, and psychological strains on women clericals. At UPR, clerical workers reported being expected to provide financial assistance for adult siblings and older parents; room and board for family members from other parts of the island; and a range of counseling and advocacy work for members of their extended family networks. Acting as intermediaries and brokers, women clerical workers track down government benefits and services in health, housing, and veterans' affairs and negotiate with the criminal justice system for incarcerated relatives. Employed women also provide home care for seriously ill family members.

As I have shown above, employment, unemployment, underemployment, and poverty are integral parts of life for many women clerical workers. Categories of class and occupation may appear statistically clear and distinct in the census data; but in clerical workers' lives, these categories break down and blend into each other, constituting different aspects of their multifaceted working-class reality. Much more research is needed in order to understand the complex linkages between employed women and those who are unemployed or out of the workforce. Clearly, the range of connections that link salaried workers with those who work in informal economic activities are profound.

Issues of Race and National Identity among Clerical Workers. Racial identity is a very complex issue in Puerto Rico. Questions on racial classification were eliminated from the United States census in 1950, making statistical analysis difficult; and social science discussion is often anecdotal and rarely systematic. Meanwhile racial categories in Puerto Rican society are fluid, contextual, and based on self-perception.[23] Thus, the existence of racism is often denied. Some Puerto Rican scholars explain this by citing the fact that under Spanish rule racial categories were never institutionalized on the island to the extent that they were in the United States. As a result, racial nomenclature is fluid and sometimes contradictory: such terms as *trigueño, moreno,* and *negro*—all describing various shades of dark skin—are used to refer to Afro–Puerto Ricans.[24] At the same time, *blanquito* ("whitey") and *muy blanquito* (very white) are used as derogatory terms for persons who project arrogance and wealth—regardless of skin color; while the words *negro* or *negra* (black) and *negrito* or *negrita* ("little black one") are intimate terms of endearment, again regardless of skin color.

The ease and cultural openness between phenotypically diverse groups is often the basis for the argument that there is no racism in Puerto Rico. Yet people sometimes refer to those "others" who still want to whiten the race or hide their own African or mulatto heritage.[25] And the majority of people I interviewed acknowledged that Puerto Rican people who would be called African-descended or black according to United States standards are concentrated in the lowest economic levels. Nevertheless, many Puerto Ricans dismiss the racial significance of that observation, arguing that it reflects class rather than racial oppression.

Racism in Puerto Rico is also a dynamic process, one that changes historically. The shift from an industrial economy to a service economy since the 1950s has created new bases for racial discrimination at work. In the manufacturing sector, where "personality" and personal connections are also important vehicles in securing employment and promotion, discrimination based on race is not as obvious since the industrial work process tends to emphasize productivity, manual dexterity, and speed over interpersonal relations. In the world of office work, on the other hand, personal attributes are listed by supervisors as the most important criteria for employment; thus, physical appearance becomes a class and race filter. This may explain why Afro–Puerto Rican women are employed in white-collar office work at a far lower rate than their proportion in the general population. When black clerical workers are employed, it tends to be at the lowest-level jobs. I myself never encountered an Afro–Puerto Rican woman in the position of executive secretary in any of the private-sector firms I visited.

Computerized office work has a particular relationship to the struggle to define national identity vis-à-vis Puerto Rico's colonial relationship to the United States. Popular discourse and political action on the question of Puerto Rico's political status was at a heightened pitch during my two years of fieldwork in 1990–91. A plebiscite had been initiated by the United States Congress in 1989 in an attempt to resolve the island's longstanding political crisis. The plebiscite process was eventually abandoned by Congress, but while it was in force, women clerical workers participated in the intense and far-reaching national debate. Clerical workers I interviewed reflected the range of political affiliations present in Puerto Rico. HEEND at UPR does not take positions on political questions, but membership is almost evenly divided between pro-commonwealth and pro-statehood forces. Many founders and union activists in HEEND, however, are *independentistas*.

At the same time, the ideological identification of computerized clerical work with notions of social progress, technological advances, and modernity tends to create a symbolic association between this field of work and the United States, regardless of the beliefs of particular workers. Clerical workers are intricately linked to the United States through technology transfer and electronic communications. Women are obliged to negotiate their way through English-language computer programs, keyboards, and instruction books imported from the United States. Daily tasks require them to use software, keyboard commands, and systems of logic constructed and printed in English. Fax machines, e-mail, and Internet systems may bring San Juan secretaries closer to the world of Wall Street finance than many working-class Puerto Ricans actually living in Manhattan. This close association with the United States also resonates with the popular-culture image of secretaries as consumers who spend all their free time in United States–style shopping malls "frittering away" their salaries on such feminine wares as clothes, makeup, and jewelry.

Clerical Workers' Strategies for Change

This section of the chapter will consider some of the social and political strategies that are empowering women clerical workers in Puerto Rico to turn management's "logic against them," as one scholar put it, in order to challenge the dominant constructs of gender and class relations in their workplaces.[26] In general, there is a belief that women have an innate fear of machinery and cannot master computers, and that they are too delicate, passive, and lacking in scientific knowledge to engage the new technology. However, the large number of women currently registered for secretarial training and computer programming courses contradicts these notions. Sessions offered by UPR's Office of Personnel were always oversubscribed. Reflecting on the new office technology, women offered sophisticated and realistic assessments. Women workers' desire to master computer skills was usually phrased as part of personal goals to "better themselves" (hay que mejorarse). They were eager to learn computer software programs and new office machinery, provided these would help them complete their tasks or enhance their dignity on the job. They opposed practices designed to monitor their productivity or increase their workload. Even those women who admitted feeling intimidated by the new technology expressed an interest in learning to use it. HEEND also encourages workers to learn the new technology. Workers did express resentment of computers when their supervisors assumed they were experts after attending only a single training session. They also expressed great frustration over the office politics and favoritism that determine the way computer resources are distributed. HEEND raised this issue in contract negotiations, demanding an equitable procedure for the distribution of new office technology.

Another arena in which supervisors invoke a contradictory gender logic to control women's labor is in the realm of personal appearance. Almost every woman I interviewed noted the pressure from supervisors and peers to participate in fashion and hairstyle competition at work. They complained about the exorbitant proportion of their salaries spent on clothes. Some managers created a mixed message by demanding a seductive style and fashion competition and then criticizing those workers who tried to conform to their wishes. With their eyes on U.S. corporate practices, some managers trivialized Puerto Rican clerical workers, saying they did not display an appropriately professional style of dress. A freelance management consultant who conducts workshops on this topic complained to me that office workers were too sensual and too "Puerto Rican." When I asked for clarification, she said women dressed in a seductive style that was "too Latin, too tropical." This creates confusion and self-doubt among women workers, leaving them unsure about their own judgments and making it easier for supervisors to assert their authority.

Workers have developed a range of responses to the "fashion question." Many women were willing participants in the office style contests; others were critical of them but found it difficult as individuals to change things. PSI stresses a preference for sedate, conservative clothes, while HEEND at UPR has no position on the issue. One of the most creative responses I found was developed by another trade union for office workers in Puerto Rico, the Union of Employees at Cruz Azul (Blue Cross, a private company not related to the United States company). The first time I saw the navy blue uniforms worn by clerical workers at this health insurance company in San Juan, I assumed it was a management policy designed to control the largely female workforce. In fact, the right to wear uniforms was a union demand. The women I interviewed at Cruz Azul explained that they finally got fed up with the intense pressure to buy fashionable and expensive clothes; the cost was prohibitive and shopping took up too much of their time. They demanded uniforms in their contract negotiations. The Cruz Azul union contract now requires the company to provide workers with two uniforms every year (a matching skirt and suit jacket). What began as a women's demand was extended to men in subsequent negotiations, after men complained about the expensive business suits they were expected to purchase. Even management now wears uniforms, although the addition of stripes and the use of different colors signal distinctions of rank.

There is no bargaining contract language on the issue of uniforms at UPR, but fashion pressure on campus generally tends to be less intense than in private-sector firms. Nevertheless, the idea of uniforms is starting to catch on. Two women I interviewed at the main UPR campus in Río Piedras commissioned a seamstress to make uniforms for them in 1992. The woman who initiated the idea is an evangelical Protestant; her office mate is a radical *independentista*. Despite their political differences, both women share a frustration with the consumer culture and the high cost of office fashion. They wear uniforms four days a week, every day but Friday, explaining: "There should be one day open for choice, for color and self-expression." The uniform solution to the fashion question also allows women to remove themselves from office competition over fashion, a contest often associated with the promise of prestige and favors from the boss.

Office demeanor and telephone manners is another arena where management attempts to assert control. Managers and training consultants argue that women workers violate office protocol and the guidelines established by modern scientific management when they interject traditional Puerto Rican phrases into business conversations, such as: "*Chacha! No me diga!*" (Girl, you don't say!) and "*Ay bendito, m'hija!*" (Oh, mercy, my child!). Managers consider this style too informal and too personal. Women workers are divided on this issue. Some women agree with management; others appreciate these typical phrases as subtle affirmations of Puerto Rican culture. Women argue that they should have the right to speak like Puerto Ricans: "Why should we have to act like North Americans, as long as we get the work done?"

Conclusion

This chapter has described the role of gender, class, race, and nationality in shaping the identities of women clerical workers in Puerto Rico. Organizations of these workers are guided by different logics in their efforts to empower their constituencies. PSI functions like many similar business and professional associations. Founded and headquartered in the United States, PSI has established chapters in five different towns in Puerto Rico.[27] A number of UPR clerical workers I interviewed were PSI members in San Juan, Arecibo, Mayagüez, and Carolina. The PSI philosophy for clerical success stresses individual responsibility for upward mobility, dress codes, technical expertise, and professionalization.[28] PSI also administers a "licensed professional secretary" exam and workshops on stress management and self-esteem. A favorite PSI slogan, recorded in their literature and heard in all the group meetings is: "Act like a professional, and they will treat you like a professional."

HEEND, on the other hand, employs a dramatically different approach. As a trade union, HEEND tends to define problems as structural and to emphasize collective action. In institutional settings like UPR, where decisions are made outside the framework of individual offices, personal style and good relations with one's supervisor cannot guarantee equity on the job. One of the most important advances won by HEEND in the area of education and training is free tuition for university employees and their spouses and children. This includes release time for workers to attend daytime classes. These benefits extend to the graduate level and include free tuition at the prestigious UPR Law School. Tuition remission is often the only way women clerical workers can guarantee a full-ranging, rich education for themselves and their children (rather than an education limited to computer training or machine repair programs). HEEND argues that working-class people need to be able to study such academic subjects as history, music theory, geography, and the sciences. More than half the women I interviewed listed these benefits as one of the main reasons they remained at their jobs, even though the salaries are lower than in the private sector.

The increasing participation of women clerical workers in organizations such as HEEND and PSI has changed the nature of trade unions and professional organizations in Puerto Rico. PSI has been encouraged to move beyond its traditional style to adopt a more militant tone, talking about boycotts and picket lines during National Secretaries' Week. HEEND has expanded its collective bargaining demands to include specific, trend-setting contract language on such women's issues as sexual harassment, domestic violence, and office stress. The union has won free family health care and an on-site day-care center. In response to criticisms of women workers, the union has also adopted more inclusive language and more democratic forms for discussion, including small-group

meetings and workshops. Women clerical workers are working to transform both their offices and their organizations. In the process, they are
transforming their position as women and as workers in contemporary
Puerto Rico.

NOTES

Acknowledgments: This chapter is dedicated to the memory of Angélica Meléndez, a
founding member of the Hermandad de Empleados Exentos No Docente (the Brotherhood of Exempt, Non-Teaching Employees) trade union and an inspiration to everyone
who worked with her—*una tremenda compañera que ha estado siempre presente en la lucha.* An
earlier draft of this essay was presented at the eighteenth International Congress of the
Latin American Studies Association (LASA) in Atlanta, Georgia, in March 1994.

1. This chapter is based on my dissertation research, "From Bootstrap to Shoulder-
strap: Women Clerical Workers in Puerto Rico," for the doctoral program in anthropology
at the Graduate School and University Center of the City University of New York. Support
for my fieldwork in the years 1990–92 was provided by Intercambio, the CUNY-UPR academic exchange program at the Center for Puerto Rican Studies, Hunter College, New
York City.

2. Estado Libre Asociado de Puerto Rico, Negociado de Estadísticas sobre el Grupo
Trabajador, *Serie histórica del empleo, desempleo y grupo trabajador en Puerto Rico, 1947–1990*
(San Juan, Departamento de Trabajo y Recursos Humanos, 1991), 5.

3. For general information on women's economic participation in Operation Bootstrap, see Luz del Alba Acevedo, "Política de industrialización y cambios en el empleo femenino en Puerto Rico: 1947–1982," *Hómines* 10, no. 2 (1987): 40–69. For a more detailed
study, see Carmen A. Pérez-Herranz, "The Impact of a Development Program on Working
Women in the Garment Industry: A Study of Women and Production in Puerto Rico"
(Ph.D. diss., Rutgers University, 1990).

4. For more discussion on the demise of Operation Bootstrap, see Helen Icken Safa,
The Myth of the Male Breadwinner: Women and Industrialization in the Caribbean (Boulder,
Colo.: Westview Press, 1995), 59–97.

5. Proyecto Caribeño de Justicia y Paz, *Nuestra palabra* 3, no. 1 (1989): 1–2.

6. Linda Reyes Colón, *Desigualdad social y pobreza* (documentary film in three parts)
(Río Piedras: University of Puerto Rico, 1988).

7. Pérez-Herranz, "The Impact of a Development Program," passim.

8. Ibid., 124, 329.

9. For a historical discussion of the rising militancy among public sector workers in
Puerto Rico during the 1970s, see Liliana Cotto Morales, "Trends in the Puerto Rican Labor Movement: State Employees' Organization and Strike Militance in the First Luster of
the Seventies," *Hómines* 10, no. 2 (1987): 174–98. For specific information on the history
and class consciousness of clerical and technical workers at the University of Puerto Rico,
see Hermandad de Empleados Exentos No Docente of the University of Puerto Rico

(HEEND), *Convenio, 1989–1992: Luchamos para vencer* (1990); HEEND, *Convenio, 1986–1989: Año XV Aniversario (1972–87): Luchamos para vencer* (1986); Fernando Picó, Milton Pabón, Roberto Alejandro, *Las vallas rotas* (Río Piedras: Ediciones Huracán, 1982); Nieves Falcón et al., *Huelga y sociedad* (Río Piedras: Editorial Edil, 1982), 22, 165–66. For research from the United States that documents a similar pattern of labor militancy among university clerical workers, including trade union organizing and strikes organized by clerical and technical workers at Boston, Duke, Yale, Harvard, and Columbia Universities, see Geraldine Casey, "Text, Anti-Text, and the Need for a Class-based Hermeneutics," *Anthropology of Work Review* 12, no. 1 (1991): 3–8; Karen Brodkin Sacks, *Caring by the Hour: Women, Work, and Organizing at Duke Medical Center* (Champaign: University of Illinois Press, 1988); Cynthia Saltzman, "You Can't Eat Prestige: Women and Unions at Yale" (Ph.D. diss., Columbia University, 1988).

10. At the University of Puerto Rico, HEEND has won protection against sexual harassment and negotiated specific language on this issue in their collective bargaining agreements. HEEND supports the movement against domestic violence through education and political action. The union was an initial sponsor of Law 54, the first piece of legislation to define and offer specific protection from domestic violence in Puerto Rico. See editorial in *Claridad*, June 30, 1989, 12. For more information on domestic violence in Puerto Rico, see Comisión para los Asuntos de la Mujer, *El maltrato es un crimen* (San Juan: Comisión para los Asuntos de la Mujer, 1989). For more information on the issue of sexual harassment in the workplace, see Lourdes Martínez et al., *El hostigamiento sexual de las trabajadoras en sus centros de empleo* (Río Piedras: Universidad de Puerto Rico Centro de Investigaciones Sociales, 1986); Marya Muñoz-Vázquez and Ruth Silva Bonilla, *El hostigamiento sexual: Sus manifestaciones y características en la sociedad, en los centros de empleos, y los centros de estudios* (Río Piedras: Universidad de Puerto Rico Centro de Investigaciones Sociales, 1985).

11. Aline Frambes-Buxeda, "Ensayo fotográfico sobre la mujer puertorriqueña," *Hómines* 10, no. 2 (1987): 9–31.

12. For more information on the migration patterns among contemporary women clerical workers, see, Vilma Ortiz, "Changes in the Characteristics of Puerto Rican Migrants from 1955 to 1980," *International Migration Review* 20, no. 3 (1986): 612–28; Estado Libre Asociado de Puerto Rico, Junta de Planificación, *Indicadores socioeconómicos de la situación de las mujeres en Puerto Rico* (San Juan: Junta de Planificación, Negociado de Estadísticas, 1990).

13. Estado Libre Asociado de Puerto Rico, *Empleo por grupo ocupacional—Hembras—Años naturales (1954 al 1990)*, tables 29–32 (San Juan: Departamento de Trabajo y Recursos Humanos, 1991), 57–64.

14. In the summer of 1992, job listings posted at the Departments of Secretarial Sciences at the Río Piedras and Bayamón campuses of the UPR offered wages of $5.00 and $5.50 an hour for secretarial positions that required competency in word processing as well as English/Spanish bilingual skills.

15. The articulation of gender, race, and class has been a central focus in anthropological research on women and work throughout the 1980s. Pioneering research has traced the ways identities based on gender, race, and class have been used to mobilize women for work in the export-processing zones in Third World countries in Latin America, the Caribbean, Asia, and the Middle East. See Eleanor Leacock and Helen Safa, eds., *Women's*

Work: Development and the Division of Labor by Gender (South Hadley, Mass.: Bergin and Garvey, 1986); June Nash and Helen Safa, eds., *Women and Change in Latin America* (South Hadley, Mass.: Bergin and Garvey, 1986); June Nash and Patricia Fernández-Kelly, eds., *Women, Men and the International Division of Labor* (Albany: State University of New York Press, 1983). Scholars have also undertaken theoretical explorations of the connections and disjunctures among identities based on gender, race, and class. See, June Nash, "Cultural Parameters of Sexism and Racism in the International Divsion of Labor," in *Racism, Sexism and the World-System,* ed. Joan Smith et al. (Westport, Conn.: Greeenwood Press, 1988), 11–38; Karen Brodkin Sacks, "Towards a Unified Theory of Class, Race, and Gender," *American Ethnologist* 16, no. 3 (1989): 534–50. Anthropologists are now applying these frameworks to examine the role of women workers in the global factory and in the new international division of labor. See Frances Rothstein and Michael Blim, eds., *Anthropology and the Global Factory: Studies of Industrialization in the Late Twentieth Century* (New York: Bergin and Garvey, 1992); Kathryn Ward, ed., *Women Workers and Global Restructuring* (Ithaca: Cornell Univerity Press, 1990). These developments are characterized by the rapid mobility and restructuring of capital on an international scale, facilitated by the expansion of high-technology communications and information networks. The development of clerical work is a central feature of this worldwide process.

16. Palmira N. Ríos-González, "Women and Industrialization in Puerto Rico: Gender Division of Labor and the Demand for Female Labor in the Manufacturing Sector, 1950–1980" (Ph.D. diss., Yale University, 1990), 200.

17. Junta de Planificación de Puerto Rico, *Indicadores socioeconómicos,* tables 1, 2, 4.

18. See Idsa E. Alegría Ortega, "La representación de la mujer trabajadora en la televisión en Puerto Rico," *Hómines,* 10, no. 2 (1987): 289–93.

19. Transformations in the labor process for white collar workers were given specific consideration in the pioneering work by C. Wright Mills, *White Collar: The American Middle Classes* (Oxford: Oxford University Press, 1951). See also Barbara Garson, *The Electronic Sweatshop: How Computers Are Transforming the Office of the Future into the Factory of the Past* (New York: Simon and Schuster, 1988); Massachusetts History Workshop, *"They Can't Run the Office Without Us:" Sixty Years of Clerical Work* (Cambridge, Mass.: Massachusetts History Workshop, 1985); Mark McColloch, *White Clerical Workers in Transition: The Boom Years, 1940–1970* (Westport, Conn.: Greenwood Press, 1983).

20. Luz del Alba Acevedo, "Política de industrialización," 40–69.

21. See Frank Bonilla and Ricardo Campos, *Industry and Idleness* (New York: Center for Puerto Rican Studies, History and Migration Task Force, 1986); James L. Dietz, *Economic History of Puerto Rico: Institutional Change and Capitalist Development* (Princeton, N.J.: Princeton University Press, 1986); Pedro Angel Rivera, *Manos a la Obra: The Story Behind Operation Bootstrap* (New York: City University of New York, Center for Puerto Rican Studies, 1986).

22. This pattern follows the process of deskilling described by Harry Braverman, *Labor and Monopoly Capital: The Degradation of Work in the Twentieth Century* (New York: Monthly Review Press, 1974).

23. See, for example, *UMPUEN Informa* (Revista de la Unión de Mujeres Puertorriqueñas Negras) 2, no. 1 (1994): 2.

24. Here it is important to caution against the facile imposition of categories imposed by the United States scholarship on a very different Caribbean and Latino context. At the

same time, reliance on what ethnographers call the "natives' point of view" or "insider research" is also inadequate. It also would not be appropriate to accept the assertion that there is no racism in Puerto Rico, simply because people say so in their interviews.

25. It also finds expression in popular phrases or *refranes,* the most famous being "y tu agüella adónde 'sta?" (and your grandmother, where is she?) which chides the striver who would deny his African family ancestry in an effort to improve his social standing.

26. Karen Hossfeld, " 'Their Logic Against Them': Contradictions in Sex, Race, and Class in Silicon Valley," in *Women Workers and Global Restructuring,* ed. Kathryn Ward (Ithaca, N.Y.: Cornell University Press, 1991), 149–78.

27. Professional Secretaries International, *Visión y mundo de la secretaria: Mujer de hoy* (San Juan: PSI, 1989).

28. Universidad Interamericana, *De secretaria a gerente: Mito o realidad* (San Juan: Programa de Educación Superior Continuada, Universidad Interamericana, 1986).

ABOUT THE CONTRIBUTORS

RINA BENMAYOR was Director of the Cultural Task Force of the Centro de Estudios Puertorriqueños at Hunter College of the City University of New York (CUNY). She is currently Professor in the Department of Human CommunicationS at California State University at Monterey Bay.

EILEEN BORIS is Professor of History at Howard University. Her publication *Home to Work: Motherhood and the Politics of Industrial Homework in the United States* won the 1995 Philip Taft Prize in Labor History. Her latest publication is *Homeworkers in Global Perspective: Invisible No More*. Currently she is researching issues of gender, race, and citizenship rights.

GERALDINE J. CASEY is Director of the Women's Center at John Jay College of CUNY. She participated in the University of New York–Universidad de Puerto Rico *Intercambio* Student Exchange Program from 1990 to 1991. She is presently completing her dissertation for the Graduate School and University Center of CUNY.

ALICE COLÓN-WARREN is Associate Researcher of the Centro de Estudios, Recursos, y Servicios a la Mujer (CERES) of the Centro de Investigaciones (CIS) of the Universidad de Puerto Rico at Río Piedras. She is also coauthor of *El aborto en Puerto Rico: Ensayo bibliográfico y bibliografía anotada* and editor of "Género y mujeres puertorriqueñas," a CIS monograph.

ANA JUARBE was a member of the Centro de Estudios Puertorriqueños at Hunter College of CUNY. She is coauthor of "Responses to Poverty among Puerto Rican Women: Identity, Community, and Cultural Citizenship," Report to the Joint Committee on Contemporary Hispanic Issues of the Inter-University Program for Latino Research and the Social Science Research Council.

MARYA MUÑOZ-VÁZQUEZ is Professor in the Department of Psychology at the Universidad de Puerto Rico in Río Piedras. She is the coauthor of *El divorcio en la sociedad puertorriqueña,* and coauthor of "Hostigamiento sexual: Sus manifestaciones y características en la sociedad, centros de empleo, y centros de estudios," a CIS monograph.

ALTAGRACIA ORTIZ is Professor of History and Puerto Rican Studies at John Jay College of CUNY and Fellow at the Centro de Estudios Puertorriqueños at Hunter College of CUNY. She is the author of *Eighteenth-Century Reforms in the Caribbean* and of numerous articles on Puerto Rican women. At present she is working on a book, *Gender, Work, and Culture: A History of Puerto Rican Women.*

CARMEN A. PÉREZ-HERRANZ is Associate Professor in the Department of Anthropology of the Universidad de Puerto Rico at Río Piedras. She is presently researching issues of gender and the media among women in Puerto Rico.

VIRGINIA SÁNCHEZ KORROL is Chairperson of Puerto Rican Studies at Brooklyn College of CUNY. She is the author of *From Colonia to Community: The History of Puerto Ricans in New York City, 1917–1948* and coauthor of *The Puerto Rican Struggle: Essays in Survival.*

ROSA M. TORRUELLAS was Director of the El Barrio Literacy Program of the Centro de Estudios Puertorriqueños at Hunter College of CUNY. She was coauthor of "Responses to Poverty among Puerto Rican Women: Identity, Community, and Cultural Citizenship," Report to the Joint Committee on Contemporary Hispanic Issues of the Inter-University Program for Latino Research and the Social Science Research Council.

INDEX

AFDC (Aid to Families with Dependent Children): and American citizenship, 195; and family support, 184; and inadequate employment, 127; and labor force participation, 127. *See also* welfare

affinal relations. *See* kinship networks

African Americans: and child care, 200–201; and class status, 132; in clerical sector, 14; and discrimination, 8, 73, 77n; and education, 96; in garment industry, 8, 73, 75–76n, 77n; and ILGWU, 79n; and labor force participation, 13, 14, 75–76n, 77n, 80–81n, 115, 123; and labor reserves, 132; in management, 121; migration of, 115; and motherhood, 200; and poverty, 108, 130, 132; and service jobs, 14, 75n, 128, 133; underemployment among, 123; and unemployment, 123; and welfare, 127, 185; and women heads of household, 108

age: among clerical workers, 16, 211; and education, 143, 191; among garment workers, 16–17, 29n, 57, 70, 143, 145, 150–51, 152, 156, 159, 160; and labor force participation, 13, 205; in management, 121; and migrants, 72; among needleworkers, 41; and paternalism, 41, 146; and teachers, 94; among tobacco workers, 4; among welfare recipients, 186; and working-class consciousness, 140. *See also* elderly women

Agraciani, Sara, 34

agregados (share-croppers), 40

agricultural production, changes in, 36, 115, 144; for coffee, 3, 36; and export

trade, 36; and impact of industrialization, 162–63; numbers of workers in, 121; for sugar cane, 3, 4, 36; for tobacco, 6, 36; and women's work, 3, 162. *See also* capitalism; kinship networks; tobacco industry; wages

Alianza Obrera, 83

American Federation of Labor, 45

Americanization. *See* assimilation

Anglero, Teresa, 48

Arcelay, María Luisa, 5, 39

Arroyo, Luci, 212–13

Artes y Letras, 84–85

ASPIRA: bilingual campaign of, 100–102; Consent Decree of, 101; and study of drop-outs, 208n. *See also* education

ASPIRA vs. the Board of Education, 101

assimilation: and bilingual education, 87; and educational system in Puerto Rico, 90; and English-speaking programs, 84; and melting-pot paradigm, 88; policies of, 86; and teaching methods, 89; among white immigrant women, 200

"Atrévete," 210

Avilés, Julia, 196–97

barriada (neighborhood). *See* community

El Barrio Popular Education Program, 186

Belpré, Pura, 10

Bilingual Education Act, 101

bohío (shack). *See* household

Bonilla, Pura, 98

calados (fine needlework), 5, 55

Capetillo, Luisa, 4–5

capitalism, ix, 3, 4, 6, 36; and agricultural

works, 150; leaders in, 10, 11, 12, 84, 102–3n; and migrants, 10–11, 86; militancy of, 127; and parents, 99; and researchers, 82, 168; social reproduction of, 223; social services to, 90; Spanish language in, 83. *See also* education; environmental pollution; Latina/os; marginalization; SAT; welfare

compadrazgo system. *See* kinship networks

confectionary industry, presence of women in, 10

consumerism: among clerical workers, 227; and economic development, 157. *See also* garment industry

contracts: benefits in, 71, 80n, 151, 212, 213, 229; and ILGWU, 9, 66, 151; and immigrant labor, 69; negotiation of, 65–66, 67, 222, 223, 227–28, 229; and office attire, 227–28; and union funds, 67, 213, 215–16; and wage negotiation, 65, 69. *See also* garment industry; sexual harassment

Correa, Elizabeth, 213, 214

Cossío, Raquel, 194, 202

CPRNS (El Comité Pro-Rescate de Nuestra Salud) (Committee to Rescue Our Health): activities of, 19, 168, 169–70, 171, 174–75, 178–80; and decision-making process, 19, 173–78; failures of, 19, 177–78, 180; goals of, 18, 19, 174–76; leadership in, 19, 170–71, 172, 173, 174, 175, 176; organization in, 19, 172; origins of, 18, 172; professional advisers in, 19, 168, 169–70; and reductionist paradigm, 176–78; successes of, 19, 178–80. *See also* occupational health; professional sector

craft industries, percentages of workers in, 4, 120, 121

Cruz, Hijinia, 33, 34

Cruz, Monserrate, 172, 176

cultural citizenship. *See* cultural rights

cultural rights: among clerical workers, 219–20; definition of, 187, 201; expressions of, 198, 199; and gender roles, 203, 206; and welfare use, 21, 192, 196–201. *See also* working class

dignidad. See cultural rights

discrimination: in education, 101; and ethnicity, 1, 9, 20, 58, 64–65, 72–73; in garment industry, 1, 8–9, 57–60, 63–68, 71, 72–73, 77n, 78–79n; and gender, 1, 4, 24, 125; in ILGWU, 9–10, 58–59, 60, 64, 65, 66, 67–68, 71, 73; and immigrant labor force, 24; in labor market, 112, 120, 123, 225; in manufacturing sector, 225; and race, 2, 20, 24, 225; and service sector, 225; and wages, 113, 120; and women heads of household, 134. *See also* African Americans; gender

domestic occupation: migrant women in, 10, 195, 202; number of women in, 3, 120, 121; under Spanish colonialism, 3. *See also* children: and child labor; service sector

domestic violence, campaign against, 212, 229, 231n

double shift: burden of, 48, 140, 144, 204; among clerical workers, 217; among garment workers, 17, 152, 155, 158; among migrant women, 8; research on, 141

Dubinsky, David, 58–59, 66

earnings. *See* salaries; wages

economic development: and automation, 115; and employment, 157; and environment, 162–63; impact of, 16–24, 86, 142–43, 157, 162–63; lack of, 35, 141; in Latin America, 23; in Middle Atlantic region, 114–15; model of, 45; and women, 23–24, 141, 142–43, 157. *See also* agricultural production; capitalism; consumerism; labor reserves; Operation Bootstrap

education: and adult literacy, 20, 186; and ASPIRA conference, 100–101; and bilingualism, 1, 84, 88–89, 94, 96; and "buddy system," 87–88; among children on welfare, 202–3; and colonialism, 12, 88, 90; and community concerns, 104n; constraints in, 90, 125; differences in, 125; among different ethnic groups, 122; drop-outs in, 208n; and employment, 13, 14, 119, 125–26, 144; among garment workers, 16, 73, 159; impact of migration on, 125; and

women heads of household, 13, 14, 15, 17, 20, 106, 108–10, 113–14, 130, 134, 144, 186, 221; and women's work, 3, 21, 24, 34–35, 112, 134, 141–42, 152, 153–57, 171, 184, 187–89, 204, 217. *See also* family; needlework industry; welfare; work ethic

ILGWU (International Ladies' Garment Workers' Union): antiradicalism in, 59, 66; and delegates to annual convention, 59; funds of, 9, 67–68; and garment industry problems, 9, 66, 69, 71; and home needlework, 8, 56; in *Justice* newspaper, 68; locals in, 9, 57, 58, 60, 64, 66; organization of workers in, 9, 57, 58, 60, 79n; policies of, 65–67, 69, 70–71; and relocation of garment companies, 10, 66, 71; workers' appraisal of, 17, 67, 68, 71, 147–48, 151, 157. *See also* African Americans; contracts; discrimination; home needlework industry: campaign against; language; Latina/os; patrimony; white women
immigrant labor: among Asians, 69, 71, 73; among Europeans, 8–9, 56, 58, 64, 65, 67, 73, 115; among Haitians, 71; among Latin Americans, 24, 69, 71, 73, 115, 128, 129, 133; restriction of, 9, 36, 115; shortages of, 71. *See also* garment industry
immigration. *See* migration
income levels: among clerical workers, 223; of migrant household, 186; among needleworkers, 39–40; of women heads of household, 107
informal economic activities: among clerical workers, 22, 217–18, 223, 224; and economic survival, 70, 112, 128; and home needlework, 27n, 112; and selling of food, 3, 210, 211; numbers in, 25n; and women on welfare, 15, 20, 196, 202
Insular Council of Unions of Needleworkers, 47, 48
international division of labor: adaptation of, 158; impact of, 141; and industrialization, 165; role of women in, 232

Jewish Labor Committee, 68
job loss: among clerical workers, 222; and economic transformations, 13; fear of, 190–91; in garment industry, 38, 58, 62–63, 70, 73, 143–44; and gender differences, 117; impact of, 126, 186, 190, 192–93; and labor force participation, 13–14, 111, 127, 133; in manufacturing sector, 13, 14, 15, 62–63, 70, 115, 204; and poverty, 129; in tobacco industry, 5, 6; and welfare, 20, 186, 190; and women heads of household, 129–32. *See also* capitalism; labor reserves
Jones Act (1917), and educational system, 88
jornaleras, 3
Jovellanos, Luisa, 189, 194, 198–99, 201

kinship networks: among agricultural workers, 17, 149; and child care, 200–201; among clerical workers, 148, 223–24; and *compadrazgo system*, 57, 149, 200–201; among garment workers, 17–18, 57, 147–51, 153, 155, 157, 158; among homeworkers, 23, 34, 35, 51; single mothers and, 130; and women on welfare, 184, 194. *See also* community

labor force participation: among clerical workers, 224; and cultural values, 126; and decline of homeworkers, 54; declines in, 13, 54n, 70, 73–74, 115, 119, 127, 128; among different ethnic groups, 116; and education, 14, 15, 119, 123, 131–32, 190; and family, 14, 204; and "female occupations," 3–4, 36; and fertility, 119; and gender, 114, 139, 141–44, 158; geographic differences in, 125, 126, 127; and homeownership, 15, 131–32; impact of, 139, 157; increases in, 14, 29n, 123; and labor market conditions, 8, 105, 114, 119, 123, 125, 127, 131; in Latin America, 24, 142; in manufacturing, 8–9, 15, 57, 60, 127, 143, 144; in Mid-Atlantic region, 13–15, 105, 106, 114, 118–19; of migrant women, 105, 115; and Operation Bootstrap, 15, 221; rates of, 13, 118–19, 126;

14, 123–25, 126, 142, 143, 209; and foreign competition, 129; and low-wage labor, 117; relocation of, 126, 140; significance of Puerto Ricans in, 126, 128–29.
See also discrimination; employment;
factories; garment industry; labor force
participation; labor reserves; managerial sector; needlework industry; Operation Bootstrap; service sector; wages
maquiladora plants, 23, 24
Marcantonio, Vito, 85
marginalization: from labor market, 114,
142, 190, 204; of women, 114, 162, 186,
204; of working class, 2
marital status: and birth control, 200; and
education, 131; changes in, 204; and
earnings, 131, 132, 133; among garment workers, 16–17, 140, 159; and
home ownership, 131; and labor force
participation, 13, 15; among needleworkers, 33, 34, 35, 39; among tobacco
workers, 4; and welfare, 20, 134, 186,
193, 194, 195, 198
Martín, Cielo, 172, 174, 175, 180
Martínez, Esther, 203
maternalist politics, 21, 47
Mathew, Alfredo, 98
meat-packing industry, workers in, 10
migrant labor. *See* immigrant labor
migration: and children, 11; and colonialism, 72; cycles of, 72, 125, 126; and economic conditions, 106, 189–90; and education, 88, 125; and garment industry,
8; and labor, 1, 2, 5, 7–13, 20, 22, 23,
24, 60, 86, 115, 187, 189; to Mid-Atlantic region, 7, 71n, 115; and needlework industry, 8; population accounts
of, 10–11; reasons for, 5, 10, 20, 22, 56,
57, 72, 86, 126, 144, 159, 187, 189, 215;
research on, 2–3; and return migrants,
29n, 72, 156; and welfare, 185; of
women, 2, 7–13, 20, 72, 115, 144; of
working-class, 2. *See also* African Americans; age; capitalism; clerical sector;
community; education; Great Depression; history; home needlework industry; household; language; Latina/os;
Operation Bootstrap; teachers; tobacco
industry

minimum wage: in garment industry, 66,
77; and homework industry, 38, 44, 45;
in needlework industry, 47, 49; regulation of, 5; and tobacco strippers, 38;
and welfare use, 191, 196
Miranda, Carmen, 99
Misión Industrial, 172
moonlighting activities. *See* informal economic activities
Mother's Day, 22, 154, 219–20
multinational corporations: and deteriorating work conditions, 141; and exploitation of workers, 23; in garment
industry, 68, 69–70, 79n; and occupational safety, 18–19; and women workers, 16–17, 24. *See also* underemployment; unemployment; wages
municipio. See community

National Association for the Advancement
of Colored People, 64, 68
National Consumers' League, 48
National Origins Act (1924), 9
National Women's Trade Union League,
44
Nazario, Dolores, 98
Needleworkers' Union, 46, 49
needlework industry: and community
workshop plan, 48, 50; decline of, 7,
50; and European imports, 36; and export trade, 6; and homework, 6, 7;
households of, 6; number of women
in, 4, 6; origins of, 36, 37; regulation
of, 7; relocation of, 50; and shops, 5, 6;
significance of, 50; training in, 37;
working conditions in, 6, 7, 8, 50. *See
also* age; children: and child labor; education; factories; gender; Great Depression; home needlework industry; income levels; labor struggles; marital
status; migration; NRA; occupational
health; poverty; unemployment; wages;
white women
Nehama, Saby, 59
Neruda, Pablo, 220
New Deal: and homeworkers, 35; and
NRA, 7, 33–34, 43–44
NIOSH (National Institute of Occupational Safety and Health), 167